THE THEORY and PRACTICE of PERSPECTIVE

G. A. STOREY

DOVER PUBLICATIONS, INC.
Mineola, New York

Bibliographical Note

This Dover edition, first published in 2006, is an unabridged, slightly altered republication of the edition published by Oxford at the Clarendon Press, Oxford, 1910. In the Dover edition, the foldout illustration between pp. 58 and 59 of the original has been reproduced as a double-page spread, with a somewhat reduced image. Likewise, the foldout illustration between pp. 170 and 171 of the original has been reproduced as a turnpage, with a somewhat reduced image.

International Standard Book Number: 0-486-44907-6

Manufactured in the United States of America
Dover Publications, Inc., 31 East 2nd Street, Mineola, N.Y. 11501

DEDICATED

TO

SIR EDWARD J. POYNTER

BARONET

PRESIDENT OF THE ROYAL ACADEMY

IN TOKEN OF FRIENDSHIP

AND REGARD

PREFACE

It is much easier to understand and remember a thing when a reason is given for it, than when we are merely shown how to do it without being told why it is so done ; for in the latter case, instead of being assisted by reason, our real help in all study, we have to rely upon memory or our power of imitation, and to do simply as we are told without thinking about it. The consequence is that at the very first difficulty we are left to flounder about in the dark, or to remain inactive till the master comes to our assistance.

Now in this book it is proposed to enlist the reasoning faculty from the very first : to let one problem grow out of another and to be dependent on the foregoing, as in geometry, and so to explain each thing we do that there shall be no doubt in the mind as to the correctness of the proceeding. The student will thus gain the power of finding out any new problem for himself, and will therefore acquire a true knowledge of perspective.

CONTENTS

BOOK I

BOOK II

BOOK III

BOOK IV

BOOK FIRST

THE NECESSITY OF THE STUDY OF PERSPECTIVE TO PAINTERS, SCULPTORS, AND ARCHITECTS

LEONARDO DA VINCI tells us in his celebrated *Treatise on Painting* that the young artist should first of all learn perspective, that is to say, he should first of all learn that he has to depict on a flat surface objects which are in relief or distant one from the other; for this is the simple art of painting. Objects appear smaller at a distance than near to us, so by drawing them thus we give depth to our canvas. The outline of a ball is a mere flat circle, but with proper shading we make it appear round, and this is the perspective of light and shade.

'The next thing to be considered is the effect of the atmosphere and light. If two figures are in the same coloured dress, and are standing one behind the other, then they should be of slightly different tone, so as to separate them. And in like manner, according to the distance of the mountains in a landscape and the greater or less density of the air, so do we depict space between them, not only making them smaller in outline, but less distinct.'[1]

Sir Edwin Landseer used to say that in looking at a figure in a picture he liked to feel that he could walk round it, and this exactly expresses the impression that the true art of painting should make upon the spectator.

There is another observation of Leonardo's that it is well I should here transcribe; he says: 'Many are desirous of learning to draw, and are very fond of it, who are notwithstanding void of a proper disposition for it. This may be known by their want of perseverance; like boys who draw everything in a hurry, never finishing or shadowing.' This shows they do not care for their work, and all instruction is thrown away upon them. At the present time there is too much of this 'everything in a hurry',

[1] Leonardo da Vinci's *Treatise on Painting*.

and beginning in this way leads only to failure and disappointment. These observations apply equally to perspective as to drawing and painting.

Unfortunately, this study is too often neglected by our painters, some of them even complacently confessing their ignorance of it; while the ordinary student either turns from it with distaste, or only endures going through it with a view to passing an examination, little thinking of what value it will be to him in working out his pictures. Whether the manner of teaching perspective is the cause of this dislike for it, I cannot say; but certainly most of our English books on the subject are anything but attractive.

All the great masters of painting have also been masters of perspective, for they knew that without it, it would be impossible to carry out their grand compositions. In many cases they were even inspired by it in choosing their subjects. When one looks at those sunny interiors, those corridors and courtyards by De Hooghe, with their figures far off and near, one feels that their charm consists greatly in their perspective, as well as in their light and tone and colour. Or if we study those Venetian masterpieces by Paul Veronese, Titian, Tintoretto, and others, we become convinced that it was through their knowledge of perspective that they gave such space and grandeur to their canvases.

I need not name all the great artists who have shown their interest and delight in this study, both by writing about it and practising it, such as Albert Dürer and others, but I cannot leave out our own Turner, who was one of the greatest masters in this respect that ever lived; though in his case we can only judge of the results of his knowledge as shown in his pictures, for although he was Professor of Perspective at the Royal Academy in 1807—over a hundred years ago—and took great pains with the diagrams he prepared to illustrate his lectures, they seemed to the students to be full of confusion and obscurity; nor am I aware that any record of them remains, although they must have contained some valuable teaching, had their author possessed the art of conveying it.

However, we are here chiefly concerned with the necessity of this study, and of the necessity of starting our work with it.

Before undertaking a large composition of figures, such as the 'Wedding-feast at Cana', by Paul Veronese, or 'The School of Athens', by Raphael, the artist should set out his floors, his walls, his colonnades, his balconies, his steps, &c., so that he may know where to place his personages, and to measure their different sizes according to their distances; indeed, he must make his stage and his scenery before he introduces his actors. He can then proceed with his composition, arrange his groups and the accessories with ease, and above all with correctness. But I have noticed that some of our cleverest painters will arrange their figures to please the eye, and when fairly advanced with their work will call in an expert, to (as they call it) put in their perspective for them, but as it does not form part of their original composition, it involves all sorts of difficulties and vexatious alterings and rubbings out, and even then is not always satisfactory. For the expert may not be an artist, nor in sympathy with the picture, hence there will be a want of unity in it; whereas the whole thing, to be in harmony, should be the conception of one mind, and the perspective as much a part of the composition as the figures.

If a ceiling has to be painted with figures floating or flying in the air, or sitting high above us, then our perspective must take a different form, and the point of sight will be above our heads instead of on the horizon; nor can these difficulties be overcome without an adequate knowledge of the science, which will enable us to work out for ourselves any new problems of this kind that we may have to solve.

Then again, with a view to giving different effects or impressions in this decorative work, we must know where to place the horizon and the points of sight, for several of the latter are sometimes required when dealing with large surfaces such as the painting of walls, or stage scenery, or panoramas depicted on a cylindrical canvas and viewed from the centre thereof, where a fresh point of sight is required at every twelve or sixteen feet.

Without a true knowledge of perspective, none of these things can be done. The artist should study them in the great compositions of the masters, by analysing their pictures and seeing how and for what reasons they applied their knowledge. Rubens put low horizons to most of his large figure-subjects, as in 'The Descent from the Cross', which not only gave grandeur to his designs, but, seeing they were to be placed above the eye, gave a more natural appearance to his figures. The Venetians often put the horizon almost on a level with the base of the picture or edge of the frame, and sometimes even below it; as in 'The Family of Darius at the Feet of Alexander', by Paul Veronese, and 'The Origin of the "Via Lactea"', by Tintoretto, both in our National Gallery. But in order to do all these things, the artist in designing his work must have the knowledge of perspective at his fingers' ends, and only the details, which are often tedious, should he leave to an assistant to work out for him.

We must remember that the line of the horizon should be as nearly as possible on a level with the eye, as it is in nature; and yet one of the commonest mistakes in our exhibitions is the bad placing of this line. We see dozens of examples of it, where in full-length portraits and other large pictures intended to be seen from below, the horizon is placed high up in the canvas instead of low down; the consequence is that compositions so treated not only lose in grandeur and truth, but appear to be toppling over, or give the impression of smallness rather than bigness. Indeed, they look like small pictures enlarged, which is a very different thing from a large design. So that, in order to see them properly, we should mount a ladder to get upon a level with their horizon line (see Fig. 66, double-page illustration).

We have here spoken in a general way of the importance of this study to painters, but we shall see that it is of almost equal importance to the sculptor and the architect.

A sculptor student at the Academy, who was making his drawings rather carelessly, asked me of what use perspective was to a sculptor. 'In the first place,' I said, 'to reason out apparently difficult problems, and to find how easy they become, will improve your mind; and in the second, if you have to do monumental work, it will teach you the exact size to make your figures according to the height they are to be placed, and also the boldness with which they should be treated to give them their full effect.'

He at once acknowledged that I was right, proved himself an efficient pupil, and took much interest in his work.

I cannot help thinking that the reason our public monuments so often fail to impress us with any sense of grandeur is in a great measure owing to the neglect of the scientific study of perspective. As an illustration of what I mean, let the student look at a good engraving or photograph of the Arch of Constantine at Rome, or the Tombs of the Medici, by Michelangelo, in the sacristy of San Lorenzo at Florence. And then, for an example of a mistake in the placing of a colossal figure, let him turn to the Tomb of Julius II in San Pietro in Vinculis, Rome, and he will see that the figure of Moses, so grand in itself, not only loses much of its dignity by being placed on the ground instead of in the niche above it, but throws all the other figures out of proportion or harmony, and was quite contrary to Michelangelo's intention. Indeed, this tomb, which was to have been the finest thing of its kind ever done, was really the tragedy of the great sculptor's life.

The same remarks apply in a great measure to the architect as to the sculptor. The old builders knew the value of a knowledge of perspective, and, as in the case of Serlio, Vignola, and others, prefaced their treatises on architecture with chapters on geometry and perspective. For it showed them how to give proper proportions to their buildings and the details thereof; how to give height and importance both to the interior and exterior ; also to give the right sizes of windows, doorways, columns, vaults, and other parts, and the various heights they should make their towers, walls, arches, roofs, and so forth. One of the most beautiful examples of the application of this knowledge to architecture is the Campanile of the Cathedral, at Florence, built by Giotto and Taddeo Gaddi, who were painters as well as architects. Here it will be seen that the height of the windows is increased as they are placed higher up in the building, and the top windows or openings into the belfry are about six times the size of those in the lower story.

WHAT IS PERSPECTIVE?

PERSPECTIVE is a subtle form of geometry; it represents figures and objects not as they are but as we see them in space, whereas geometry represents figures not as we see them but

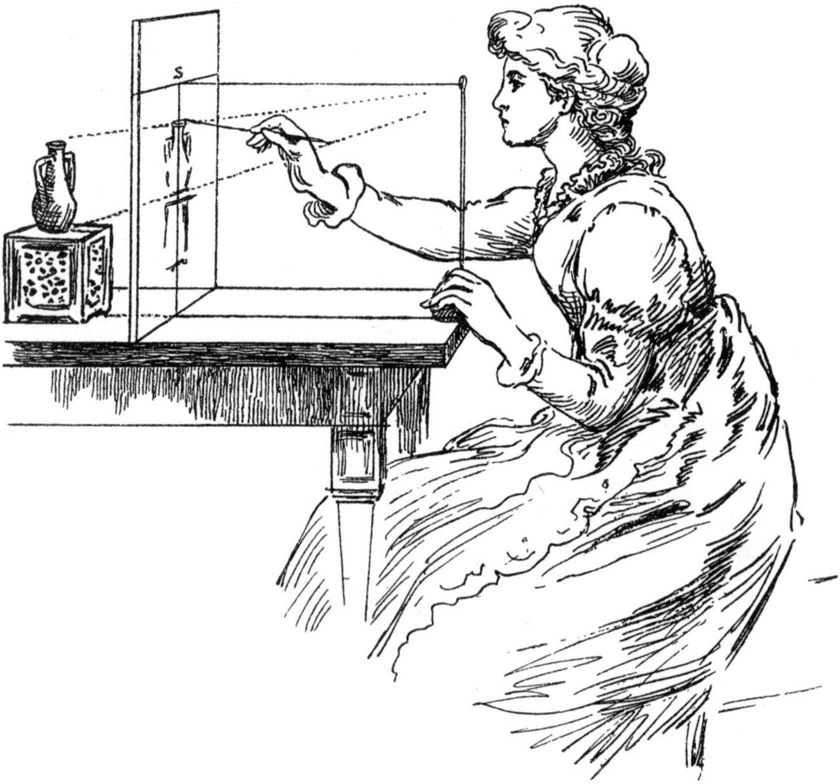

FIG. 1.

as they are. When we have a front view of a figure such as a square, its perspective and geometrical appearance is the same, and we see it as it really is, that is, with all its sides equal and all its angles right angles, the perspective only varying in size according to the distance we are from it; but if we place that square flat on the table and look at it sideways or at an angle, then we become conscious of certain changes in its form —the side farthest from us appears shorter than that near to us,

FIG. 2.

and all the angles are different. Thus A (Fig. 2) is a geometrical square and B is the same square seen in perspective.

The science of perspective gives the dimensions of objects seen in space as they appear to the eye of the spectator, just as a perfect tracing of those objects on a sheet of glass placed vertically between him and them would do; indeed its very name is derived from *perspicere*, to see through. But as no tracing done by hand could possibly be mathematically correct, the mathematician teaches us how by certain points and measurements we may yet give a perfect image of them. These images are called projections, but the artist calls them pictures. In

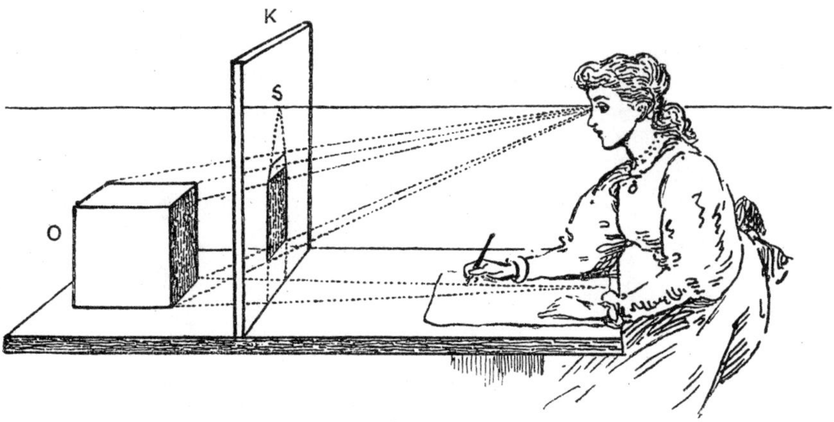

FIG. 3.

this sketch K is the vertical transparent plane or picture, O is a cube placed on one side of it. The young student is the spectator on the other side of it, the dotted lines drawn from the corners of the cube to the eye of the spectator are the visual rays, and the points on the transparent picture plane where these visual rays pass through it indicate the perspective position of those points on the picture. To find these points is the main object or duty of linear perspective.

Perspective up to a certain point is a pure science, not depending upon the accidents of vision, but upon the exact laws of reasoning. Nor is it to be considered as only pertaining to the craft of the painter and draughtsman. It has an intimate connexion with our mental perceptions and with the ideas that are impressed upon the brain by the appearance of all that surrounds us. If we saw everything as depicted by plane geometry, that is, as a map, we should have no difference of view, no variety of ideas, and we should live in a world of unbearable monotony; but as we see everything in perspective, which is infinite in its variety of aspect, our minds are subjected to countless phases of thought, making the world around us constantly interesting, so it is devised that we shall see the infinite wherever we turn, and marvel at it, and delight in it, although perhaps in many cases unconsciously.

In perspective, as in geometry, we deal with parallels, squares, triangles, cubes, circles, &c.; but in perspective the same figure takes an endless variety of forms, whereas in geometry it has but one. Here are three equal geometrical squares: they are all

FIG. 4.

alike. Here are three equal perspective squares, but all varied

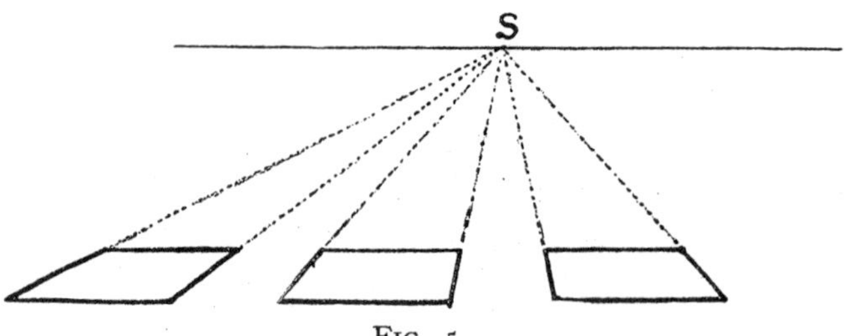

FIG. 5.

in form; and the same figure changes in aspect as often as we view it from a different position. A walk round the dining-room table will exemplify this.

It is in proving that, notwithstanding this difference of appearance, the figures do represent the same form, that much of our work consists; and for those who care to exercise their reasoning powers it becomes not only a sure means of knowledge, but a study of the greatest interest.

Perspective is said to have been formed into a science about the fifteenth century. Among the names mentioned by the unknown but pleasant author of *The Practice of Perspective*, written by a Jesuit of Paris in the eighteenth century, we find Albert Dürer, who has left us some rules and principles in the fourth book of his *Geometry*; Jean Cousin, who has an express treatise on the art wherein are many valuable things; also Vignola, who altered the plans of St. Peter's left by Michelangelo; Serlio, whose treatise is one of the best I have seen of these early writers; Du Cerceau, Serigati, Solomon de Cause, Marolois, Vredemont; Guidus Ubaldus, who first introduced foreshortening; the Sieur de Vaulizard, the Sieur Dufarges, Joshua Kirby, for whose *Method of Perspective made Easy* (?) Hogarth drew the well-known frontispiece; and lastly, the above-named *Practice of Perspective* by a Jesuit of Paris, which is very clear and excellent as far as it goes, and was the book used by Sir Joshua Reynolds.[1] But nearly all these authors treat chiefly of parallel perspective, which they do with clearness and simplicity, and also mathematically, as shown in the short treatise in Latin by Christian Wolff, but they scarcely touch upon the more difficult problems of angular and oblique perspective. Of modern books, those to which I am most indebted are the *Traité Pratique de Perspective* of M. A. Cassagne (Paris, 1873), which is thoroughly artistic, and full of pictorial examples admirably done; and to M. Henriet's *Cours Rational de Dessin*. There are many other foreign books of excellence, notably M. Thibault's *Perspective*, and some German and Swiss books, and yet, notwithstanding this imposing array of authors, I venture to say that many new features and original

[1] There is another book called *The Jesuit's Perspective* which I have not yet seen, but which I hear is a fine work.

problems are presented in this book, whilst the old ones are not neglected. As, for instance, How to draw figures at an angle without vanishing points (see p. 141, Fig. 162, &c.), a new method of angular perspective which dispenses with the cumbersome setting out usually adopted, and enables us to draw figures at any angle without vanishing lines, &c., and is almost, if not quite, as simple as parallel perspective (see p. 133, Fig. 150, &c.). How to measure distances by the square and diagonal, and to draw interiors thereby (p. 128, Fig. 144). How to explain the theory of perspective by ocular demonstration, using a vertical sheet of glass with strings, placed on a drawing-board, which I have found of the greatest use (see p. 29, Fig. 29). Then again, I show how all our perspective can be done inside the picture; that we can measure any distance into the picture from a foot to a mile or twenty miles (see p. 86, Fig. 94); how we can draw the Great Pyramid, which stands on thirteen acres of ground, by putting it 1,600 feet off (Fig. 224), &c., &c. And while preserving the mathematical science, so that all our operations can be proved to be correct, my chief aim has been to make it easy of application to our work and consequently useful to the artist.

The Egyptians do not appear to have made any use of linear perspective. Perhaps it was considered out of character with their particular kind of decoration, which is to be looked upon as picture writing rather than pictorial art; a table, for instance, would be represented like a ground-plan and the objects upon it in elevation or standing up. A row of chariots with their horses and drivers side by side were placed one over the other, and although the Egyptians had no doubt a reason for this kind of representation, for they were grand artists, it seems to us very primitive; and indeed quite young beginners who have never drawn from real objects have a tendency to do very much the same thing as this ancient people did, or even to emulate the mathematician and represent things not as they appear but as they are, and will make the top of a table an almost upright square and the objects upon it as if they would fall off.

No doubt the Greeks had correct notions of perspective, for the paintings on vases, and at Pompeii and Herculaneum, which were either by Greek artists or copied from Greek pictures, show some knowledge, though not complete knowledge, of this science. Indeed, it is difficult to conceive of any great artist making his perspective very wrong, for if he can draw the human figure as the Greeks did, surely he can draw an angle.

The Japanese, who are great observers of nature, seem to have got at their perspective by copying what they saw, and, although they are not quite correct in a few things, they convey the idea of distance and make their horizontal planes look level, which are two important things in perspective. Some of their landscapes are beautiful; their trees, flowers, and foliage exquisitely drawn and arranged with the greatest taste; whilst there is a character and go about their figures and birds, &c., that can hardly be surpassed. All their pictures are lively and intelligent and appear to be executed with ease, which shows their authors to be complete masters of their craft.

The same may be said of the Chinese, although their perspective is more decorative than true, and whilst their taste is exquisite their whole art is much more conventional and traditional, and does not remind us of nature like that of the Japanese.

We may see defects in the perspective of the ancients, in the mediaeval painters, in the Japanese and Chinese, but are we always right ourselves? Even in celebrated pictures by old and modern masters there are occasionally errors that might easily have been avoided, if a ready means of settling the difficulty were at hand. We should endeavour then to make this study as simple, as easy, and as complete as possible, to show clear evidence of its correctness (according to its conditions), and at the same time to serve as a guide on any and all occasions that we may require it.

To illustrate what is perspective, and as an experiment that any one can make, whether artist or not, let us stand at a window that looks out on to a courtyard or a street or a garden, &c., and trace with a paint-brush charged with Indian ink or water-colour the outline of whatever view there happens to be outside, being careful to keep the eye always in the same place by means of a rest; when this is dry, place a piece of drawing-paper over it and trace through with a pencil. Now we will rub out the tracing on the glass, which is sure to be rather clumsy, and, fixing our paper down on a board, proceed to draw the scene before us, using the main lines of our tracing as our guiding lines.

If we take pains over our work, we shall find that, without troubling ourselves much about rules, we have produced a perfect perspective of perhaps a very difficult subject. After practising for some little time in this way we shall get accustomed to what are called perspective deformations, and soon be able to dispense with the glass and the tracing altogether and to sketch straight from nature, taking little note of perspective beyond fixing the point of sight and the horizontal-line; in fact, doing what every artist does when he goes out sketching.

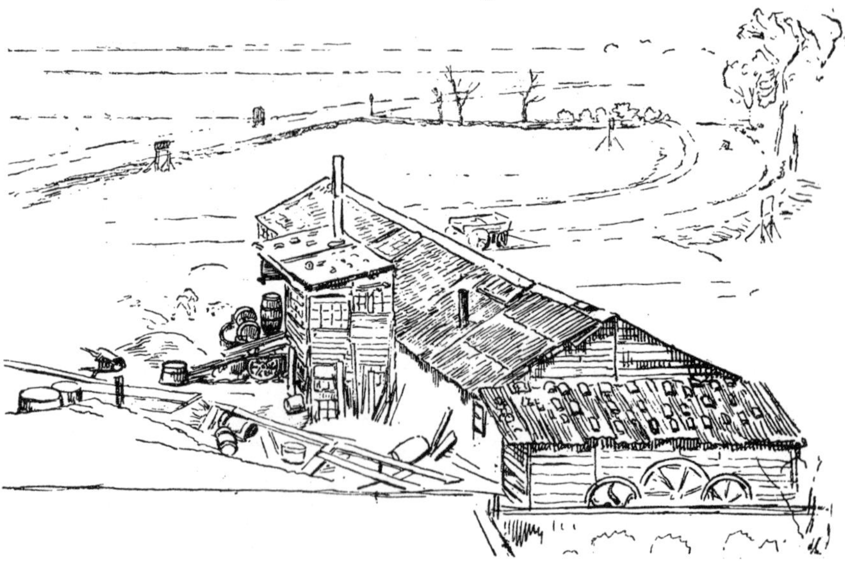

FIG. 6. This is a much reduced reproduction of a drawing made on my studio window in this way some twenty years ago, when the builder started covering the fields at the back with rows and rows of houses.

THE THEORY OF PERSPECTIVE

Definitions

I

Fig. 7. In this figure, AKB represents the picture or transparent vertical plane through which the objects to be represented can be seen, or on which they can be traced, such as the cube C.

The line HD is the **Horizontal-line** or **Horizon,** the chief line in perspective, as upon it are placed the principal points to which

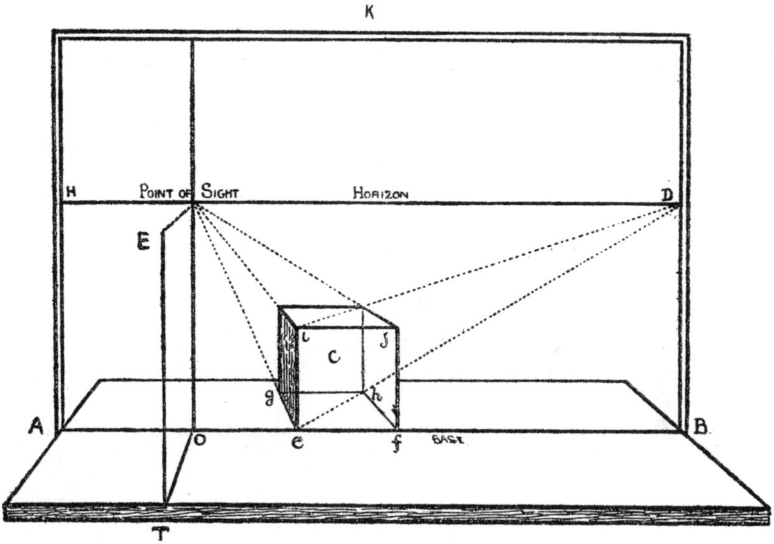

FIG. 7.

our perspective lines are drawn. First, the **Point of Sight** and next D, the **Point of Distance.** The chief vanishing points and measuring points are also placed on this line.

Another important line is AB, the **Base** or **Ground line,** as it is on this that we measure the width of any object to be represented, such as *ef*, the base of the square *efgh*, on which the cube C is raised. E is the position of the eye of the spectator, being drawn in perspective, and is called the **Station-point.**

Note that the perspective of the board, and the line SE, is not the same as that of the cube in the picture AKB, and also that so much of the board which is behind the picture plane partially represents the **Perspective-plane,** supposed to be perfectly level and to extend from the base line to the horizon. Of this we shall speak further on. In nature it is not really level, but partakes in extended views of the rotundity of the earth, though in small areas such as ponds the roundness is infinitesimal.

Fig. 8. This is a side view of the previous figure, the picture

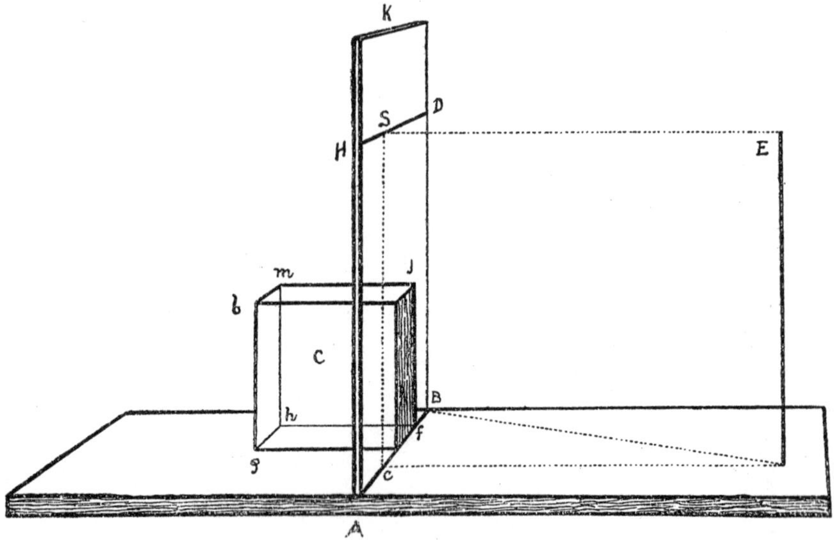

FIG. 8.

plane K being represented edgeways, and the line SE its full length. It also shows the position of the eye in front of the point of sight S. The horizontal-line HD and the base or ground-line AB are represented as receding from us, and in that case are called vanishing lines, a not quite satisfactory term.

It is to be noted that the cube C is placed close to the transparent picture plane, indeed touches it, and that the square *fj* faces the spectator E, and although here drawn in perspective it appears to him as in the other figure. Also, it is at the same time a perspective and a geometrical figure, and can therefore be measured with the compasses. Or in other words, we can touch the square *fj*, because it is on the surface of the picture, but we cannot touch the square *ghmb* at the other end of the cube and can only measure it by the rules of perspective.

II

The Point of Sight, the Horizon, and the Point of Distance

There are three things to be considered and understood before we can begin a perspective drawing. First, the position of the eye in front of the picture, which is called the **Station-point,** and of course is not in the picture itself, but its position is indicated by a point on the picture which is exactly opposite the

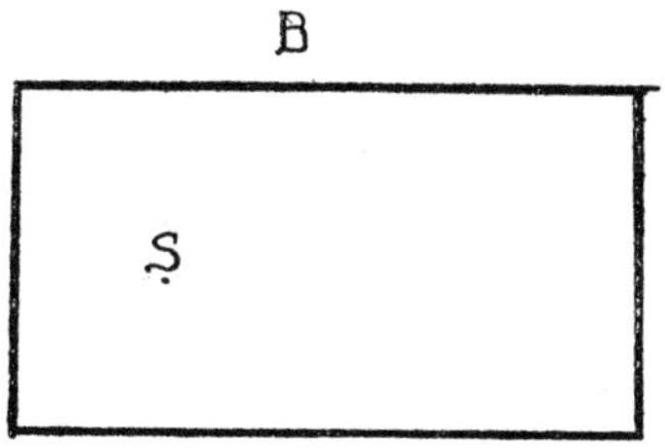

Fig. 9.

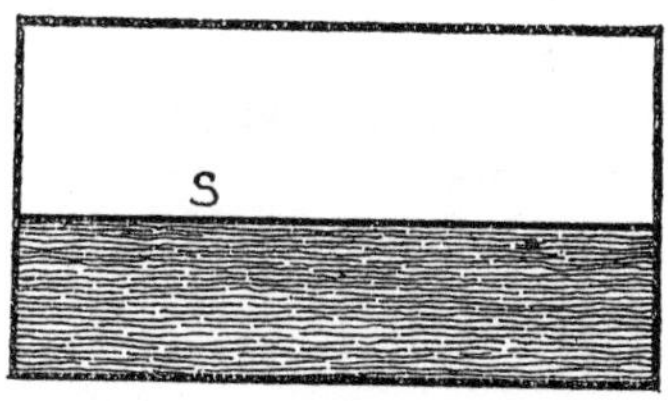

Fig. 10.

eye of the spectator, and is called the **Point of Sight,** or **Principal Point,** or **Centre of Vision,** but we will keep to the first of these.

If our picture plane is a sheet of glass, and is so placed that we can see the landscape behind it or a sea-view, we shall find that the distant line of the horizon passes through that point of sight, and we therefore draw a line on our picture which exactly corresponds with it, and which we call the **Horizontal-line** or **Horizon.**[1] The height of the horizon then depends entirely upon the position of the eye of the spectator: if he rises, so does the horizon; if he stoops or descends to lower ground, so does the horizon follow his movements. You may sit in a boat on a calm sea, and the horizon will be as low down as you are, or you may go to the top of a high cliff, and still the horizon will be on the same level as your eye.

[1] In a sea-view, owing to the rotundity of the earth, the real horizontal line is slightly below the sea line, which is noted in Chapter I.

This is an important line for the draughtsman to consider, for the effect of his picture greatly depends upon the position of the horizon. If you wish to give height and dignity to a mountain or a building, the horizon should be low down, so that these things may appear to tower above you. If you wish to show a wide expanse of landscape, then you must survey it from a height. In a composition of figures, you select your horizon according to the subject, and with a view to help the grouping. Again, in portraits and decorative work to be placed high up, a low horizon is desirable, but I have already spoken of this subject in the chapter on the necessity of the study of perspective.

III

Point of Distance

Fig. 11. The distance of the spectator from the picture is of great importance; as the distortions and disproportions arising from too near a view are to be avoided, the object of drawing being to make things look natural; thus, the floor should look level, and not as if it were running up hill—the top of a table flat, and not on a slant, as if cups and what not, placed upon it, would fall off.

In this figure we have a geometrical or ground plan of two squares at different distances from the picture, which is represented by the line KK. The spectator is first at A, the corner of the near square A*cd*. If from A we draw a diagonal of that square and produce it to the line KK (which may represent the horizontal-line in the picture), where it intersects that line at A· marks the distance that the spectator is from the point of sight S. For it will be seen that line SA equals line SA·. In like manner, if the spectator is at B, his distance from the point S is also found on the horizon by means of the diagonal BB′, so that all lines or diagonals at 45° are drawn to the point of distance (see Rule 6).

Figs. 12 and 13. In these two figures the difference is shown between the effect of the short-distance point A· and the long-distance point B·; the first, A*cd*, does not appear to lie so flat on the ground as the second square, B*ef*.

From this it will be seen how important it is to choose the

right point of distance: if we take it too near the point of sight, as in Fig. 12, the square looks unnatural and distorted. This,

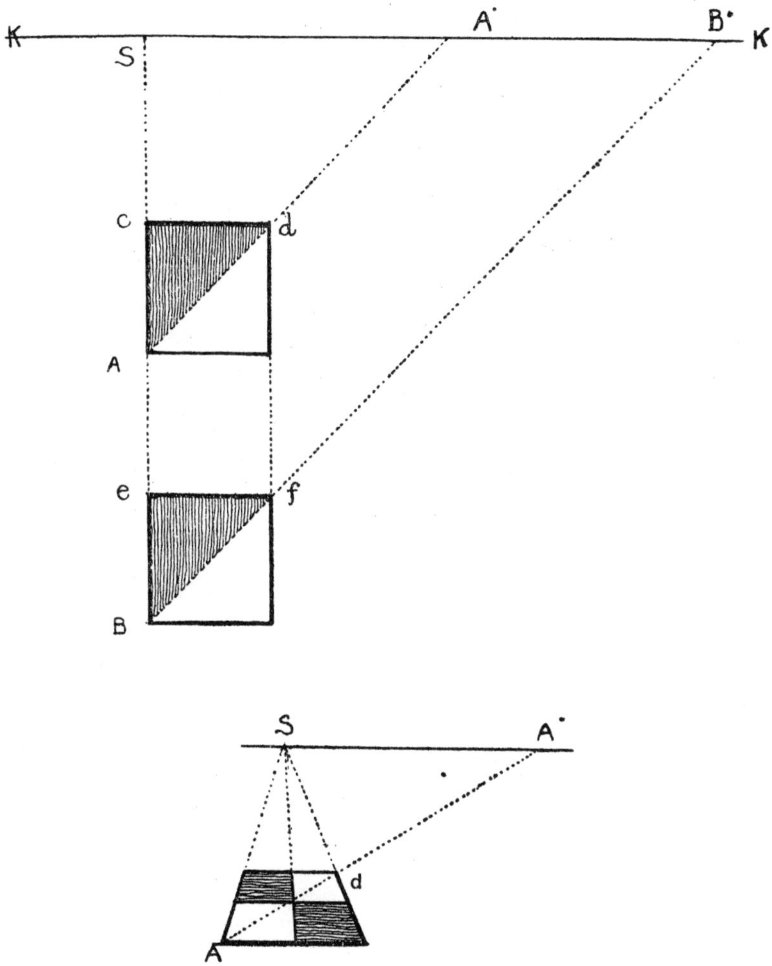

FIG. 12.

I may note, is a common fault with photographs taken with a wide-angle lens, which throws everything out of proportion, and will make the east end of a church or a cathedral appear higher than the steeple or tower; but as soon as we make our line of distance sufficiently long, as at Fig. 13, objects take their right proportions and no distortion is noticeable.

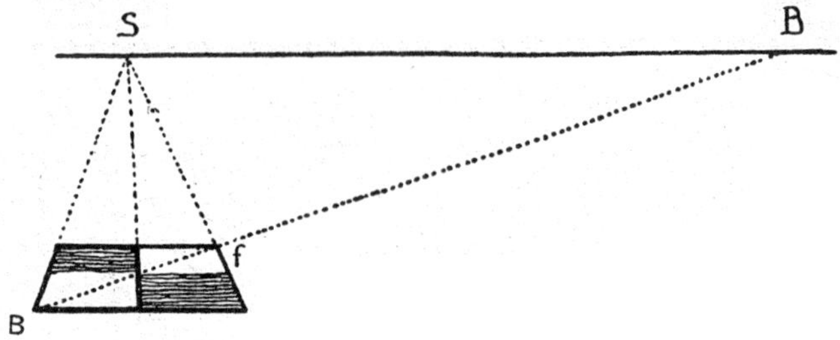

FIG. 13.

In some books on perspective we are told to make the angle of vision 60°, so that the distance SD (Fig. 14) is to be rather less than the length or height of the picture, as at A. The French recommend an angle of 28°, and to make the distance about double the length of the picture, as at B (Fig. 15), which is far more agreeable. For we must remember that the distance-point is not only the point from which we are supposed to make our tracing on the vertical transparent plane, or a point transferred

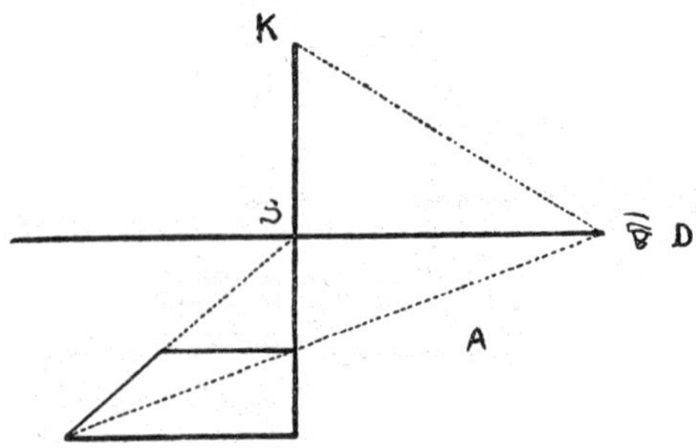

FIG. 14.

to the horizon to make our measurements by, but it is also the point in front of the canvas that we view the picture from, called the station-point. It is ridiculous, then, to have it so close that we must almost touch the canvas with our noses before we can see its perspective properly.

Now a picture should look right from whatever distance we

view it, even across the room or gallery, and of course in decorative work and in scene-painting a long distance is necessary.

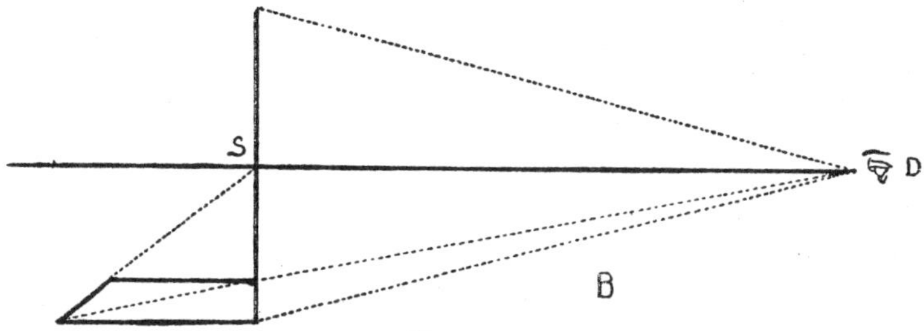

FIG. 15.

We need not, however, tie ourselves down to any hard and fast rule, but should choose our distance according to the impression

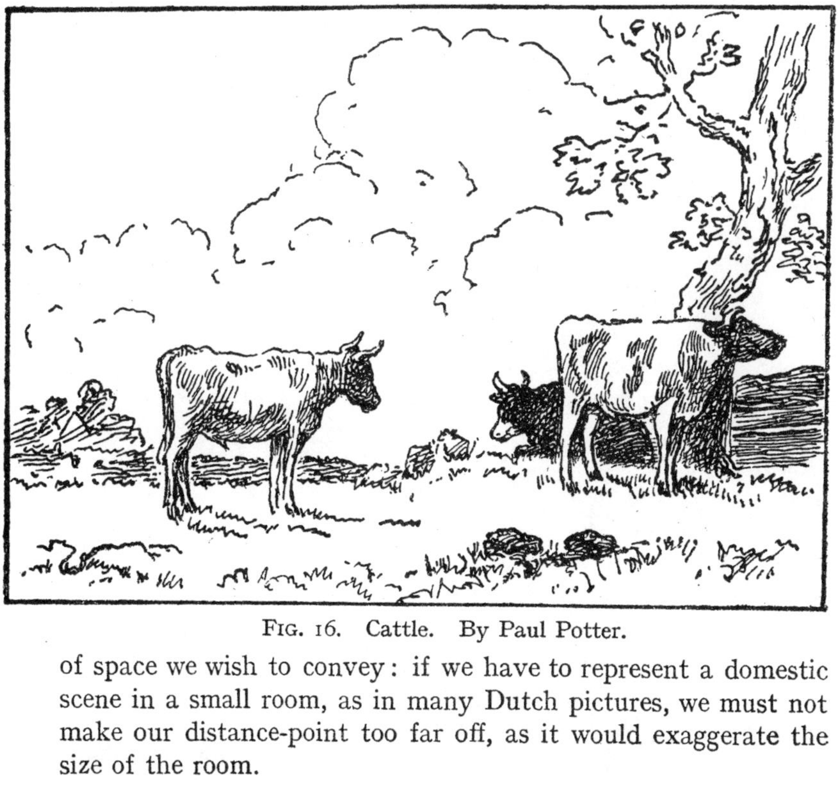

FIG. 16. Cattle. By Paul Potter.

of space we wish to convey: if we have to represent a domestic scene in a small room, as in many Dutch pictures, we must not make our distance-point too far off, as it would exaggerate the size of the room.

The height of the horizon is also an important consideration in the composition of a picture, and so also is the position of the point of sight, as we shall see farther on.

In landscape and cattle pictures a low horizon often gives space and air, as in this sketch from a picture by Paul Potter—where the horizontal-line is placed at one quarter the height of the canvas. Indeed, a judicious use of the laws of perspective is a great aid to composition, and no picture ever looks right unless these laws are attended to. At the present time too little attention is paid to them; the consequence is that much of the art of the day reflects in a great measure the monotony of the snap-shot camera, with its everyday and wearisome commonplace.

IV

Perspective of a Point, Visual Rays, &c.

We perceive objects by means of the visual rays, which are imaginary straight lines drawn from the eye to the various points of the thing we are looking at. As those rays proceed from the pupil of the eye, which is a circular opening, they form themselves into a cone called the **Optic Cone,** the base of which increases in proportion to its distance from the eye, so that the larger the view which we wish to take in, the farther must we be removed from it. The diameter of the base of this cone, with the visual rays drawn from each of its extremities to the eye, form the angle of vision, which is wider or narrower according to the distance of this diameter.

Now let us suppose a visual ray EA to be directed to some small object on the floor, say the head of a nail, A (Fig. 17). If we interpose between this nail and our eye a sheet of glass, K, placed vertically on the floor, we continue to see the nail through the glass, and it is easily understood that its perspective appearance thereon is the point *a*, where the visual ray passes through it. If now we trace on the floor a line AB from the nail to the spot B, just under the eye, and from the point *o*, where this line passes through or under the glass, we raise a perpendicular *o*S, that perpendicular passes through the precise point that the visual ray passes through. The line AB traced on the floor is the horizontal trace of the visual ray, and it will be seen that the point *a* is situated on the vertical raised from this horizontal trace.

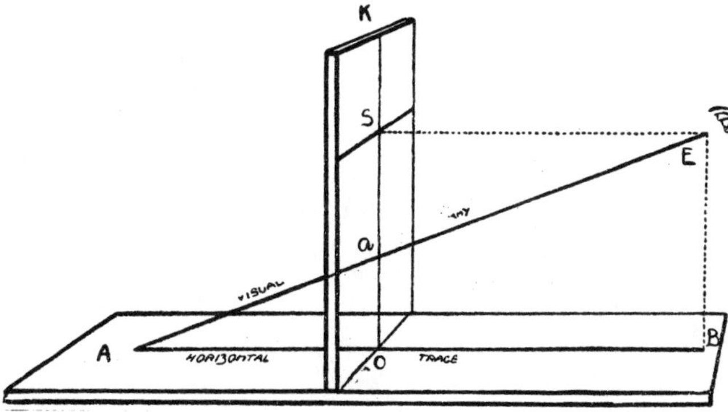

FIG. 17.

V

TRACE AND PROJECTION

If from any line A or B or C (Fig. 18), &c., we drop perpendiculars from different points of those lines on to a horizontal plane, the intersections of those verticals with the plane will be

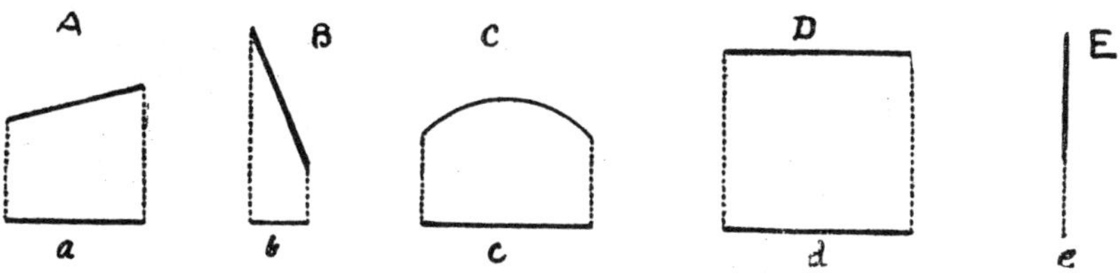

FIG. 18.

on a line called the horizontal trace or projection of the original line. We may liken these projections to sun-shadows when the sun is in the meridian, for it will be remarked that the trace does not represent the length of the original line, but only so much of it as would be embraced by the verticals dropped from each end of it, and although line A is the same length as line B its horizontal trace is longer than that of the other; that the projection of a curve (C) in this upright position is a straight line, that of a horizontal line (D) is equal to it, and the projection of a perpendicular or vertical (E) is a point only. The projections of lines or points can likewise be shown on a vertical plane, but in that case we draw lines parallel to the horizontal plane, and by this means we can get the position of a point in space; and by the assistance of perspective, as will be shown farther on, we can carry out the most difficult propositions of descriptive geometry and of the geometry of planes and solids.

The position of a point in space is given by its projection on a vertical and a horizontal plane—

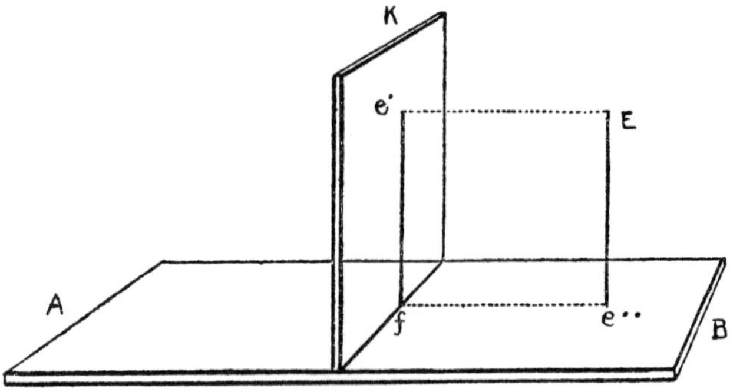

FIG. 19.

Thus *e·* is the projection of E on the vertical plane K, and *e··* is the projection of E on the horizontal plane; *fe··* is the horizontal trace of the plane *f*E, and *e·f* is the trace of the same plane on the vertical plane K.

VI

Scientific Definition of Perspective

The projections of the extremities of a right line which passes through a vertical plane being given, one on either side of it, to find the intersection of that line with the vertical plane. AE (Fig. 20) is the right line. The projection of its extremity A on the vertical plane is *a·*, the projection of E, the other extremity, is *e·*. AS is the horizontal trace of AE, and *a·e·* is its trace on the vertical plane. At point *f*, where the horizontal trace intersects the base B*c* of the vertical plane, raise perpendicular *f*P till it cuts *a*·*e*· at point P, which is the point required. For it is at the same time on the given line AE and the vertical plane K.

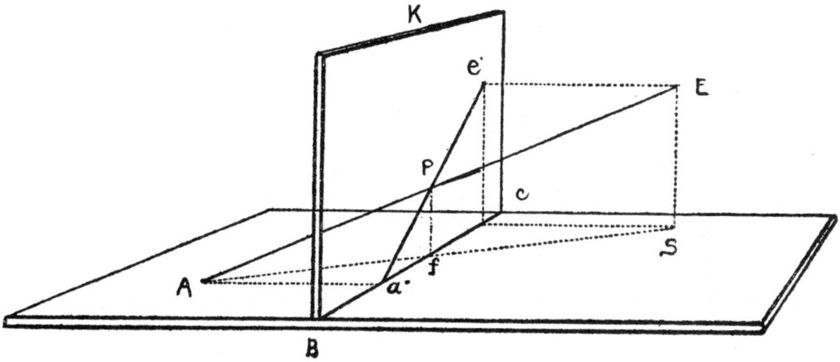

FIG. 20.

This figure is similar to the previous one, except that the extremity A of the given line is raised from the ground, but the same demonstration applies to it.

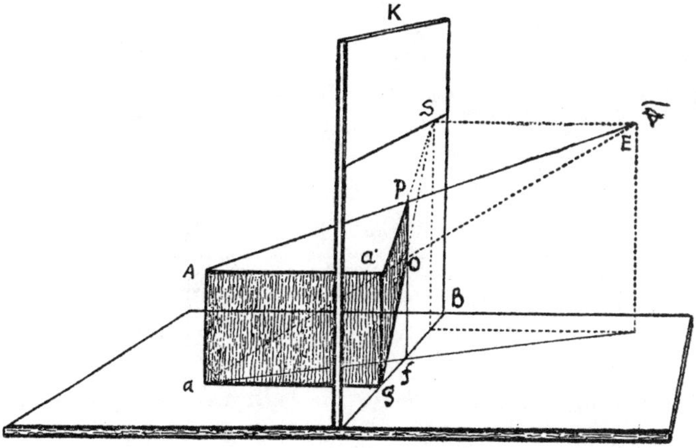

FIG. 21.

And now let us suppose the vertical plane K to be a sheet of glass, and the given line AE to be the visual ray passing from

the eye to the object A on the other side of the glass. Then if E is the eye of the spectator, its projection on the picture is S, the point of sight.

If I draw a dotted line from E to little *a*, this represents another visual ray, and *o*, the point where it passes through the picture, is the perspective of little *a*. I now draw another line from *g* to S, and thus form the shaded figure *ga*·P*o*, which is the perspective of *a*A*a*·*g*.

Let it be remarked that in the shaded perspective figure the lines *a*·P and *go* are both drawn towards S, the point of sight, and that they represent parallel lines A*a*· and *ag*, which are at right angles to the picture plane. This is the most important fact in perspective, and will be more fully explained farther on, when we speak of retreating or so-called vanishing lines.

RULES

VII

The Rules and Conditions of Perspective

The conditions of linear perspective are somewhat rigid. In the first place, we are supposed to look at objects with one eye only; that is, the visual rays are drawn from a single point, and not from two. Of this we shall speak later on. Then again, the eye must be placed in a certain position, as at E (Fig. 22), at a given height from the ground, S·E, and at a given distance from the picture, as SE. In the next place, the picture or picture plane itself must be vertical and perpendicular to the ground or horizontal plane, which plane is supposed to be as level as a billiard-table, and to extend from the base line, *ef*, of the picture to the horizon, that is, to infinity, for it does not partake of the rotundity of the earth.

We can only work out our propositions and figures in space with mathematical precision by adopting such conditions as the above. But afterwards the artist or draughtsman may modify and suit them to a more elastic view of things; that is, he can make his figures separate from one another, instead of their outlines coming close together as they do when we look at them with only one eye. Also he will allow for the unevenness of the ground and the roundness of our globe; he may even move his head and his eyes, and use both of them, and in fact make himself

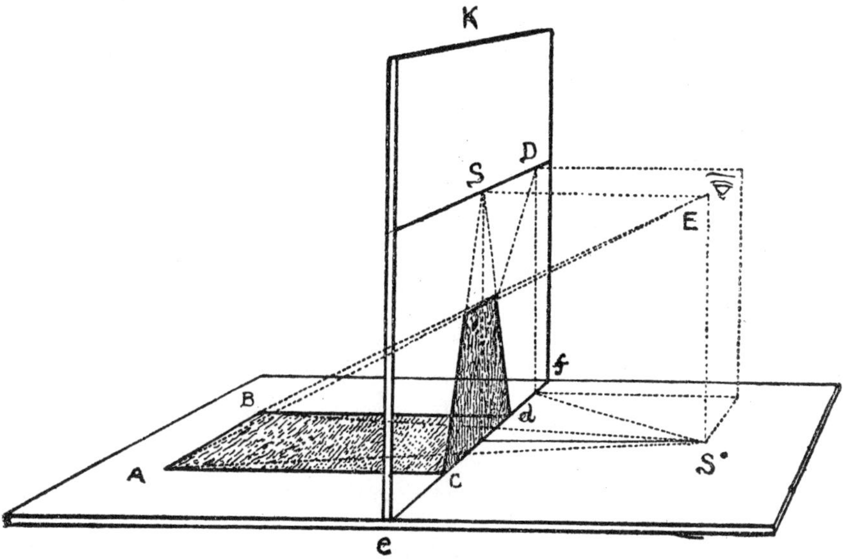

FIG. 22.

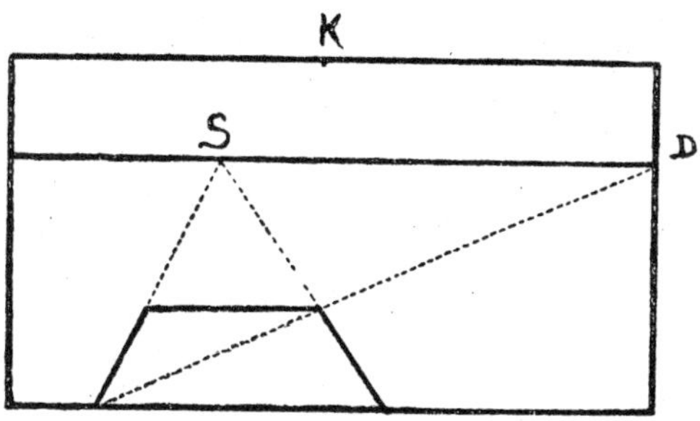

FIG. 23. Front view of above figure.

quite at his ease when he is out sketching, for Nature does all his perspective for him. At the same time, a knowledge of this rigid perspective is the sure and unerring basis of his freehand drawing.

Rule 1

All straight lines remain straight in their perspective appearance.[1]

Rule 2

Vertical lines remain vertical in perspective, and are divided in the same proportion as AB (Fig. 24), the original line, and *a·b·*, the perspective line, and if the one is divided at O the other is divided at *o·* in the same way.

It is not an uncommon error to suppose that the vertical lines of a high building should converge towards the top; so they

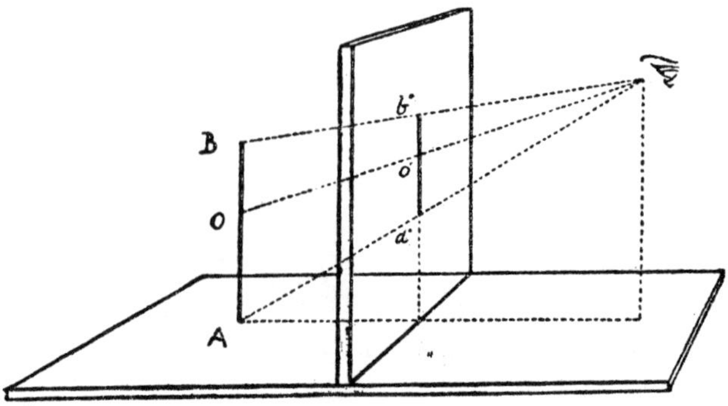

Fig. 24.

would if we stood at the foot of that building and looked up, for then we should alter the conditions of our perspective, and our point of sight, instead of being on the horizon, would be up in the sky. But if we stood sufficiently far away, so as to bring the whole of the building within our angle of vision, and the point of sight down to the horizon, then these same lines would appear perfectly parallel, and the different stories in their true proportion.

Rule 3

Horizontals parallel to the base of the picture are also parallel to that base in the picture. Thus *a·b·* (Fig. 25) is parallel to AB,

[1] Some will tell us that Nature abhors a straight line, that all long straight lines in space appear curved, &c., owing to certain optical conditions; but this is not apparent in short straight lines, so if our drawing is small it would be wrong to curve them; if it is large, like a scene or diorama, the same optical condition which applies to the line in space would also apply to the line in the picture.

and to GL, the base of the picture. Indeed, the same argument may be used with regard to horizontal lines as with verticals.

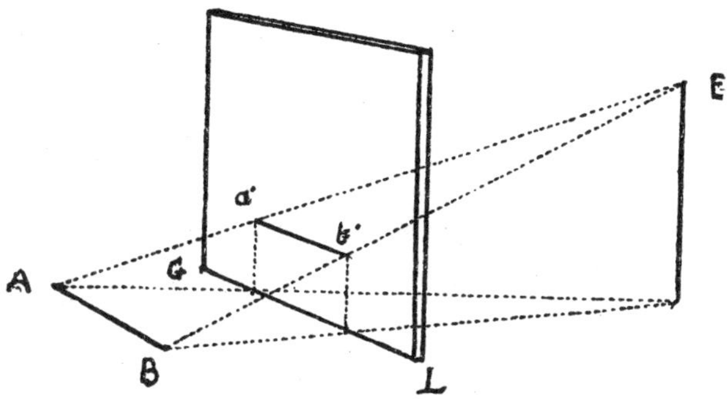

FIG. 25.

If we look at a straight wall in front of us, its top and its rows of bricks, &c., are parallel and horizontal; but if we look along it sideways, then we alter the conditions, and the parallel lines converge to whichever point we direct the eye.

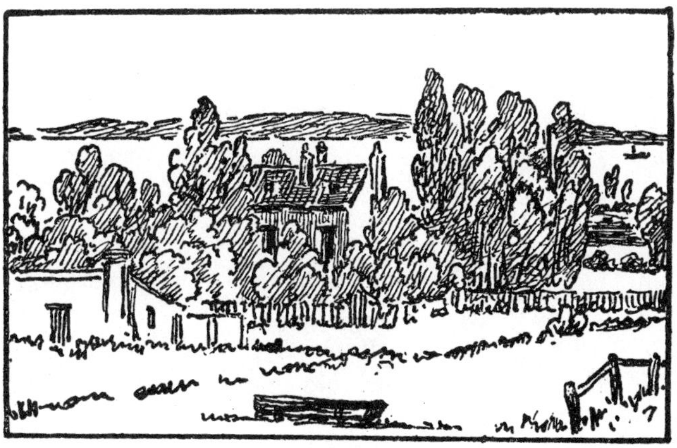

FIG. 26.

This rule is important, as we shall see when we come to the consideration of the perspective vanishing scale. Its use may be illustrated by this sketch, where the houses, walls, &c., are parallel to the base of the picture. When that is the case, then objects exactly facing us, such as windows, doors, rows of boards, or of bricks or palings, &c., are drawn with their horizontal lines parallel to the base; hence it is called parallel perspective.

RULE 4

All lines situated in a plane that is parallel to the picture plane diminish in proportion as they become more distant, but do not undergo any perspective deformation; and remain in the same relation and proportion each to each as the original lines. This is called the front view.

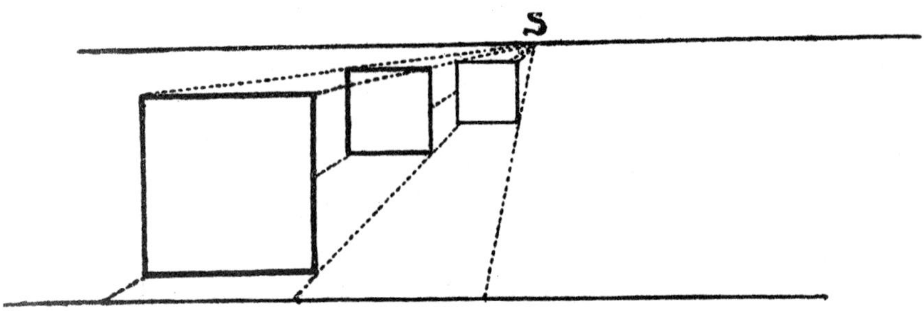

FIG. 27.

RULE 5

All horizontals which are at right angles to the picture plane are drawn to the point of sight.

Thus the lines AB and CD (Fig. 28) are horizontal or parallel to the ground plane, and are also at right angles to the picture plane K. It will be seen that the perspective lines B*a*', DC', must, according to the laws of projection, be drawn to the point of sight.

This is the most important rule in perspective (see Fig. 7 at beginning of Definitions).

An arrangement such as there indicated is the best means of illustrating this rule. But instead of tracing the outline of the square or cube on the glass, as there shown, I have a hole drilled through at the point S (Fig. 29), which I select for the point of sight, and through which I pass two loose strings A and B, fixing their ends at S.

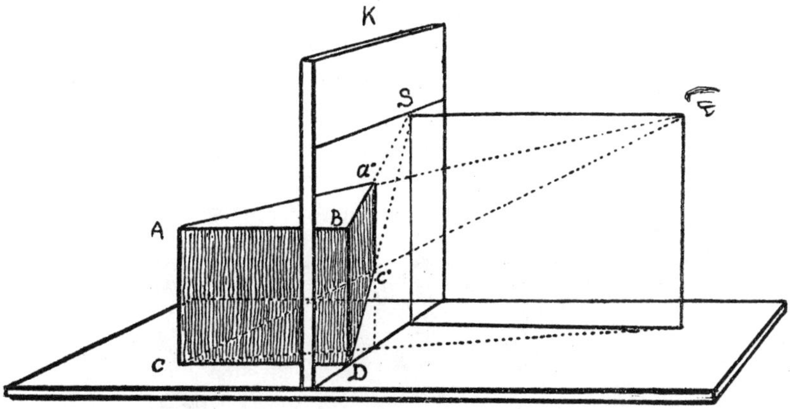

FIG. 28.

As SD represents the distance the spectator is from the glass or picture, I make string SA equal in length to SD. Now if the pupil takes this string in one hand and holds it at right angles to the

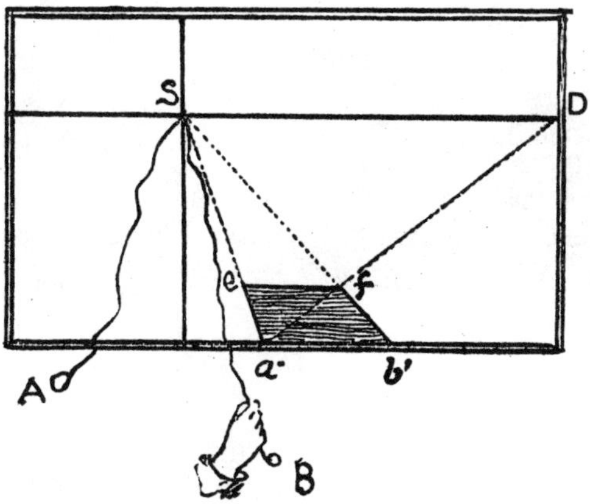

FIG. 29.

glass, that is, exactly in front of S, and then places one eye at the end A (of course with the string extended), he will be at the proper distance from the picture. Let him then take the other string, SB, in the other hand, and apply it to point *b′* where the square touches the glass, and he will find that it exactly tallies with the side *b′f* of the square *a·b′fe*. If he applies the same string to *a·*, the other corner of the square, his string will exactly tally or cover the side *a·e*, and he will thus have ocular demonstration of this important rule.

In this little picture (Fig. 30) in parallel perspective it will be seen that the lines which retreat from us at right angles to the picture plane are directed to the point of sight S.

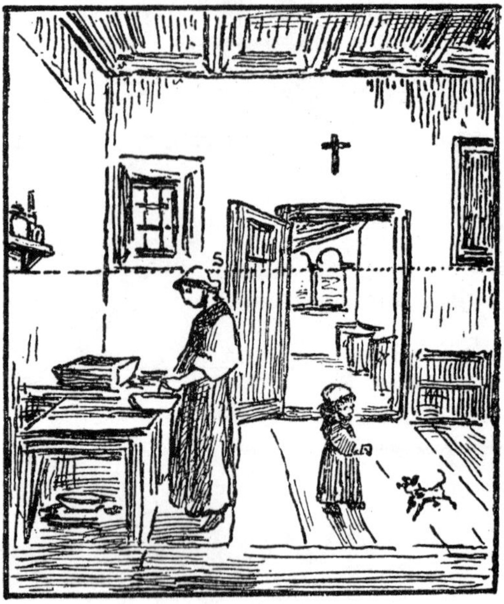

FIG. 30.

RULE 6

All horizontals which are at 45°, or half a right angle to the picture plane, are drawn to the point of distance.

We have already seen that the diagonal of the perspective square, if produced to meet the horizon on the picture, will mark on that horizon the distance that the spectator is from the point of sight (see definition, p. 16). This point of distance becomes then the measuring point for all horizontals at right angles to the picture plane.

Thus in Fig. 31 lines AS and BS are drawn to the point of sight S, and are therefore at right angles to the base AB. AD being drawn to D (the distance-point), is at an angle of 45° to the base AB, and AC is therefore the diagonal of a square. The line 1C is made parallel to AB, consequently A1CB is a square in perspective. The line BC, therefore, being one side of that square, is equal to

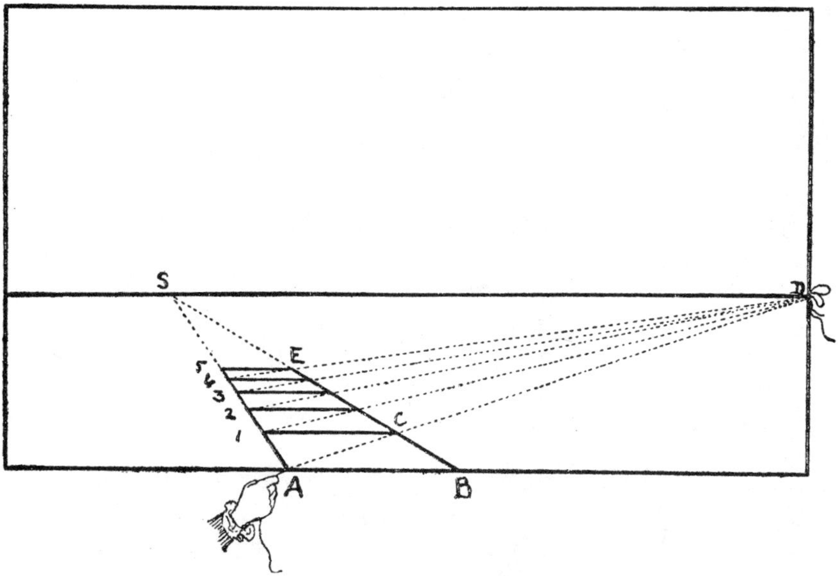

FIG. 31.

AB, another side of it. So that to measure a length on a line drawn to the point of sight, such as BS, we set out the length required, say BA, on the base-line, then from A draw a line to the point of distance, and where it cuts BS at C is the length required. This can be repeated any number of times, say five, so that in this figure BE is five times the length of AB.

RULE 7

All horizontals forming any other angles but the above are drawn to some other points on the horizontal line. If the angle is greater than half a right angle (Fig. 32), as EBG, the point is within the point of distance, as at V′. If it is less, as ABV″, then it is beyond the point of distance, and consequently farther from the point of sight.

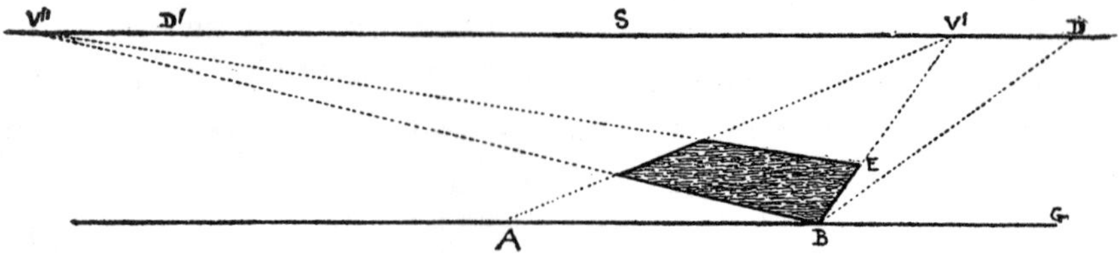

FIG. 32.

In Fig. 32, the dotted line BD, drawn to the point of distance D, is at an angle of 45° to the base AG. It will be seen that the line BV′ is at a greater angle to the base than BD; it is therefore drawn to a point V′, within the point of distance and nearer to the point of sight S. On the other hand, the line BV″ is at a more acute angle, and is therefore drawn to a point some way beyond the other distance point.

Note.—When this vanishing point is a long way outside the picture, the architects make use of a centrolinead, and the painters fix a long string at the required point, and get their perspective lines by that means, which is very inconvenient. But I will show you later on how you can dispense with this trouble by a very simple means, with equally correct results.

RULE 8

Lines which incline upwards have their vanishing points above the horizontal line, and those which incline downwards, below it. In both cases they are on the vertical which passes through the vanishing point (S) of their horizontal projections.

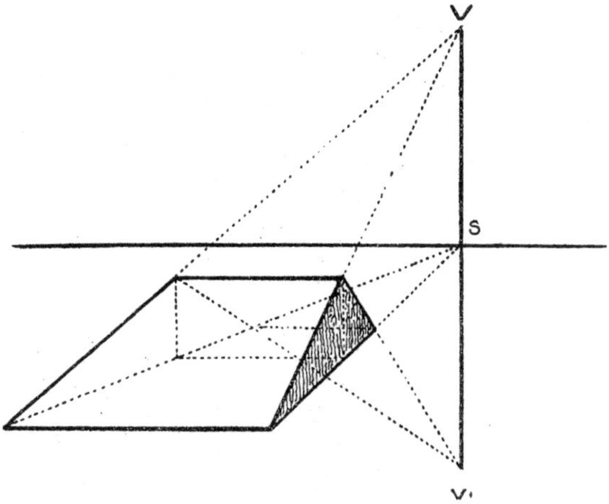

FIG. 33.

This rule is useful in drawing steps, or roads going uphill and downhill.

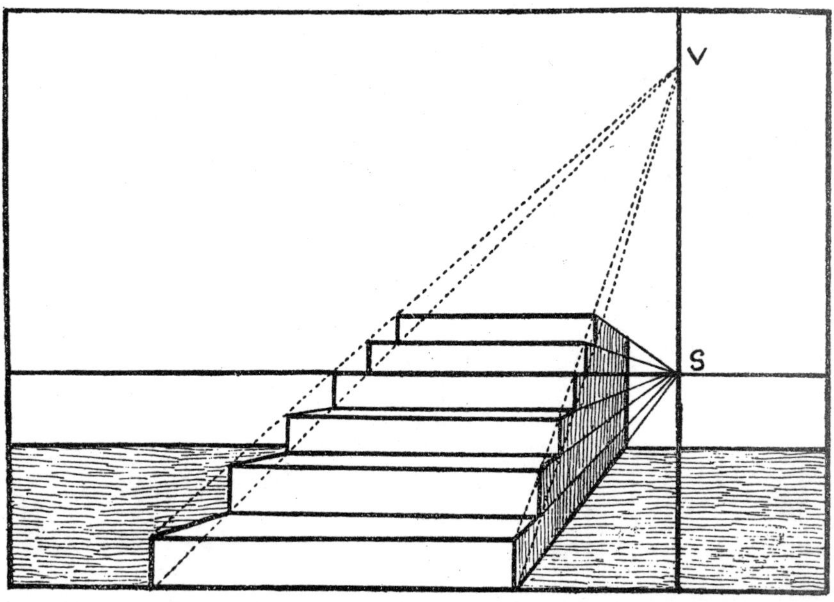

FIG. 34.

RULE 9

The farther a point is removed from the picture plane the nearer does its perspective appearance approach the horizontal line so long as it is viewed from the same position. On the

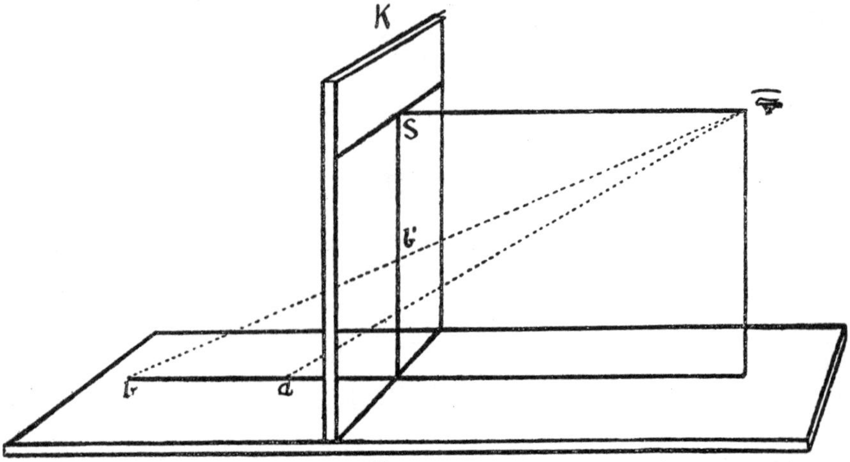

FIG. 35.

contrary, if the spectator retreats from the picture plane K (which we suppose to be transparent), the point remaining at the same place, the perspective appearance of this point will approach the ground-line in proportion to the distance of the spectator.

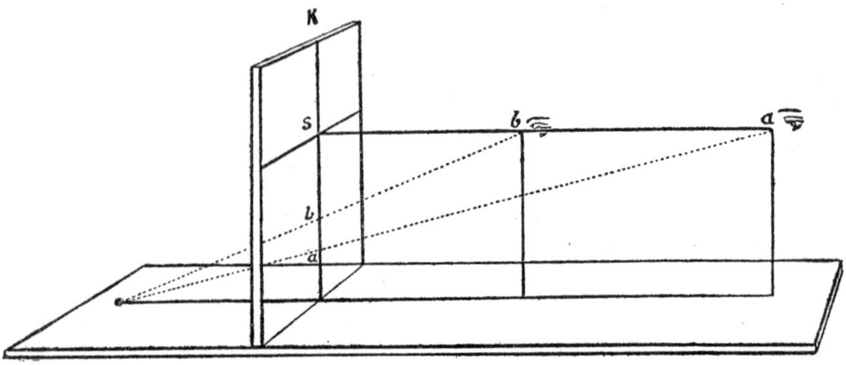

FIG. 36.

The spectator at two different distances from the picture.

Therefore the position of a given point in perspective above the ground-line or below the horizon is in proportion to the distance of the spectator from the picture, or the picture from the point.

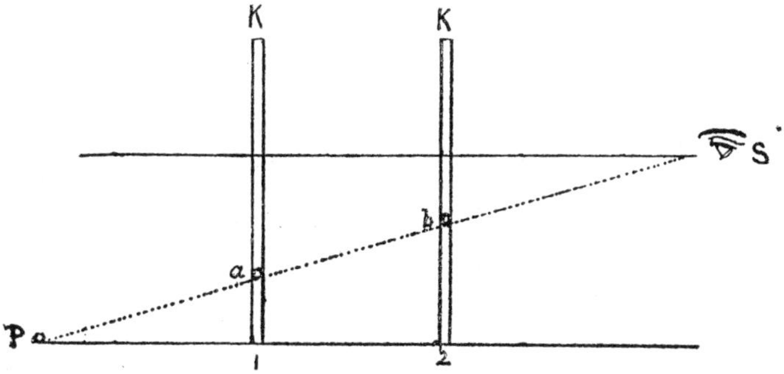

FIG. 37.

The picture at two different distances from the point.

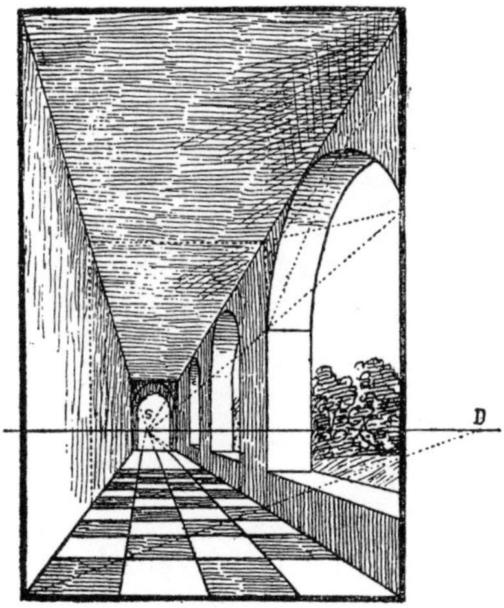

FIG. 38.

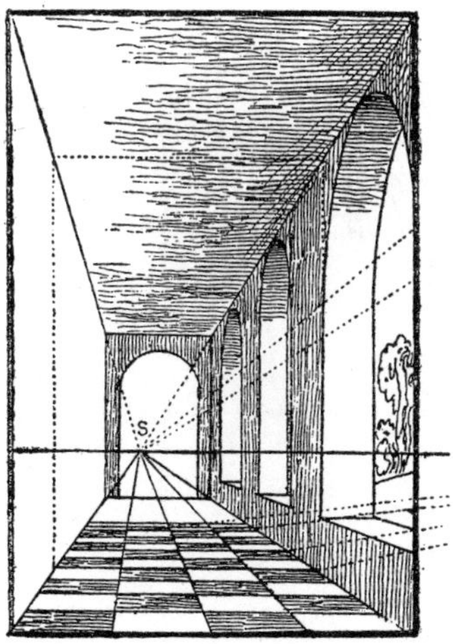

FIG. 39.

Figures 38 and 39 are two views of the same gallery from different distances. In Fig. 38, where the distance is too short, there is a want of proportion between the near and far objects, which is corrected in Fig. 39 by taking a much longer distance.

Rule 10

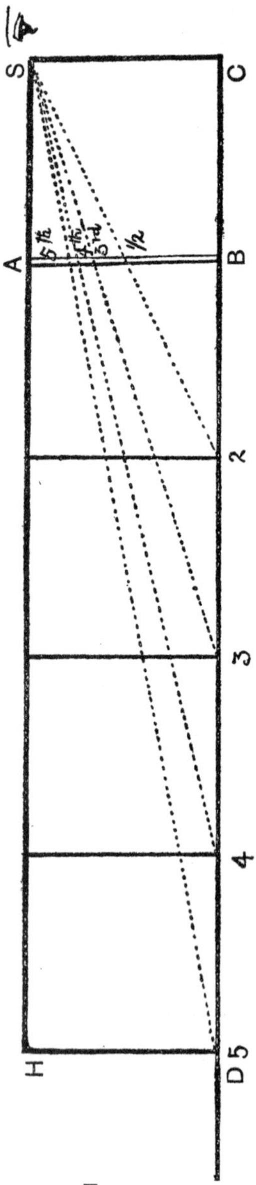

Fig. 40.

Horizontals in the same plane which are drawn to the same point on the horizon are parallel to each other.

This is a very important rule, for all our perspective drawing depends upon it. When we say that parallels are drawn to the same point on the horizon it does not imply that they meet at that point, which would be a contradiction; perspective parallels never reach that point, although they appear to do so. Fig. 40 will explain this.

Suppose S to be the spectator, AB a transparent vertical plane which represents the picture seen edgeways, and HS and DC two parallel lines, mark off spaces between these parallels equal to SC, the height of the eye of the spectator, and raise verticals 2, 3, 4, 5, &c., forming so many squares. Vertical line 2 viewed from S will appear on AB but half its length, vertical 3 will be only a third, vertical 4 a fourth, and so on, and if we multiplied these spaces *ad infinitum* we must keep on dividing the line AB by the same number. So if we suppose AB to be a yard high and the distance from one vertical to another to be also a yard, then if one of these were a thousand yards away its representation at AB would be the thousandth part of a yard, or ten thousand yards away, its representation at AB would be the ten-thousandth part, and whatever the distance it must always be something; and therefore HS and DC, however far they may be produced and however close they may appear to get, can never meet.

Fig. 41 is a perspective view of the same figure—but more extended. It will be seen that a line drawn from the tenth up-

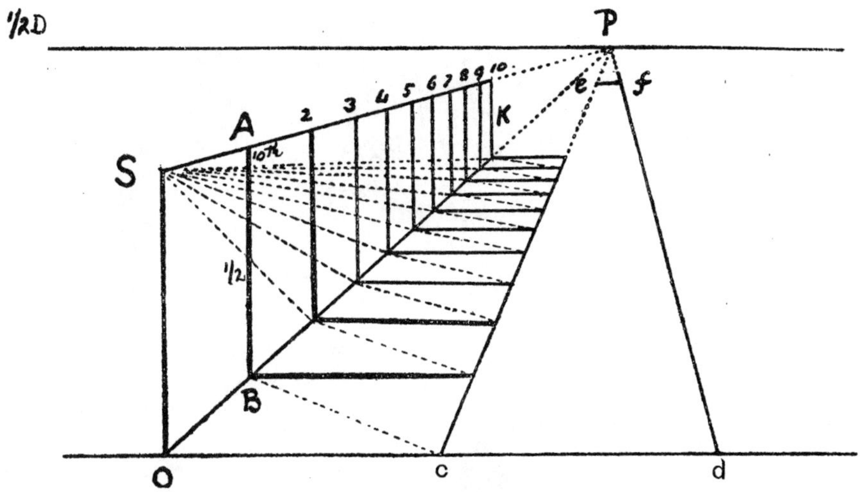

FIG. 41.

right K to S cuts off a tenth of AB. We look then upon these two lines SP, OP, as the sides of a long parallelogram of which SK is the diagonal, as *cefd*, the figure on the ground, is also a parallelogram.

The student can obtain for himself a further illustration of this rule by placing a looking-glass on one of the walls of his studio and then sketching himself and his surroundings as seen therein.

He will find that all the horizontals at right angles to the glass will converge to his own eye. This rule applies equally to lines which are at an angle to the picture plane as to those that are at right angles or perpendicular to it, as in Rule 7. It also applies to those on an inclined plane, as in Rule 8.

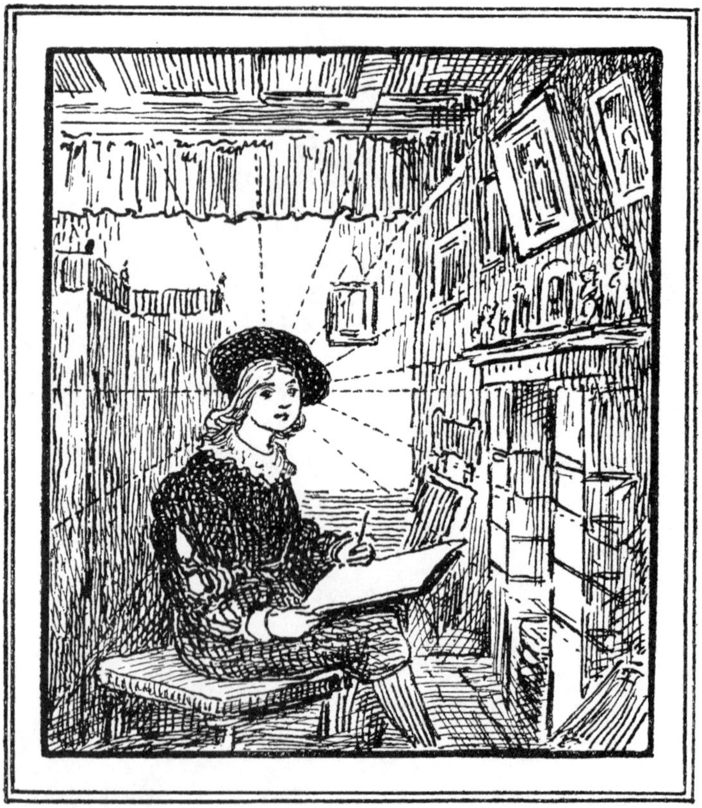

FIG. 42. Sketch of artist in studio.

With the above rules and a clear notion of the definitions and conditions of perspective, we should be able to work out any proposition or any new figure that may present itself. At any rate, a thorough understanding of these few pages will make the labour now before us simple and easy. I hope, too, it may be found interesting. There is always a certain pleasure in deceiving and being deceived by the senses, and in optical and other illusions, such as making things appear far off that are quite near, in making a picture of an object on a flat surface to look as if it stood out and in relief by a kind of magic. But there is, I think, a still greater pleasure than this, namely, in invention and in overcoming difficulties—in finding out how to do things for ourselves by our reasoning faculties, in originating or being original, as it were. Let us now see how far we can go in this respect.

VIII

A Table or Index of the Rules of Perspective

The rules here set down have been fully explained in the previous pages, and this table is simply for the student's ready reference.

Rule 1

All straight lines remain straight in their perspective appearance.

Rule 2

Vertical lines remain vertical in perspective.

Rule 3

Horizontals parallel to the base of the picture are also parallel to that base in the picture.

Rule 4

All lines situated in a plane that is parallel to the picture plane diminish in proportion as they become more distant, but do not undergo any perspective deformation. This is called the front view.

Rule 5

All horizontal lines which are at right angles to the picture plane are drawn to the point of sight.

Rule 6

All horizontals which are at 45° to the picture plane are drawn to the point of distance.

Rule 7

All horizontals forming any other angles but the above are drawn to some other points on the horizontal line.

Rule 8

Lines which incline upwards have their vanishing points above the horizon, and those which incline downwards, below it. In both cases they are on the vertical which passes through the vanishing point of their ground-plan or horizontal projections.

Rule 9

The farther a point is removed from the picture plane the nearer does it appear to approach the horizon, so long as it is viewed from the same position.

Rule 10

Horizontals in the same plane which are drawn to the same point on the horizon are perspectively parallel to each other.

BOOK SECOND

THE PRACTICE OF PERSPECTIVE

In the foregoing book we have explained the theory or science of perspective; we now have to make use of our knowledge and to apply it to the drawing of figures and the various objects that we wish to depict.

The first of these will be a square with two of its sides parallel to the picture plane and the other two at right angles to it, and which we call

IX

The Square in Parallel Perspective

From a given point on the base line of the picture draw a line at right angles to that base. Let P be the given point on the

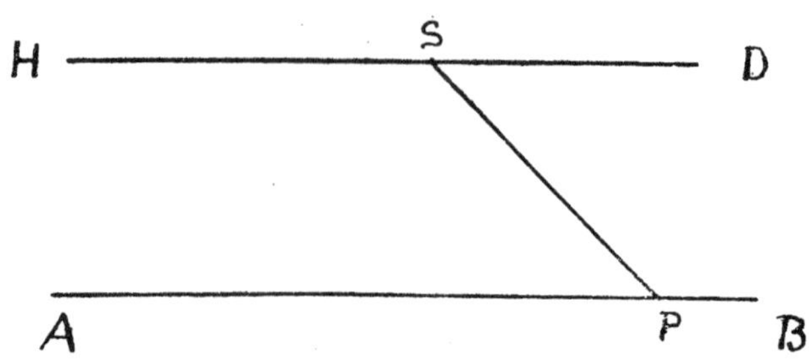

Fig. 43.

base line AB, and S the point of sight. We simply draw a line along the ground to the point of sight S, and this line will be at right angles to the base, as explained in Rule 5, and consequently angle APS will be equal to angle SPB, although it does not look so here. This is our first difficulty, but one that we shall soon get over.

In like manner we can draw any number of lines at right angles to the base, or we may suppose the point P to be placed

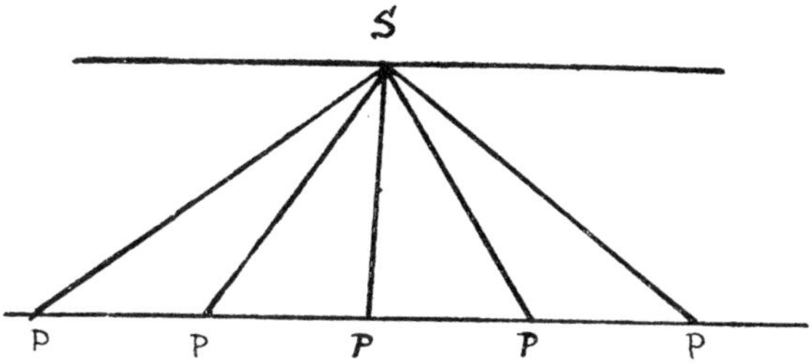

FIG. 44.

at so many different positions, our only difficulty being to conceive these lines to be parallel to each other. See Rule 10.

X

THE DIAGONAL

From a given point on the base line draw a line at 45°, or half a right angle, to that base. Let P be the given point. Draw

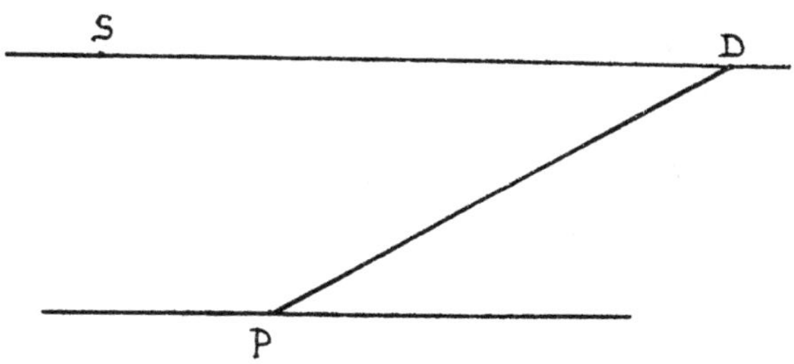

FIG. 45.

a line from P to the point of distance D and this line PD will be at an angle of 45°, or at the same angle as the diagonal of a square. See definitions.

XI

THE SQUARE

Draw a square in parallel perspective on a given length on the base line. Let *ab* be the given length. From its two extremities *a* and *b* draw *a*S and *b*S to the point of sight S. These two lines will be at right angles to the base (see Fig. 43). From *a* draw diagonal *a*D to point of distance D; this line will be 45°

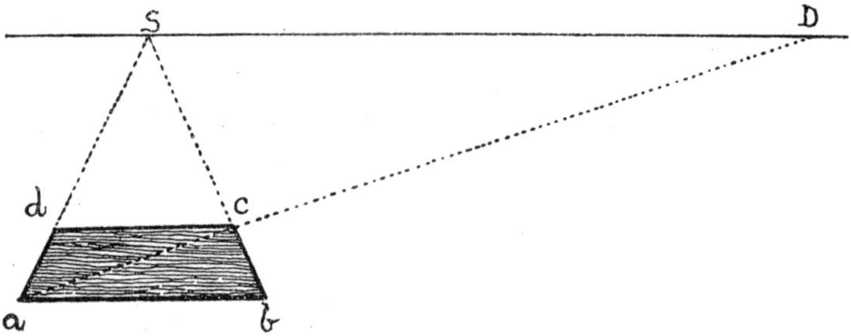

FIG. 46.

to base. At point *c*, where it cuts *b*S, draw *dc* parallel to *ab* and *abcd* is the square required.

We have here proceeded in much the same way as in drawing a geometrical square (Fig. 47), by drawing two lines AE and BC at right angles to a given line, AB, and from A, drawing the diagonal AC at 45° till it cuts BC at C, and then through C drawing EC parallel to AB. Let it be remarked that because the two

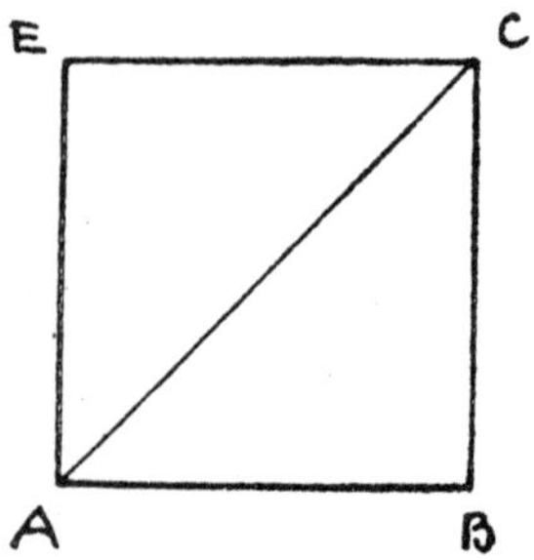

FIG. 47.

perspective lines (Fig. 48) AS and BS are at right angles to the base, they must consequently be parallel to each other, and therefore are perspectively equidistant, so that all lines parallel to AB and lying between them, such as *ad*, *cf*, &c., must be equal.

So likewise all diagonals drawn to the point of distance, which are contained between these parallels, such as A*d*, *af*, &c., must be equal. For all straight lines which meet at any point on the horizon are perspectively parallel to each other, just as two geometrical parallels crossing two others at any angle, as at

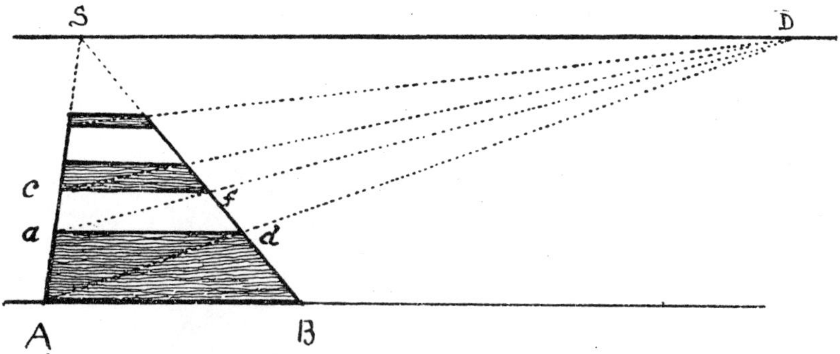

FIG. 48.

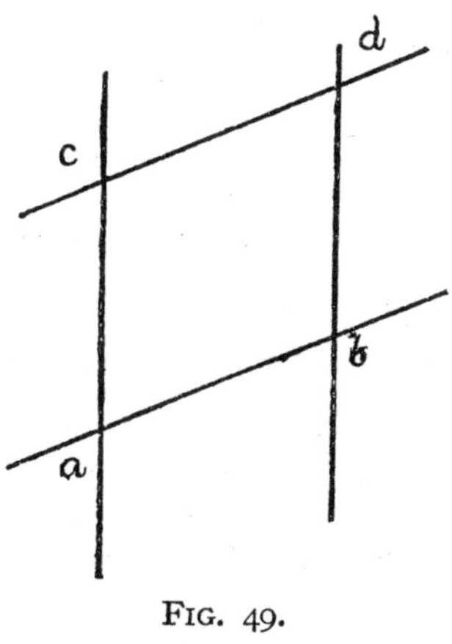

FIG. 49.

Fig. 49. Note also (Fig. 48) that all squares formed between the two vanishing lines AS, BS, and by the aid of these diagonals, are also equal, and further, that any number of squares such as are shown in this figure (Fig. 50), formed in the same way and having equal bases, are also equal; and the nine squares contained in the square *abcd* being equal, they divide each side of the larger square into three equal parts.

From this we learn how we can measure any number of given

lengths, either equal or unequal, on a vanishing or retreating line which is at right angles to the base; and also how we can

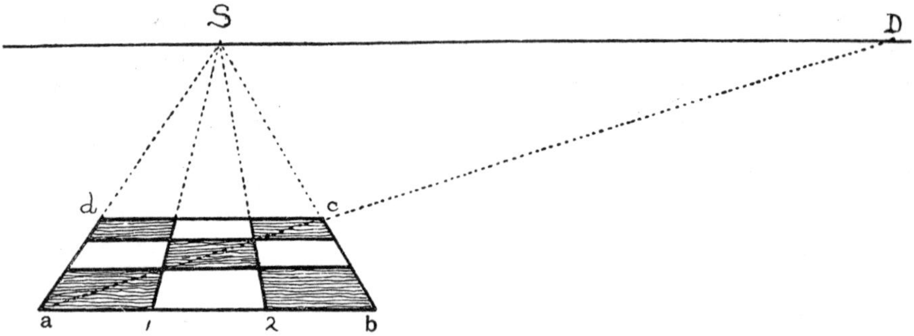

FIG. 50.

measure any width or number of widths on a line such as *dc*, that is, parallel to the base of the picture, however remote it may be from that base.

XII

GEOMETRICAL AND PERSPECTIVE FIGURES CONTRASTED

As at first there may be a little difficulty in realizing the resemblance between geometrical and perspective figures, and also about certain expressions we make use of, such as horizontals, perpendiculars, parallels, &c., which look quite different in perspective, I will here make a note of them and also place side by side the two views of the same figures.

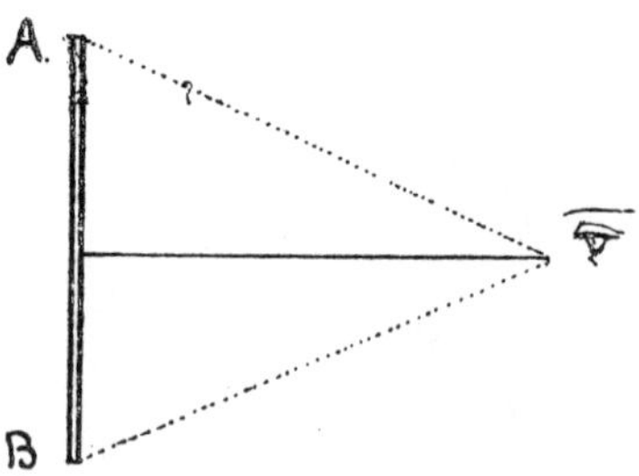

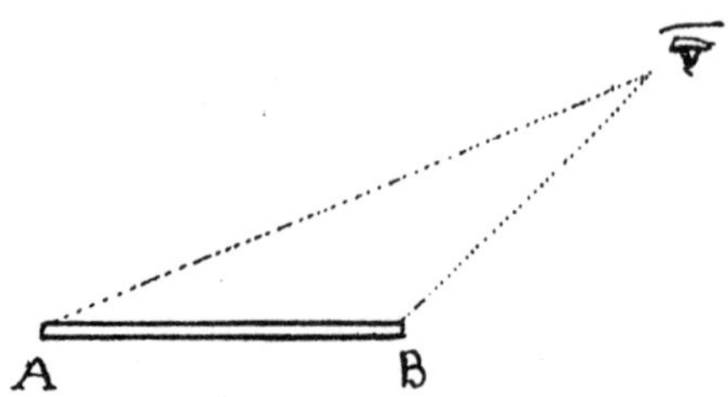

FIG. 51 A. The geometrical view. FIG. 51 B. The perspective view.

FIG. 51 C. A geometrical square.

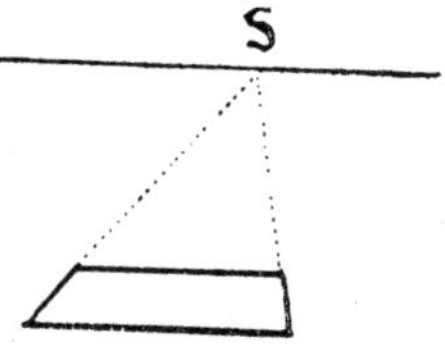

FIG. 51 D. A perspective square.

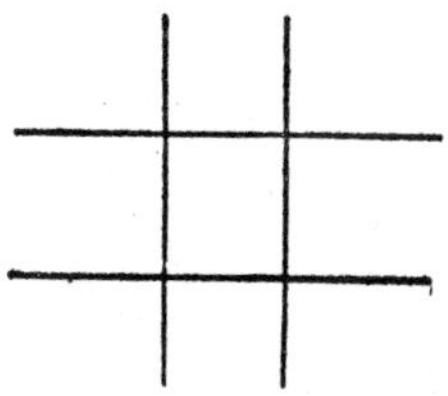

FIG. 51 E. Geometrical parallels.

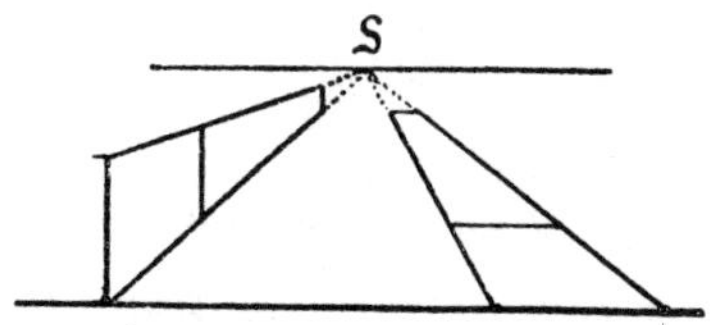

FIG. 51 F. Perspective parallels.

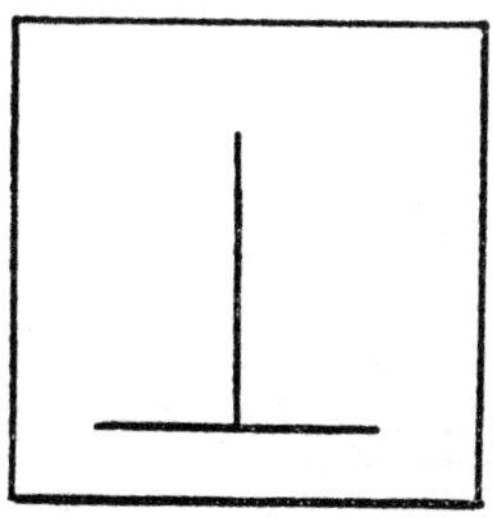

FIG. 51 G. Geometrical perpendicular.

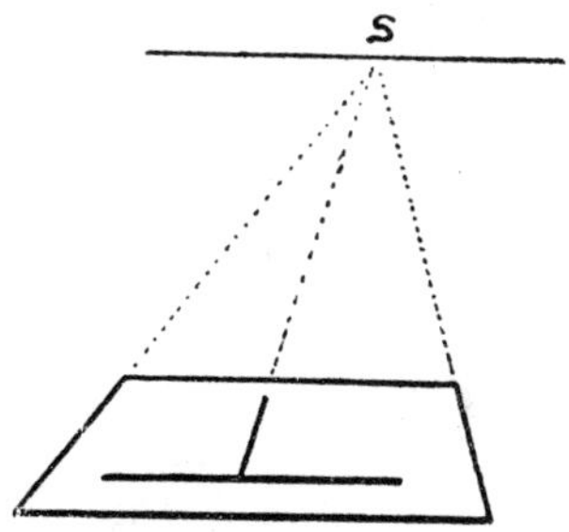

FIG. 51 H. Perspective perpendicular.

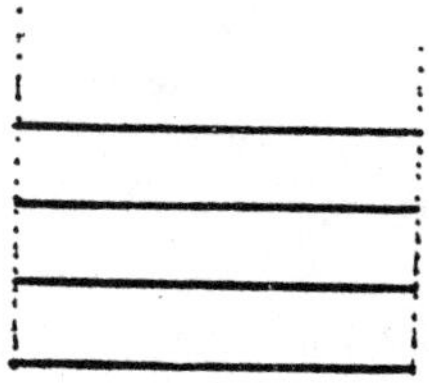

FIG. 51 I. Geometrical equal lines.

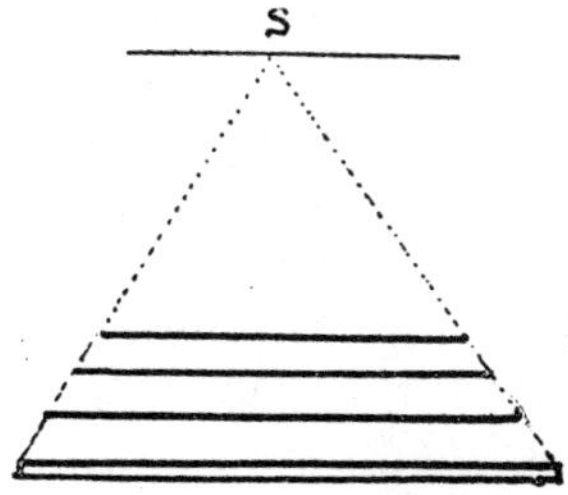

FIG. 51 J. Perspective equal lines.

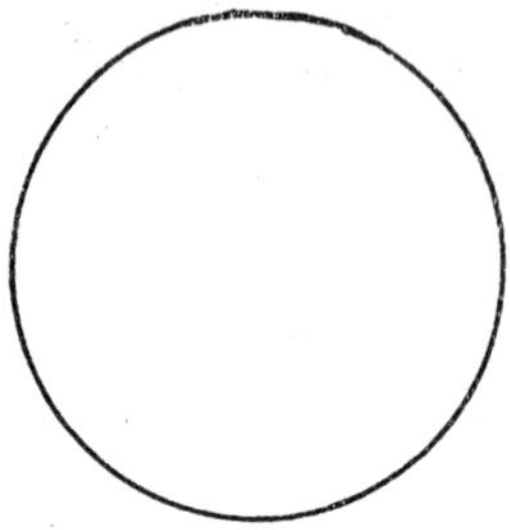

FIG. 51 K. A geometrical circle.

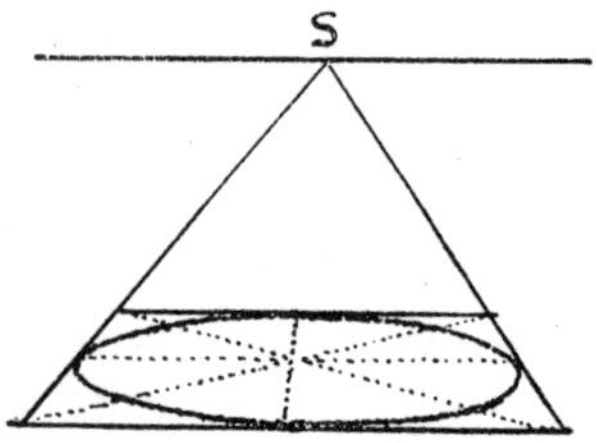

FIG. 51 L. A perspective circle.

XIII

OF CERTAIN TERMS MADE USE OF IN PERSPECTIVE

Of course when we speak of **Perpendiculars** we do not mean verticals only, but straight lines at right angles to other lines in any position. Also in speaking of **lines** a right or **straight line** is to be understood; or when we speak of **horizontals** we mean

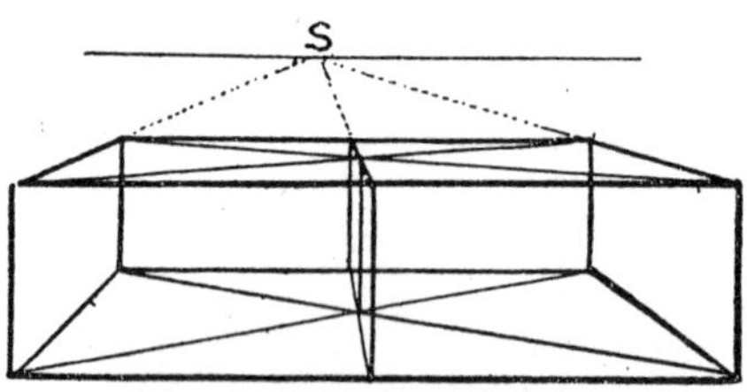

FIG. 52. Horizontals.

all straight lines that are parallel to the perspective plane, such as those on Fig. 52, no matter what direction they take so long as they are level. They are not to be confused with the horizon or horizontal-line.

There are one or two other terms used in perspective which are not satisfactory because they are confusing, such as vanishing lines and vanishing points. The French term, *fuyante* or *lignes fuyantes*, or going-away lines, is more expressive; and *point de fuite*, instead of vanishing point, is much better. I have occasionally called the former retreating lines, but the simple meaning is, lines that are not parallel to the picture plane; but a vanishing line implies a line that disappears, and a vanishing point implies a point that gradually goes out of sight. Still, it is difficult to alter terms that custom has endorsed. All we can do is to use as few of them as possible.

XIV

How to Measure Vanishing or Receding Lines

Divide a vanishing line which is at right angles to the picture plane into any number of given measurements. Let SA be the

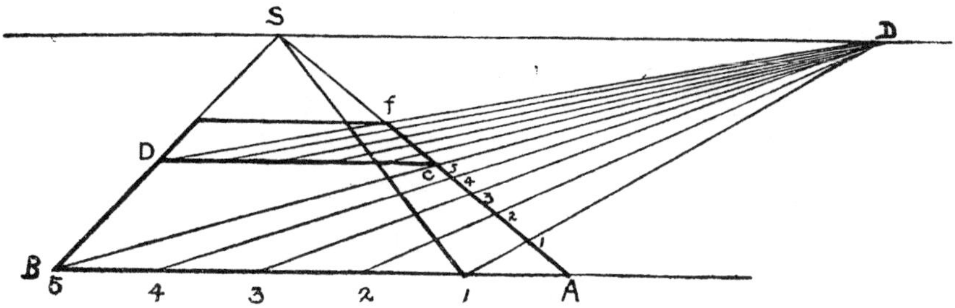

FIG. 53.

given line. From A measure off on the base line the divisions required, say five of 1 foot each; from each division draw diagonals to point of distance D, and where these intersect the line AC the corresponding divisions will be found. Note that as lines AB and AC are two sides of the same square they are necessarily equal, and so also are the divisions on AC equal to those on AB.

The line AB being the base of the picture, it is at the same time a perspective line and a geometrical one, so that we can use it as a scale for measuring given lengths thereon, but should there not be enough room on it to measure the required number we draw a second line, DC, which we divide in the same proportion and proceed to divide *cf*. This geometrical figure gives, as it were, a bird's-eye view or ground-plan of the above.

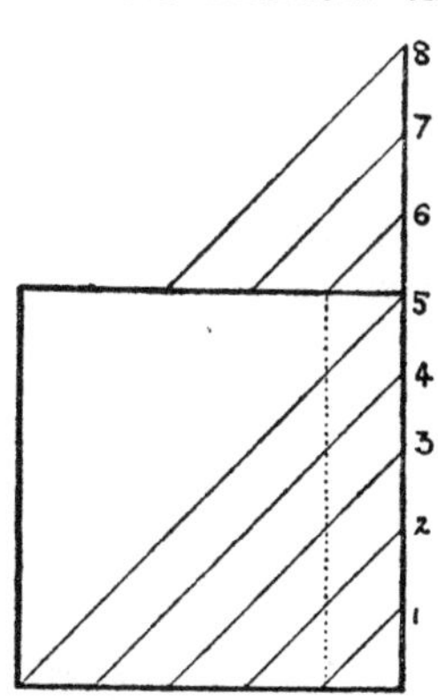

FIG. 54.

XV

How to Place Squares in Given Positions

Draw squares of given dimensions at given distances from the base line to the right or left of the vertical line, which passes through the point of sight.

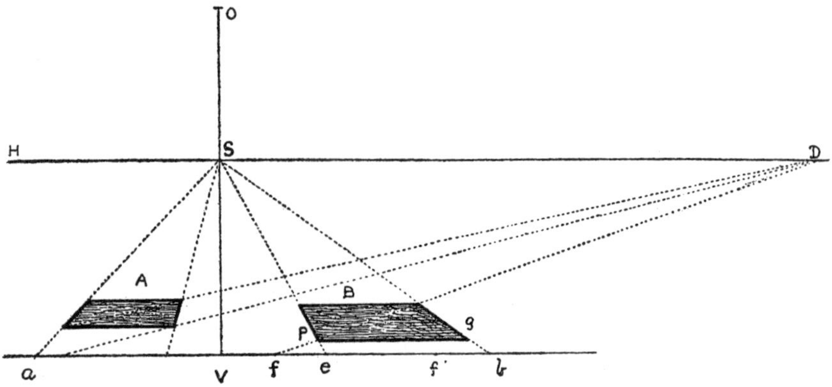

Fig. 55.

Let *ab* (Fig. 55) represent the base line of the picture divided into a certain number of feet; HD the horizon, VO the vertical. It is required to draw a square 3 feet wide, 2 feet to the right of the vertical, and 1 foot from the base.

First measure from V, 2 feet to *e*, which gives the distance from the vertical. Second, from *e* measure 3 feet to *b*, which gives the width of the square; from *e* and *b* draw *e*S, *b*S, to point of sight. From either *e* or *b* measure 1 foot to the left, to *f* or *f*·. Draw *f*D to point of distance, which intersects *e*S at P, and gives the required distance from base. Draw P*g* and B parallel to the base, and we have the required square.

Square A to the left of the vertical is 2½ feet wide, 1 foot from the vertical and 2 feet from the base, and is worked out in the same way.

Note.—It is necessary to know how to work to scale, especially in architectural drawing, where it is indispensable, but in working out our propositions and figures it is not always desirable. A given length indicated by a line is generally sufficient for our requirements. To work out every problem to scale is not only tedious and mechanical, but wastes time, and also takes the mind of the student away from the reasoning out of the subject.

XVI

How to Draw Pavements, &c.

Divide a vanishing line into parts varying in length.

Let BS· be the vanishing line: divide it into 4 long and 3 short spaces; then proceed as in the previous figure. If we draw

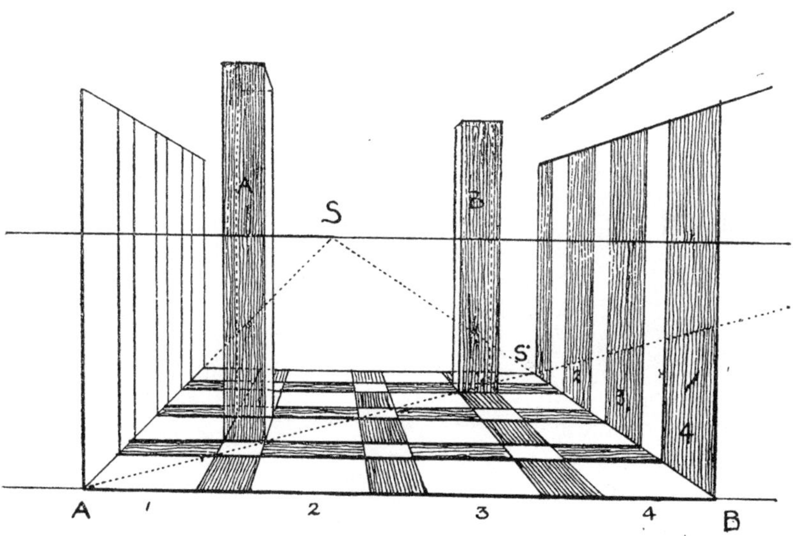

Fig. 56.

horizontals through the points thus obtained and from these raise verticals, we form, as it were, the interior of a building in which we can place pillars and other objects.

Or we can simply draw the plan of the pavement as in this figure.

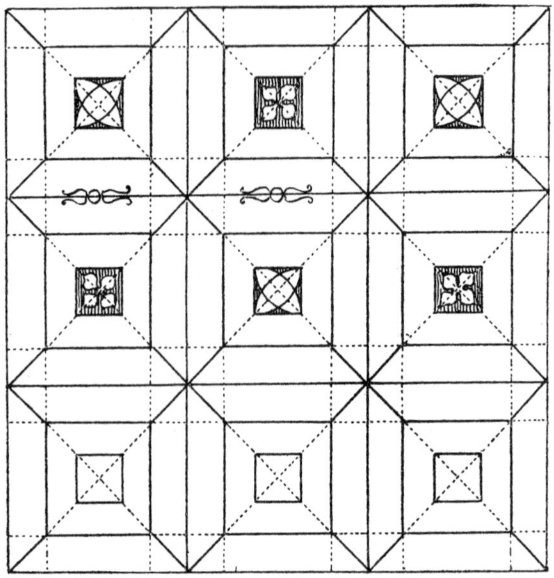

FIG. 57.

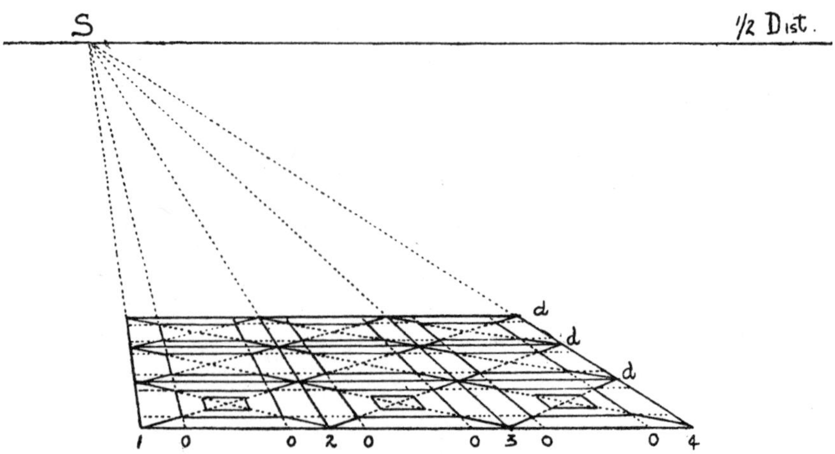

FIG. 58.

And then put it into perspective.

XVII

Of Squares placed Vertically and at Different Heights, or the Cube in Parallel Perspective

On a given square raise a cube.

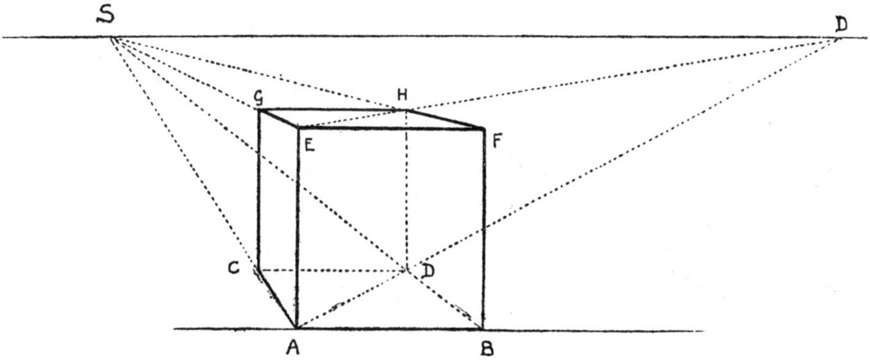

Fig. 59.

ABCD is the given square; from A and B raise verticals AE, BF, equal to AB; join EF. Draw ES, FS, to point of sight; from C and D raise verticals CG, DH, till they meet vanishing lines ES, FS, in G and H, and the cube is complete.

XVIII

The Transposed Distance

The transposed distance is a point D· on the vertical VD·, at exactly the same distance from the point of sight as is the point of distance on the horizontal line.

It will be seen by examining this figure that the diagonals of the squares in a vertical position are drawn to this vertical distance-point, thus saving the necessity of taking the measurements first on the base line, as at CB, which in the case of distant objects, such as the farthest window, would be very inconvenient. Note that the windows at K are twice as high as they are wide.

Of course these or any other objects could be made of any proportion.

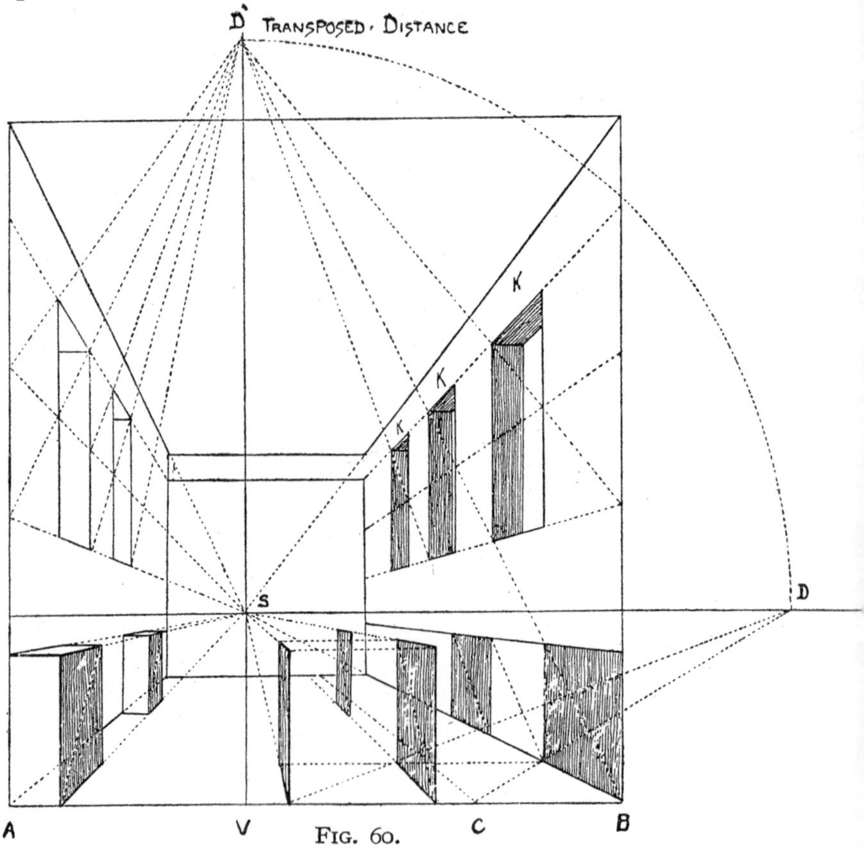

FIG. 60.

XIX

THE FRONT VIEW OF THE SQUARE AND OF THE PROPORTIONS OF FIGURES AT DIFFERENT HEIGHTS

According to Rule 4, all lines situated in a plane parallel to the picture plane diminish in length as they become more distant, but remain in the same proportions each to each as the original lines; as squares or any other figures retain the same form. Take the two squares ABCD, *abcd* (Fig. 61), one inside the other; although moved back from square EFGH they retain the same form. So in dealing with figures of different heights, such as statuary

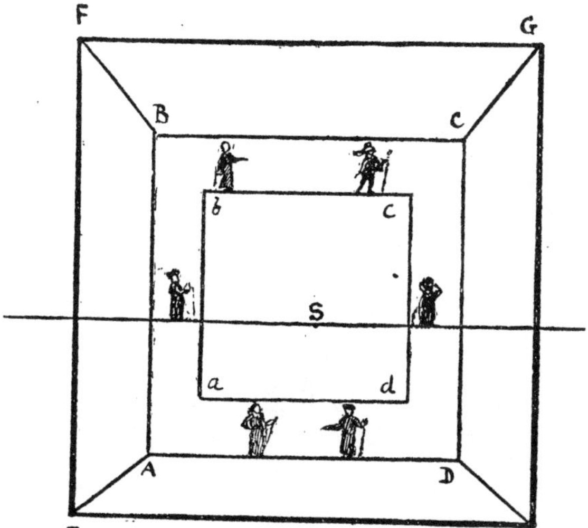

FIG. 61.

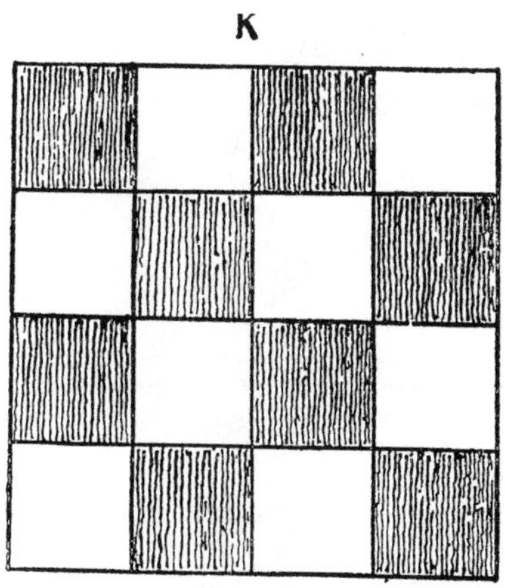

FIG. 62.

or ornament in a building, if actually equal in size, so must we represent them.

In this square K, with the checker pattern, we should not think of making the top squares smaller than the bottom ones; so it is with figures.

This subject requires careful study, for, as pointed out in our opening chapter, there are certain conditions under which

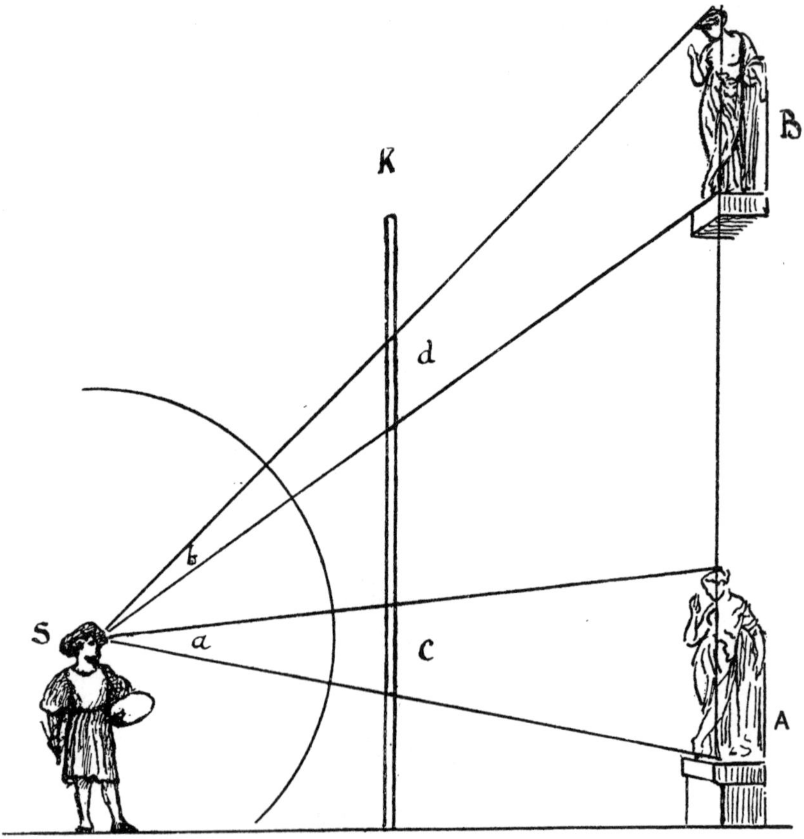

FIG. 63.

we have to modify and greatly alter this rule in large decorative work.

In Fig. 63 the two statues A and B are the same size. So if traced through a vertical sheet of glass, K, as at *c* and *d*, they would also be equal; but as the angle *b* at which the upper one is seen is smaller than angle *a*, at which the lower figure or statue is seen, it will appear smaller to the spectator (S) both in reality and in the picture.

But if we wish them to appear the same size to the spectator who is viewing them from below, we must make the angles *a* and *b* (Fig. 64), at which they are viewed, both equal. Then draw lines

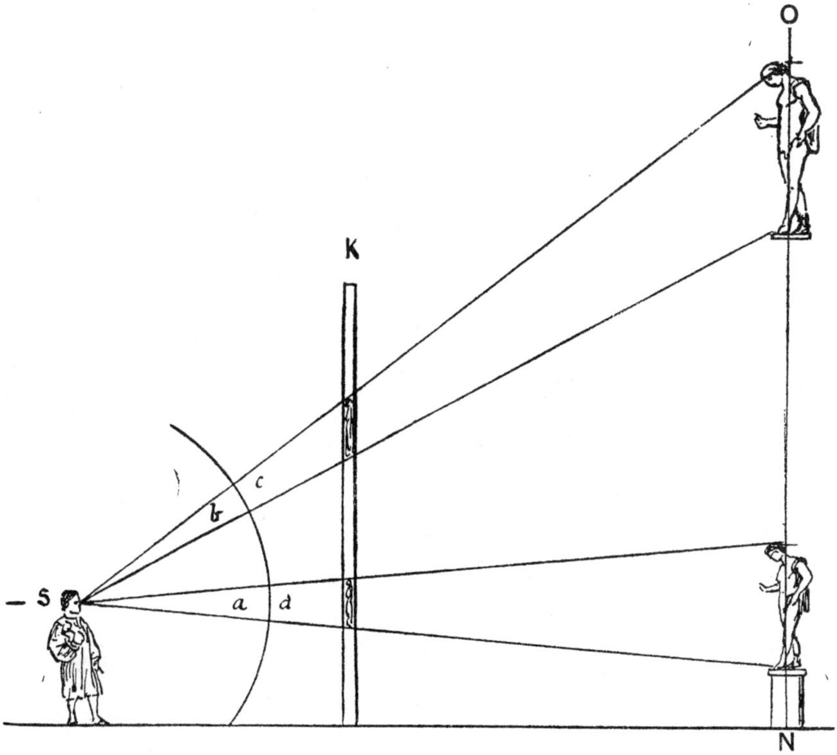

FIG. 64.

through equal arcs, as at *c* and *d*, till they cut the vertical NO (representing the side of the building where the figures are to be placed). We shall then obtain the exact size of the figure at that height, which will make it look the same size as the lower one, N. The same rule applies to the picture K, when it is of large proportions. As an example in painting, take Michelangelo's large altar-piece in the Sistine Chapel, 'The Last Judgement'; here the figures forming the upper group, with our Lord in judgement surrounded by saints, are about four times the size, that is, about twice the height, of those at the lower part of the fresco. The figures on the ceiling of the same chapel are studied not only according to their height from the pavement, which is 60 ft., but to suit the arched form of it. For instance, the head of the figure of Jonah at the end over the altar is thrown back in the design, but owing to the curvature in the architecture is actually more forward than the feet. Then again, the prophets and

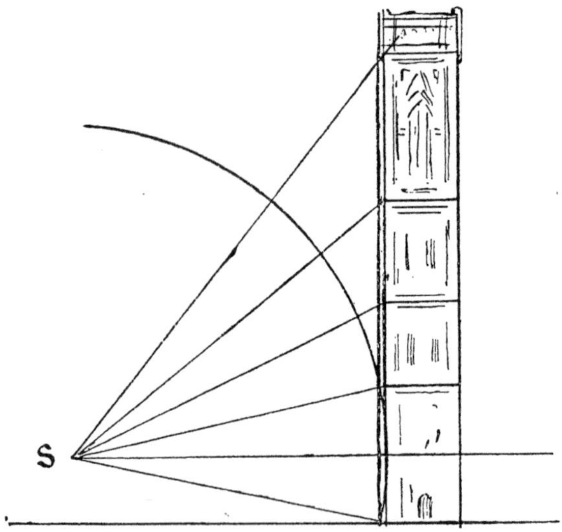

FIG. 65.

sybils seated round the ceiling, which are perhaps the grandest figures in the whole range of art, would be 18 ft. high if they stood up; these, too, are not on a flat surface, so that it required great knowledge to give them their right effect.

Of course, much depends upon the distance we view these statues or paintings from. In interiors, such as churches, halls, galleries, &c., we can make a fair calculation, such as the length of the nave, if the picture is an altar-piece—or say, half the length; so also with statuary in niches, friezes, and other architectural ornaments. The nearer we are to them, and the more we have to look up, the larger will the upper figures have to be; but if these are on the outside of a building that can be looked at from a long distance, then it is better not to have too great a difference.

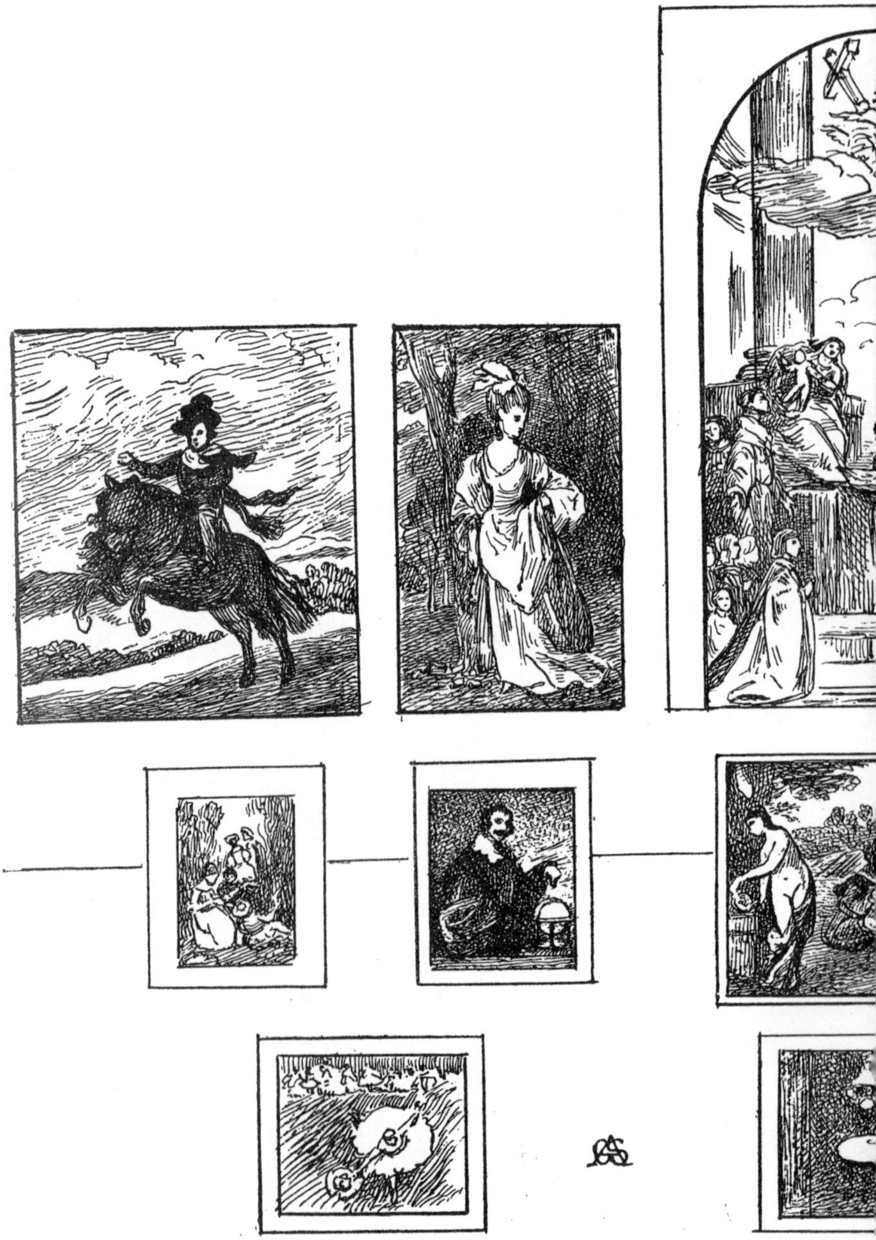

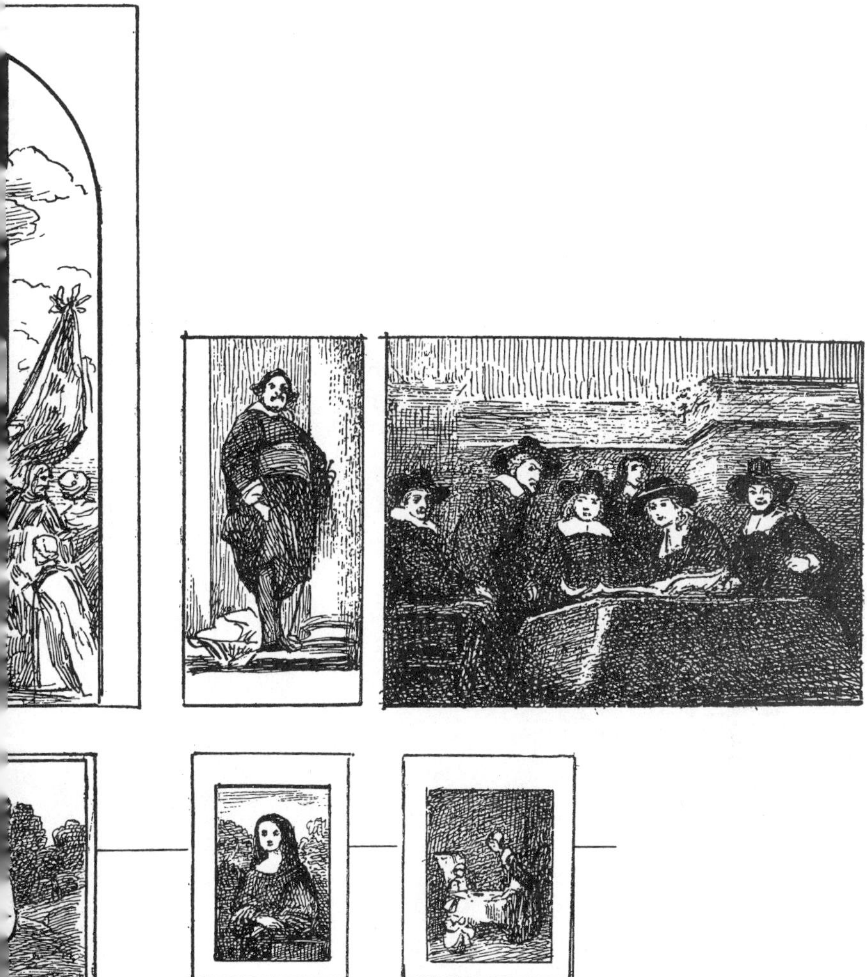
1909.

For the farther we recede the more equal are the angles at which we view the objects at their different stages, so that in each case we may have to deal with, we must consider the conditions attending it.

These remarks apply also to architecture in a great measure. Buildings that can only be seen from the street below, as pictures in a narrow gallery, require a different treatment from those out in the open, that are to be looked at from a distance. In the former case the same treatment as the Campanile at Florence is in some cases desirable, but all must depend upon the taste and judgement of the architect in such matters. All I venture to do here is to call attention to the subject, which seems as a rule to be ignored, or not to be considered of importance. Hence the many mistakes in our buildings, and the unsatisfactory and mean look of some of our public monuments.

XX

Of Pictures that are Painted according to the Position they are to Occupy

In this double-page illustration of the wall of a picture-gallery, I have, as it were, hung the pictures in accordance with the style in which they are painted and the perspective adopted by their painters. It will be seen that those placed on the line level with the eye have their horizon lines fairly high up, and are not suited to be placed any higher. The Giorgione in the centre, the Monna Lisa to the right, and the Velasquez and Watteau to the left, are all pictures that fit that position; whereas the grander compositions above them are so designed, and are so large in conception, that we gain in looking up to them.

Note how grandly the young prince on his pony, by Velasquez, tells out against the sky, with its low horizon and strong contrast of light and dark; nor does it lose a bit by being placed where it is, over the smaller pictures.

The Rembrandt, on the opposite side, with its burgomasters in black hats and coats and white collars, is evidently intended and painted for a raised position, and to be looked up to, which is evident from the perspective of the table. The grand Titian in the centre, an altar-piece in one of the churches in Venice (here reversed), is also painted to suit its elevated position, with low horizon and figures telling boldly against the sky. Those placed low down are modern French pictures, with the horizon high up and almost above their frames, but placed on the ground they fit into the general harmony of the arrangement.

It seems to me it is well, both for those who paint and for those who hang pictures, that this subject should be taken into consideration. For it must be seen by this illustration that a bigger style is adopted by the artists who paint for high places in palaces or churches than by those who produce smaller easel-pictures intended to be seen close. Unfortunately, at our picture exhibitions, we see too often that nearly all the works, whether on large or small canvases, are painted for the line, and that those which happen to get high up look as if they were toppling over, because they have such a high horizontal line; and instead of the figures telling against the sky, as in this picture of the 'Infant' by Velasquez, the Reynolds, and the fat man treading on a flag, we have fields or sea or distant landscape almost to the top of the frame, and all, so methinks, because the perspective is not sufficiently considered.

Note.—Whilst on this subject, I may note that the painter in his large decorative work often had difficulties to contend with, which arose from the form of the building or the shape of the wall on which he had to place his frescoes. Painting on the ceiling was no easy task, and Michelangelo, in a humorous sonnet addressed to Giovanni da Pistoya, gives a burlesque portrait of himself while he was painting the Sistine Chapel:—

"*I'ho già fatto un gozzo in questo stento.*"

Now have I such a goitre 'neath my chin
That I am like to some Lombardic cat,
My beard is in the air, my head i' my back,
My chest like any harpy's, and my face
Patched like a carpet by my dripping brush.
Nor can I see, nor can I budge a step;
My skin though loose in front is tight behind,
And I am even as a Syrian bow.
Alas! methinks a bent tube shoots not well;
So give me now thine aid, my Giovanni.

At present that difficulty is got over by using large strong canvas, on which the picture can be painted in the studio and afterwards placed on the wall.

However, the other difficulty of form has to be got over also. A great portion of the ceiling of the Sistine Chapel, and notably the prophets and sibyls, are painted on a curved surface, in which case a similar method to that explained by Leonardo da Vinci has to be adopted.

In Chapter CCCI he shows us how to draw a figure twenty-four braccia high upon a wall twelve braccia high. (The braccia is 1 ft. $10\frac{7}{8}$ in.). He first draws the figure upright, then from the various points draws lines to a point F on the floor of the building, marking their intersections on the profile of the wall somewhat in the manner we have indicated, which serve as guides in making the outline to be traced.

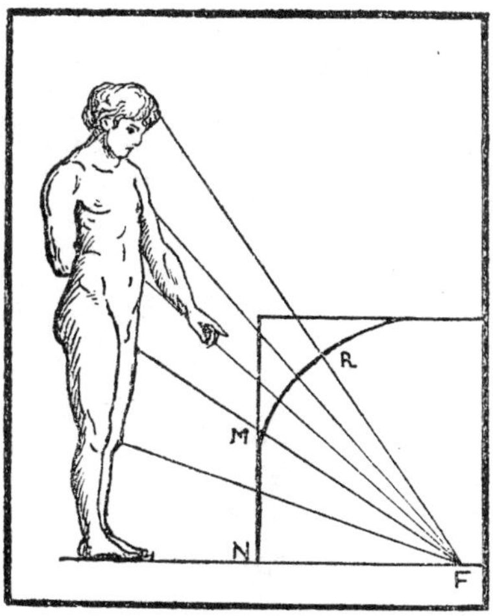

FIG. 67.

'Draw upon part of wall MN half the figure you mean to represent, and the other half upon the cove above (MR).' Leonardo da Vinci's *Treatise on Painting*.

XXI

Interiors

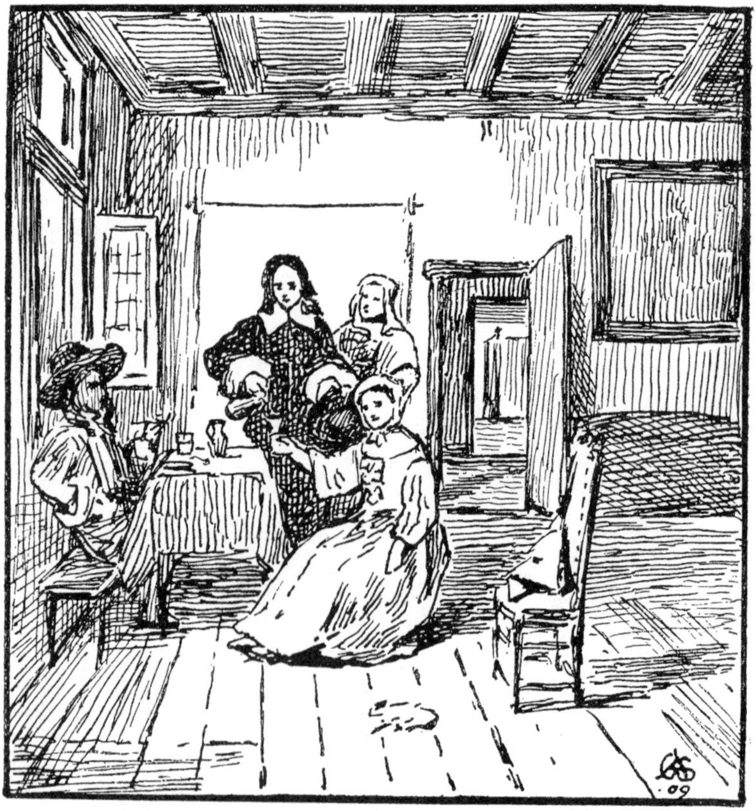

Fig. 68. Interior by de Hoogh.

To draw the interior of a cube we must suppose the side facing us to be removed or transparent. Indeed, in all our figures which represent solids we suppose that we can see through them, and in most cases we mark the hidden portions with dotted lines. So also with all those imaginary lines which conduct the eye to the various vanishing points, and which the old writers called 'occult'.

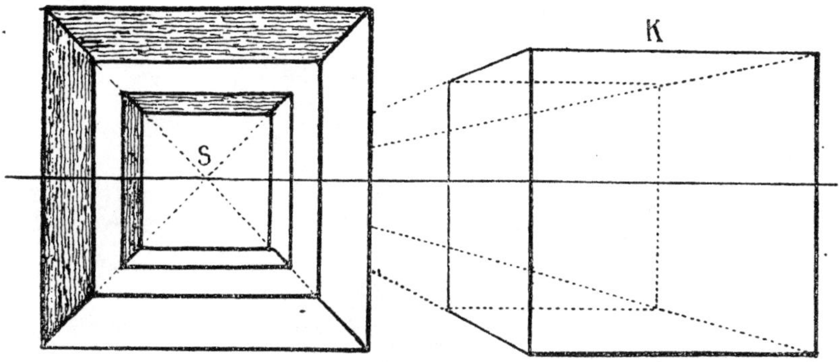

FIG. 69.

When the cube is placed below the horizon (as in Fig. 59), we see the top of it; when on the horizon, as in the above (Fig. 69), if the side facing us is removed we see both top and bottom of it, or if a room, we see floor and ceiling, but otherwise we should see but one side (that facing us), or at most two sides. When the cube is above the horizon we see underneath it.

We shall find this simple cube of great use to us in architectural subjects, such as towers, houses, roofs, interiors of rooms, &c.

In this little picture by de Hoogh we have the application of the perspective of the cube and other foregoing problems.

XXII

The Square at an Angle of 45°

When the square is at an angle of 45° to the base line, then its sides are drawn respectively to the points of distance, DD, and one of its diagonals which is at right angles to the base is drawn to the point of sight S, and the other *ab*, is parallel to that base or ground line.

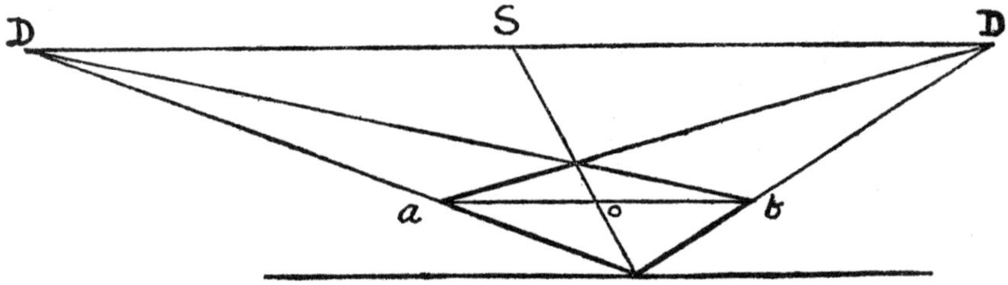

Fig. 70.

To draw a pavement with its squares at this angle is but an amplification of the above figure. Mark off on base equal distances, 1, 2, 3, &c., representing the diagonals of required squares, and from each of these points draw lines to points of distance DD′.

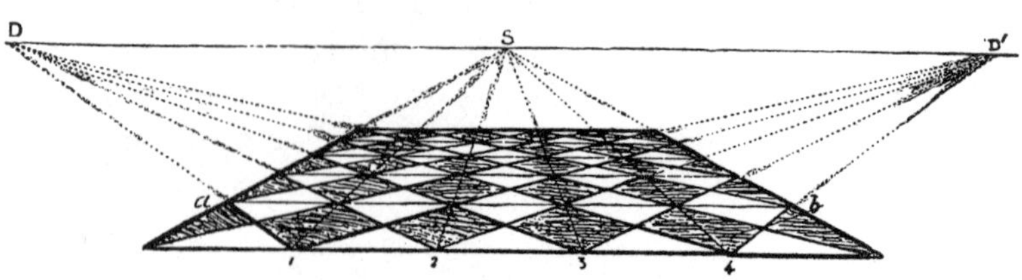

Fig. 71.

These lines will intersect each other, and so form the squares of the pavement; to ensure correctness, lines should also be drawn from these points 1, 2, 3, to the point of sight S, and also horizontals parallel to the base, as *ab*.

XXIII

The Cube at an Angle of 45°

Having drawn the square at an angle of 45°, as shown in the previous figure, we find the length of one of its sides, *dh*, by drawing a line, SK, through *h*, one of its extremities, till it cuts the

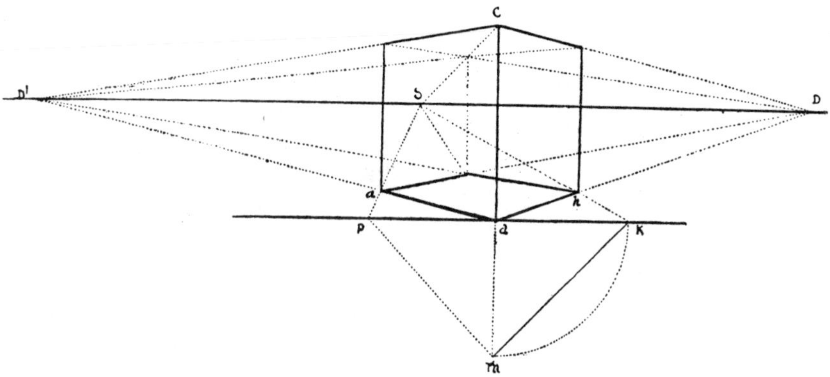

Fig. 72.

base line at K. Then, with the other extremity *d* for centre and *d*K for radius, describe a quarter of a circle K*m*; the chord thereof *m*K will be the geometrical length of *dh*. At *d* raise vertical *d*C equal to *m*K, which gives us the height of the cube, then raise verticals at *a*, *h*, &c., their height being found by drawing CD and CD′ to the two points of distance, and so completing the figure.

XXIV

Pavements Drawn by Means of Squares at 45°

The square at 45° will be found of great use in drawing pavements, roofs, ceilings, &c. In Figs. 73, 74 it is shown how

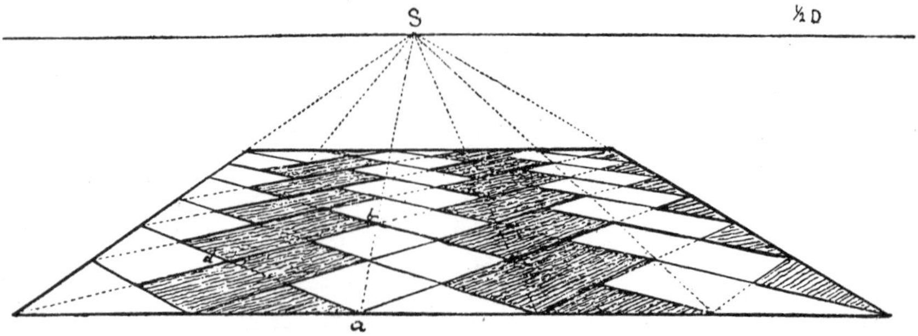

Fig. 73.

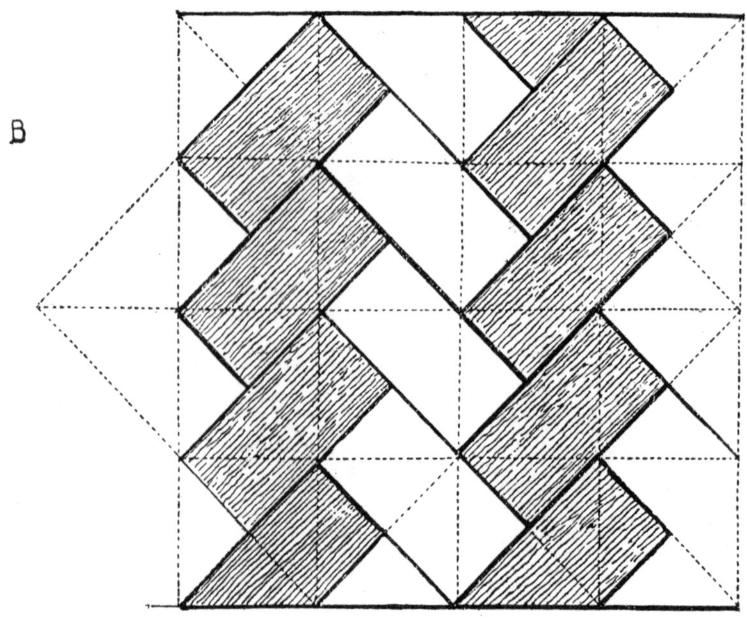

Fig. 74.

having set out one square it can be divided into four or more equal squares, and any figure or tile drawn therein. Begin by making a geometrical or ground plan of the required design, as at Figs. 74 and 75, where we have bricks placed at right angles

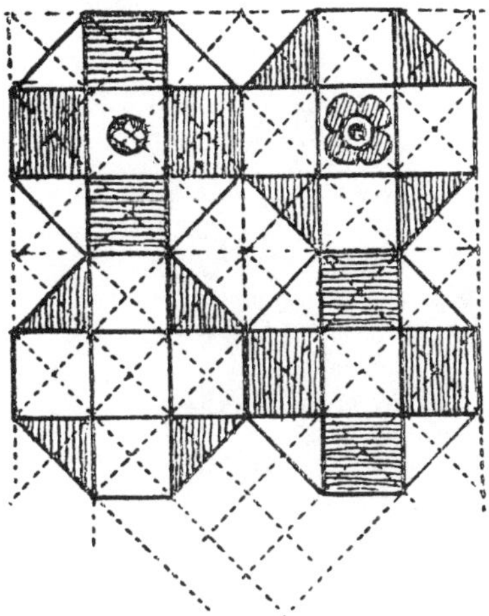

FIG. 75.

to each other in rows, a common arrangement in brick floors, or tiles of an octagonal form as at Fig. 75.

XXV

The Perspective Vanishing Scale

The vanishing scale, which we shall find of infinite use in our perspective, is founded on the facts explained in Rule 10. We

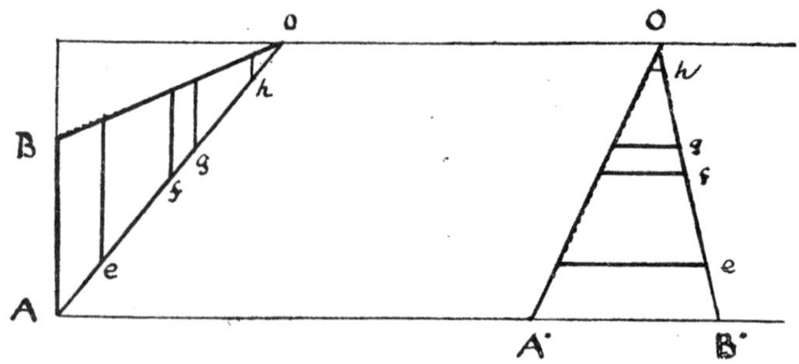

Fig. 76.

there find that all horizontals in the same plane, which are drawn to the same point on the horizon, are perspectively parallel to each other, so that if we measure a certain height or width on the picture plane, and then from each extremity draw lines to any convenient point on the horizon, then all the perpendiculars drawn between these lines will be perspectively equal, however much they may appear to vary in length.

Let us suppose that in this figure (76) AB and A·B· each represent 5 feet. Then in the first case all the verticals, as *e*, *f*, *g*, *h*, drawn between AO and BO represent 5 feet, and in the second case all the horizontals *e*, *f*, *g*, *h*, drawn between A·O and B·O also represent 5 feet each. So that by the aid of this scale we can give the exact perspective height and width of any object in the picture, however far it may be from the base line, for of course we can increase or diminish our measurements at AB and A·B· to whatever length we require.

As it may not be quite evident at first that the points O may be taken at random, the following figure will prove it.

XXVI

The Vanishing Scale can be Drawn to any Point on the Horizon

From AB (Fig. 77) draw AO, BO, thus forming the scale, raise

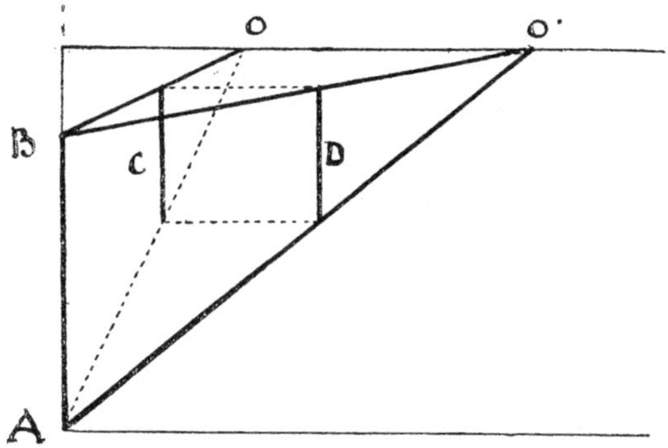

Fig. 77.

vertical C. Now form a second scale from AB by drawing AO· BO·, and therein raise vertical D at an equal distance from the base. First, then, vertical C equals AB, and secondly vertical D equals AB, therefore C equals D, so that either of these scales will measure a given height at a given distance.

(See axioms of geometry.)

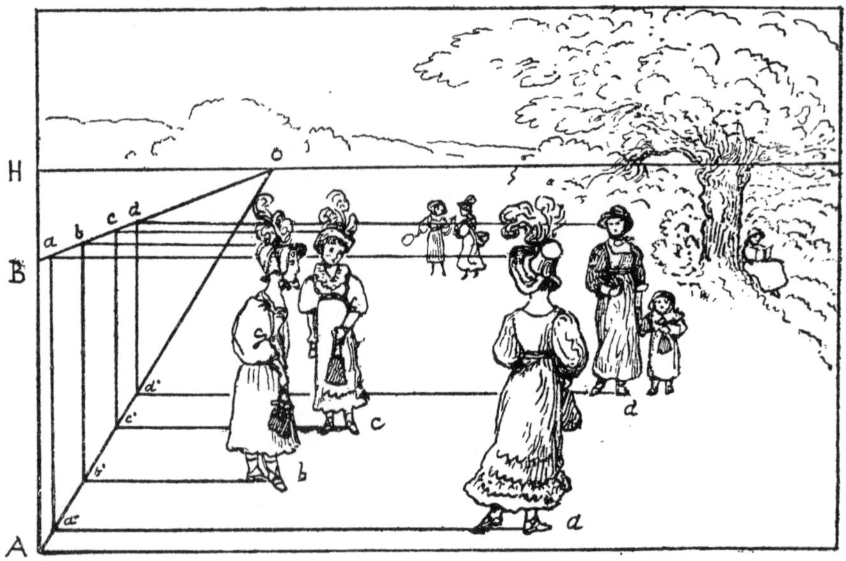

FIG. 79. Schoolgirls.

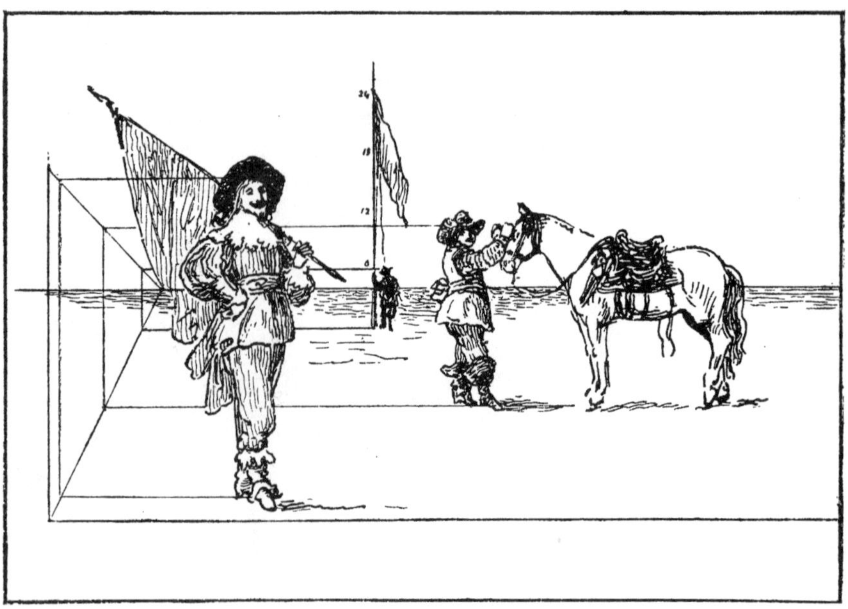

FIG. 80. Cavaliers.

XXVII

Application of Vanishing Scales to Drawing Figures

In this figure we have marked off on a level plain three or four points *a*, *b*, *c*, *d*, to indicate the places where we wish to stand

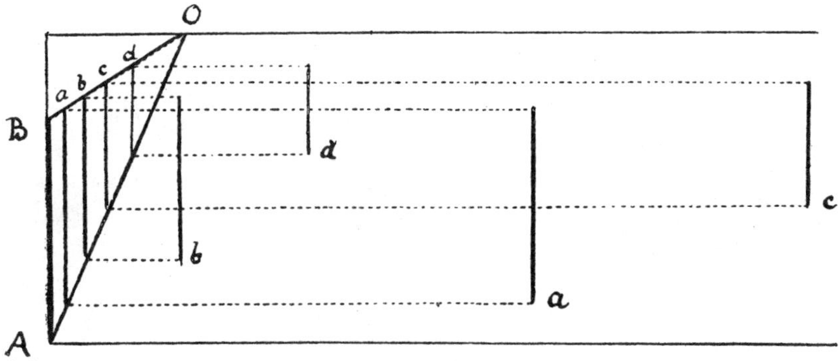

Fig. 78.

our figures. AB represents their average height, so we have made our scale AO, BO, accordingly. From each point marked we draw a line parallel to the base till it reaches the scale. From the point where it touches the line AO, raise perpendicular as *a*, which gives the height required at that distance, and must be referred back to the figure itself.

XXVIII

How to Determine the Heights of Figures on a Level Plane

First Case.

This is but a repetition of the previous figure, excepting that we have substituted these schoolgirls for the vertical lines. If we wish to make some taller than the others, and some shorter, we can easily do so, as must be evident (see Fig. 79).

Note that in this first case the scale is below the horizon, so that we see over the heads of the figures, those nearest to us being the lowest down. That is to say, we are looking on this scene from a slightly raised platform.

Second Case.

To draw figures at different distances when their heads are above the horizon, or as they would appear to a person sitting on a low seat. The height of the heads varies according to the distance of the figures (Fig. 80).

Third Case.

How to draw figures when their heads are about the height of the horizon, or as they appear to a person standing on the same level or walking among them.

In this case the heads or the eyes are on a level with the horizon,

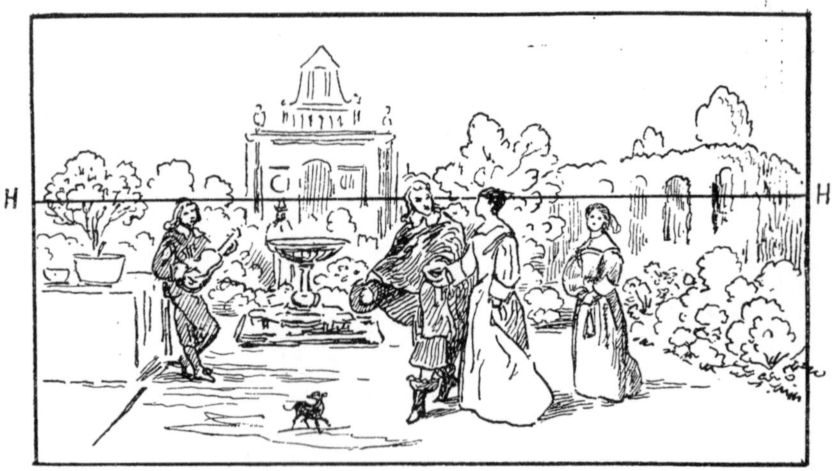

FIG. 81.

and we have little necessity for a scale at the side unless it is for the purpose of ascertaining or marking their distances from the base line, and their respective heights, which of course vary; so in all cases allowance must be made for some being taller and some shorter than the scale measurement.

XXIX

THE HORIZON ABOVE THE FIGURES

In this example from De Hoogh the doorway to the left is higher up than the figure of the lady, and the effect seems to me more pleasing and natural for this kind of domestic subject. This delightful painter was not only a master of colour, of sunlight

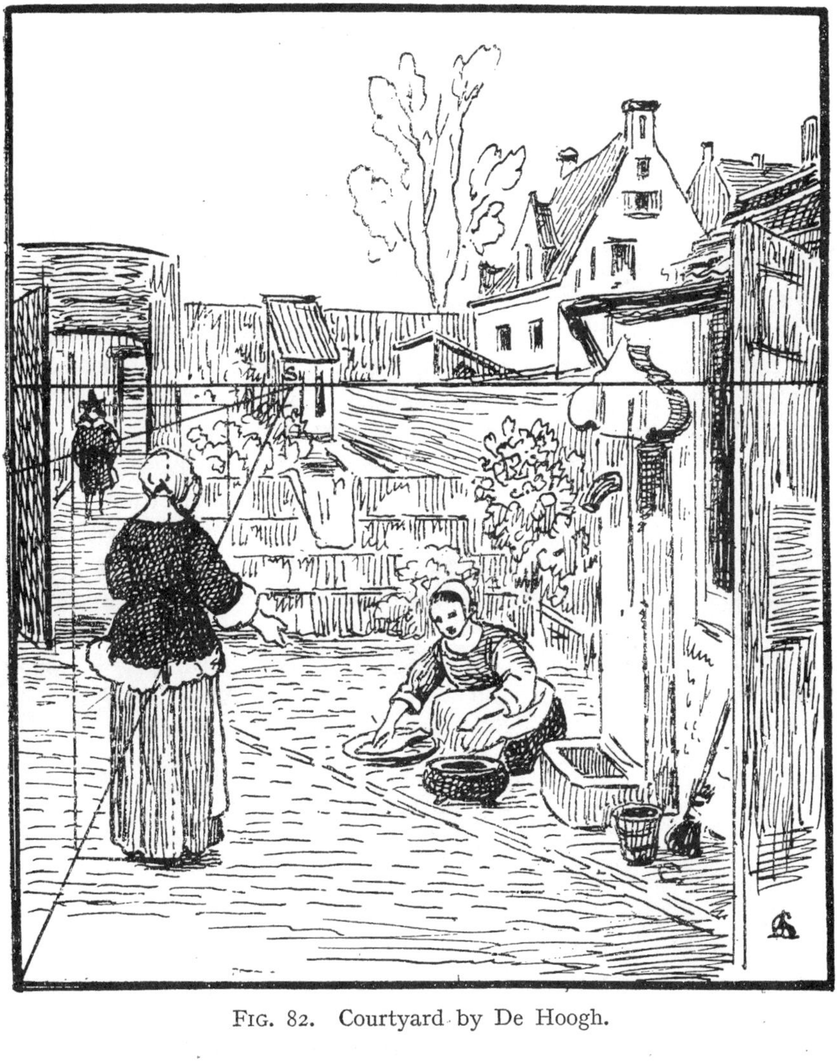

FIG. 82. Courtyard by De Hoogh.

effect, and perfect composition, but also of perspective, and thoroughly understood the charm it gives to a picture, when cunningly introduced, for he makes the spectator feel that he can walk along his passages and courtyards. Note that he frequently puts the point of sight quite at the side of his canvas, as at S, which gives almost the effect of angular perspective whilst it preserves the flatness and simplicity of parallel or horizontal perspective.

XXX

Landscape Perspective

In an extended view or landscape seen from a height, we have to consider the perspective plane as in a great measure lying above it, reaching from the base of the picture to the horizon; but of course pierced here and there by trees, mountains, buildings, &c. As a rule in such cases, we copy our perspective from nature, and do not trouble ourselves much about mathematical rules. It is as well, however, to know them, so that we may feel sure we are right, as this gives certainty to our touch and enables us to work with freedom. Nor must we, when painting from nature, forget to take into account the effects of atmosphere and the various tones of the different planes of distance, for this makes much of the difference between a good picture and a bad one; being a more subtle quality, it requires a keener artistic sense to discover and depict it. (See Figs. 95 and 103.)

If the landscape painter wishes to test his knowledge of perspective, let him dissect and work out one of Turner's pictures, or better still, put his own sketch from nature to the same test.

XXXI

Figures of Different Heights

The Chessboard

In this figure the same principle is applied as in the previous one, but the chessmen being of different heights we have to arrange the scale accordingly. First ascertain the exact height of each piece, as Q, K, B, which represent the queen, king, bishop, &c. Refer these dimensions to the scale, as shown at QKB, which will give us the perspective measurement of each piece according to the square on which it is placed.

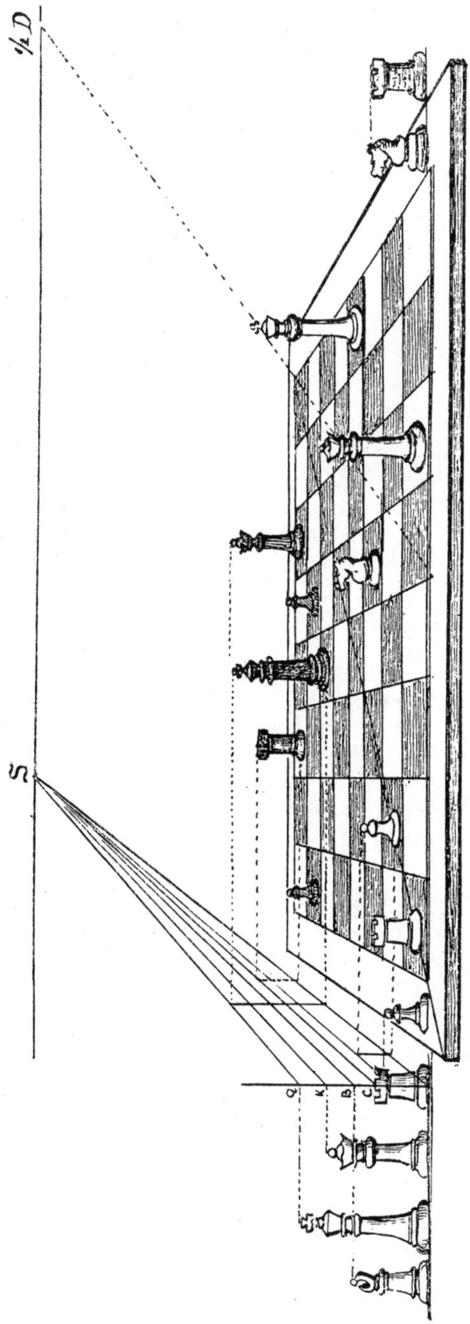

Fig. 83. Chessboard and Men.

This is shown in the above drawing (Fig. 83) in the case of

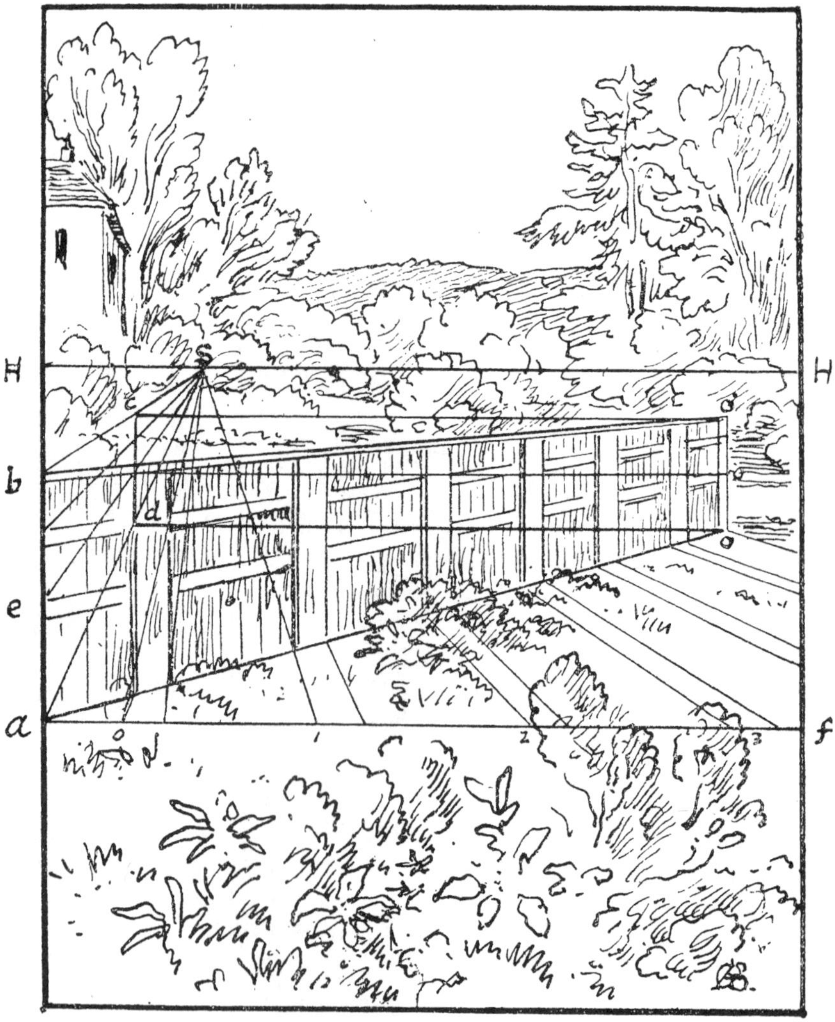

FIG. 84.

the white queen and the black queen, &c. The castle, the knight, and the pawn being about the same height are measured from the fourth line of the scale marked C.

XXXII

Application of the Vanishing Scale to Drawing Figures at an Angle when their Vanishing Points are Inaccessible or Outside the Picture

This is exemplified in the drawing of a fence (Fig. 84). Form scale *a*s, *b*s, in accordance with the height of the fence or wall to be depicted. Let *ao* represent the direction or angle at which it is placed, draw *od* to meet the scale at *d*, at *d* raise vertical *dc*, which gives the height of the fence at *oo*·. Draw lines *bo*·, *eo*, *ao*, &c., and it will be found that all these lines if produced will meet at the same point on the horizon. To divide the fence into spaces, divide base line *af* as required and proceed as already shown.

XXXIII

The Reduced Distance. How to Proceed when the Point of Distance is Inaccessible

It has already been shown that too near a point of distance is objectionable on account of the distortion and disproportion resulting from it. At the same time, the long distance-point must be some way out of the picture and therefore inconvenient. The object of the reduced distance is to bring that point within the picture.

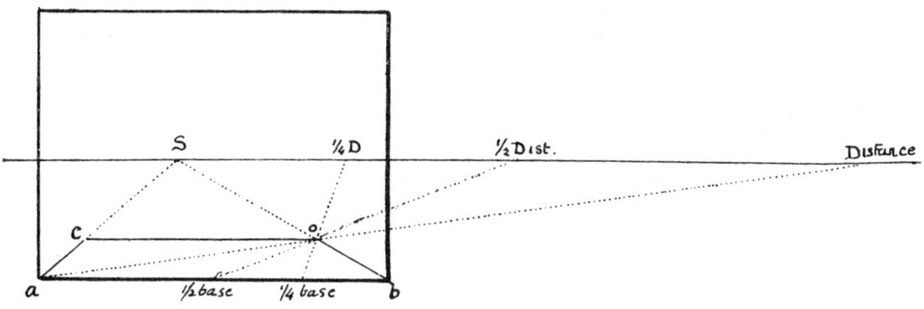

In Fig. 85 we have made the distance nearly twice the length of the base of the picture, and consequently a long way out of it. Draw S*a*, S*b*, and from *a* draw *a*D to point of distance, which cuts S*b* at *o*, and determines the depth of the square *acob*. But we can find that same point if we take half the base and draw a line from ½ base to ½ distance. But even this ½ distance-point does not come inside the picture, so we take a fourth of the base and a fourth of the distance and draw a line from ¼ base to ¼ distance. We shall find that it passes precisely through the same point *o* as the other lines *a*D, &c. We are thus able to find the required point *o* without going outside the picture.

Of course we could in the same way take an 8th or even a 16th distance, but the great use of this reduced distance, in addition to the above, is that it enables us to measure any depth into the picture with the greatest ease.

It will be seen in the next figure that without having to extend the base, as is usually done, we can multiply that base to any amount by making use of these reduced distances on the horizontal line. This is quite a new method of proceeding, and it will be seen is mathematically correct.

XXXIV

How to Draw a Long Passage or Cloister by means of the Reduced Distance

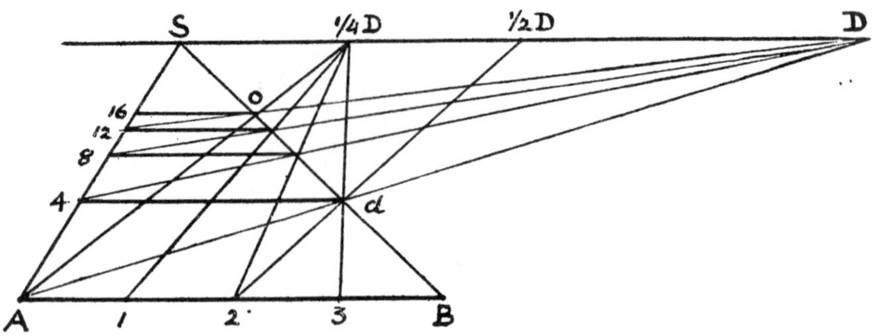

Fig. 86.

In Fig. 86 we have divided the base of the first square into four equal parts, which may represent so many feet, so that A4 and B*d* being the retreating sides of the square each represents 4 feet. But we found point ¼D by drawing 3D from ¼ base to ¼ distance, and by proceeding in the same way from each division,

A, 1, 2, 3, we mark off on SB four spaces each equal to 4 feet, in all 16 feet, so that by taking the whole base and the $\frac{1}{4}$ distance we find point O, which is distant four times the length of the base AB. We can multiply this distance to any amount by

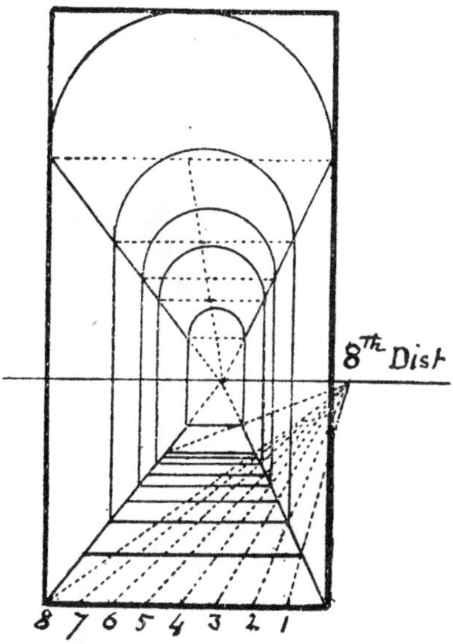

FIG. 87.

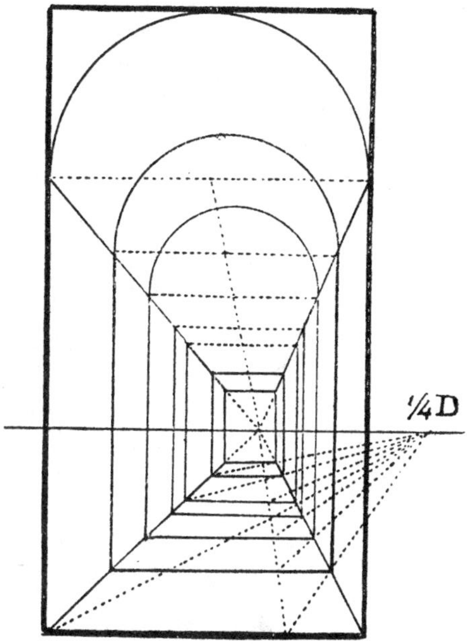

FIG. 88.

drawing other diagonals to 8th distance, &c. The same rule applies to this corridor (Fig. 87 and Fig. 88).

XXXV

How to Form a Vanishing Scale that shall give the Height, Depth, and Distance of any Object in the Picture

If we make our scale to vanish to the point of sight, as in Fig. 89, we can make SB, the lower line thereof, a measuring line for distances. Let us first of all divide the base AB into eight parts, each part representing 5 feet. From each division draw lines to 8th distance; by their intersections with SB we obtain measurements of 40, 80, 120, 160, &c., feet. Now divide the side of the picture BE in the same manner as the base, which gives us the height of 40 feet. From the side BE draw lines 5S, 15S, &c., to point of sight, and from each division on the base line also draw lines 5S, 10S, 15S, &c., to point of sight, and from each division on SB, such as 40, 80, &c., draw horizontals parallel to base. We thus obtain squares 40 feet wide, beginning at

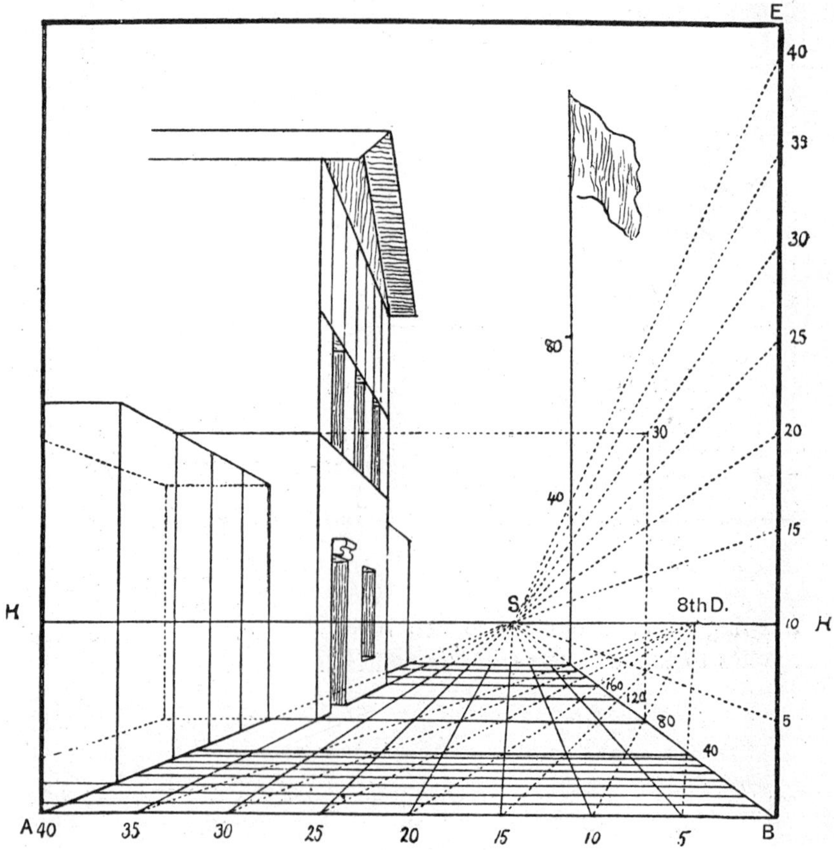

FIG. 89.

base AB and reaching as far as required. Note how the height of the flagstaff, which is 140 feet high and 280 feet distant, is obtained. So also any buildings or other objects can be measured, such as those shown on the left of the picture.

XXXVI

Measuring Scale on Ground

A simple and very old method of drawing buildings, &c., and

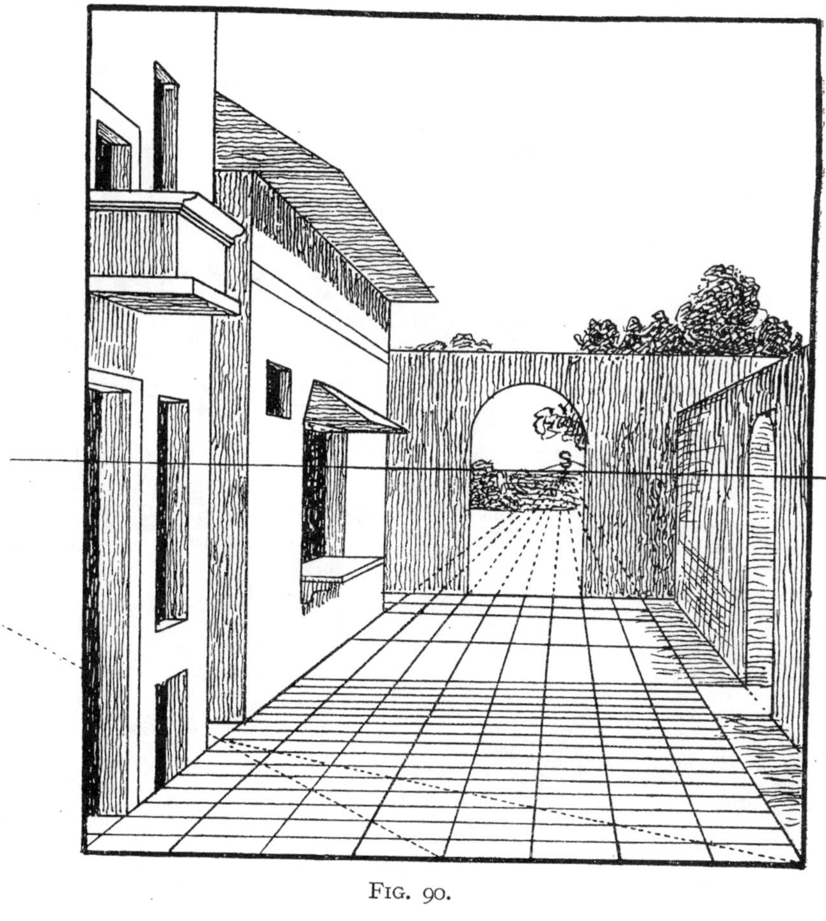

Fig. 90.

giving them their right width and height is by means of squares of a given size, drawn on the ground.

In the above sketch (Fig. 90) the squares on the ground

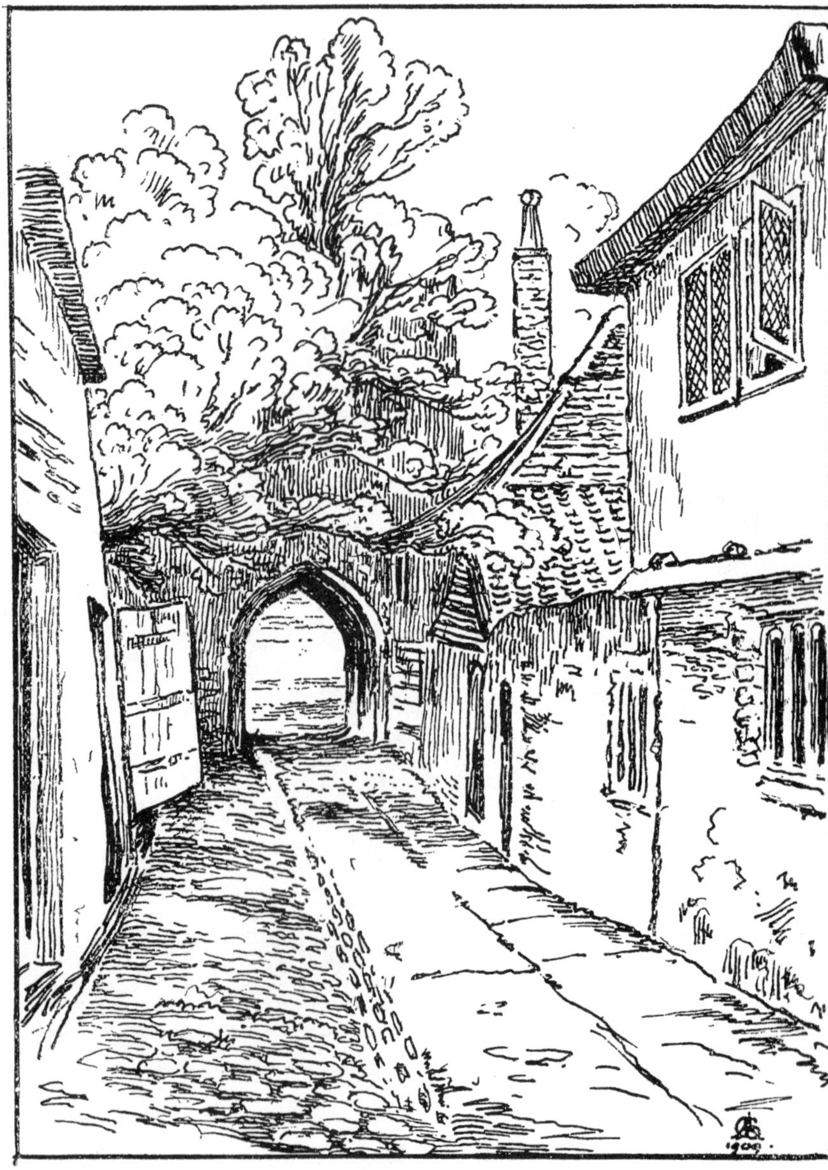

FIG. 91.
NATURAL PERSPECTIVE.

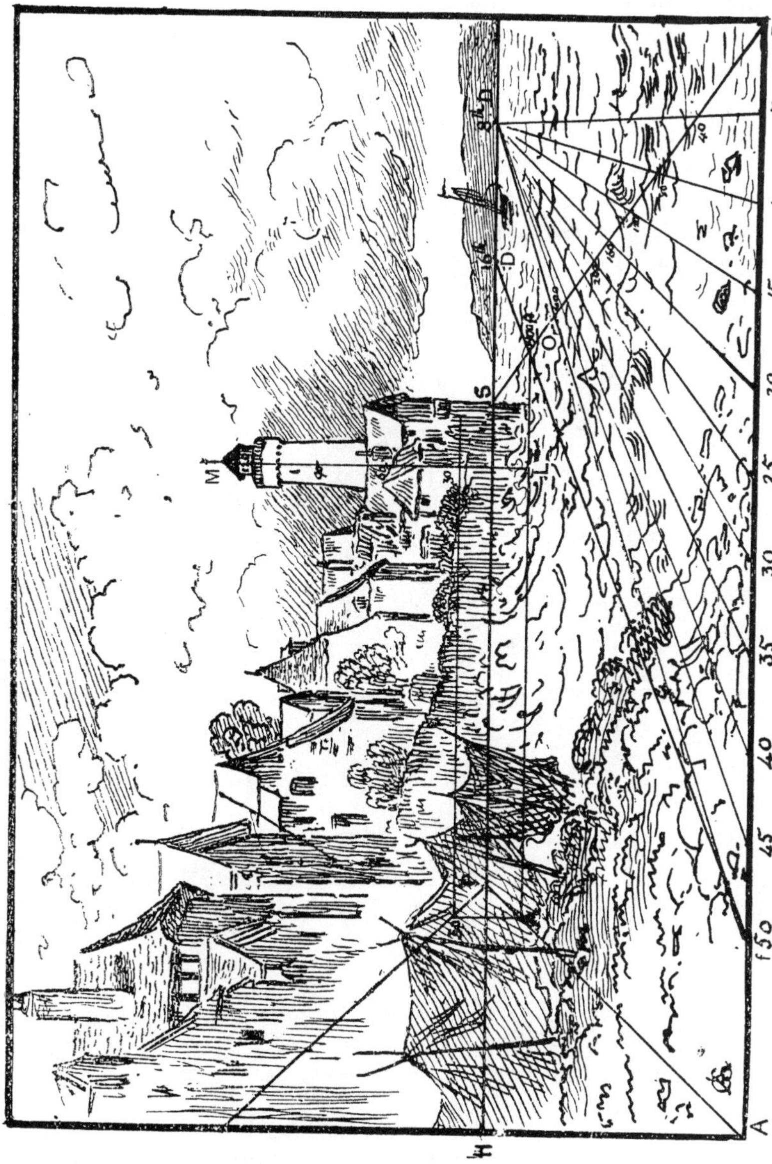

FIG. 92. Honfleur.

represent 3 feet each way, or one square yard. Taking this as our standard measure, we find the door on the left is 10 feet high, that the archway at the end is 21 feet high and 12 feet wide, and so on.

Fig. 91 is a sketch made at Sandwich, Kent, and shows a somewhat similar subject to Fig. 84, but the irregularity and freedom of the perspective gives it a charm far beyond the rigid precision of the other, while it conforms to its main laws. This sketch, however, is the real artist's perspective, or what we might term natural perspective.

XXXVII

Application of the Reduced Distance and the Vanishing Scale to Drawing a Lighthouse, &c.

Perspective of a lighthouse 135 feet high at 800 feet distance.

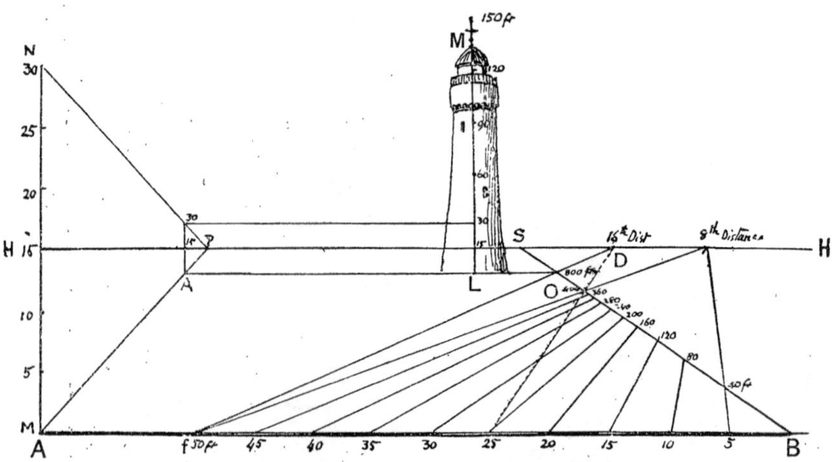

FIG. 93. Key to Fig. 92, Honfleur.

In the drawing of Honfleur (Fig. 92) we divide the base AB as in the previous figure, but the spaces measure 5 feet instead of 3 feet: so that taking the 8th distance, the divisions on the vanishing line BS measure 40 feet each, and at point O we have 400 feet of distance, but we require 800. So we again reduce the distance to a 16th. We thus multiply the base by 16. Now let us take a base of 50 feet at *f* and draw line *f*D to 16th distance; if we multiply 50 feet by 16 we obtain the 800 feet required.

The height of the lighthouse is found by means of the vanishing scale, which is 15 feet below and 15 feet above the horizon, or 30 feet from the sea-level. At L we raise a vertical LM, which shows the position of the lighthouse. Then on that vertical measure the height required as shown in the figure.

The 800 feet could be obtained at once by drawing line *f*D, or 50 feet, to 16th distance. The other measurements obtained by 8th distance serve for nearer buildings.

XXXVIII

How to Measure Long Distances such as a Mile or Upwards

The wonderful effect of distance in Turner's pictures is not to be achieved by mere measurement, and indeed can only be properly done by studying Nature and drawing her perspective as she presents it to us. At the same time it is useful to be able to test and to set out distances in arranging a composition. This latter, if neglected, often leads to great difficulties and sometimes to repainting.

To show the method of measuring very long distances we have to work with a very small scale to the foot, and in Fig. 94 I have divided the base AB into eleven parts, each part representing 10 feet. First draw AS and BS to point of sight.

From A draw AD to $\frac{1}{4}$ distance, and we obtain at 440 on line BS four times the length of AB, or 110 feet $\times$ 4 = 440 feet. Again, taking the whole base and drawing a line from A to 8th distance we obtain eight times 110 feet or 880 feet. If now we use the 16th distance we get sixteen times 110 feet, or 1,760 feet, one-third of a mile; by repeating this process, but by using the base

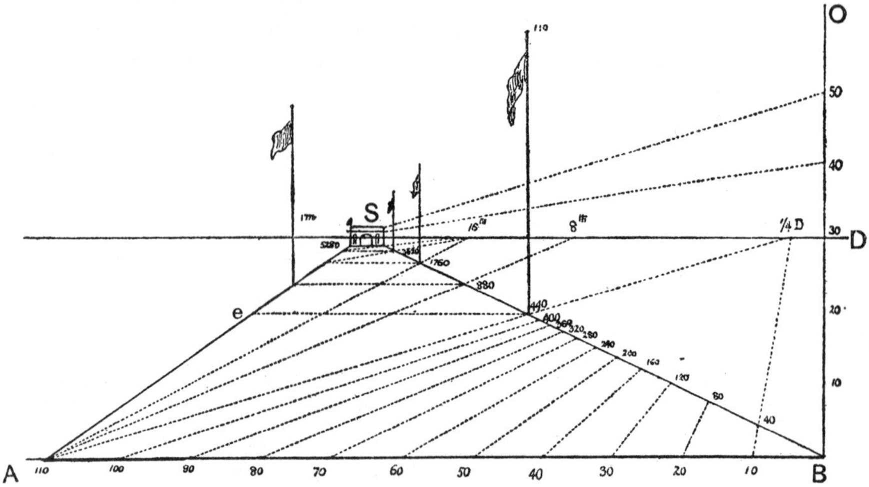

FIG. 94.

at 1,760, which is the same length in perspective as AB, we obtain 3,520 feet, and then again using the base at 3,520 and proceeding in the same way we obtain 5,280 feet, or one mile to the archway. The flags show their heights at their respective distances from the base. By the scale at the side of the picture, BO, we can measure any height above or any depth below the perspective plane.

Note.—This figure (here much reduced) should be drawn large by the student, so that the numbering, &c., may be made more distinct. Indeed, many of the other figures should be copied large, and worked out with care, as lessons in perspective

XXXIX

Further Illustration of Long Distances and Extended Views

An extended view is generally taken from an elevated position, so that the principal part of the landscape lies beneath the perspective plane, as already noted, and we shall presently treat of objects and figures on uneven ground. In the previous figure is shown how we can measure heights and depths to any extent. But when we turn to a drawing by Turner, such as the 'View from Richmond Hill', we feel that the only way to accomplish such perspective as this, is to go and draw it from nature, and even then to use our judgement, as he did, as to how much we may emphasize or even exaggerate certain features.

Note in this view the foreground on which the principal figures

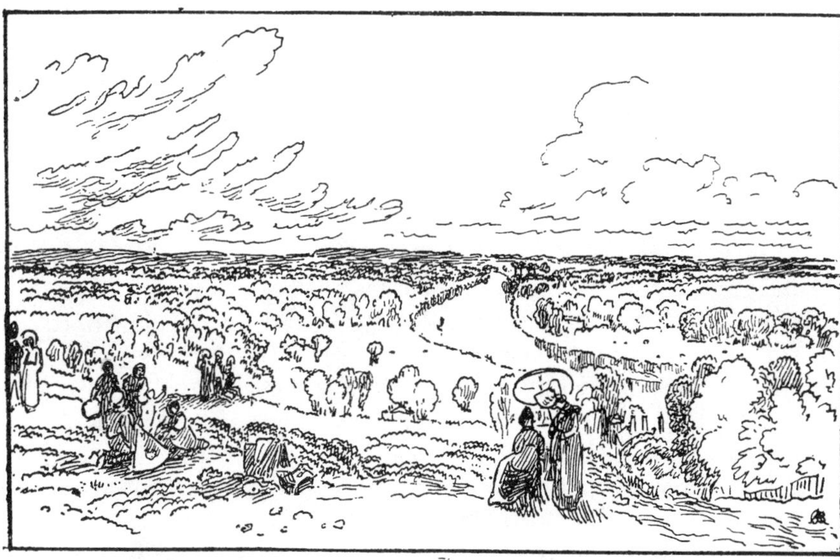

Fig. 95. Turner's View from Richmond Hill.

stand is on a level with the perspective plane, while the river and surrounding park and woods are hundreds of feet below us and stretch away for miles into the distance. The contrasts obtained by this arrangement increase the illusion of space, and the figures in the foreground give as it were a standard of measurement, and by their contrast to the size of the trees show us how far away those trees are.

XL

How to Ascertain the Relative Heights of Figures on an Inclined Plane

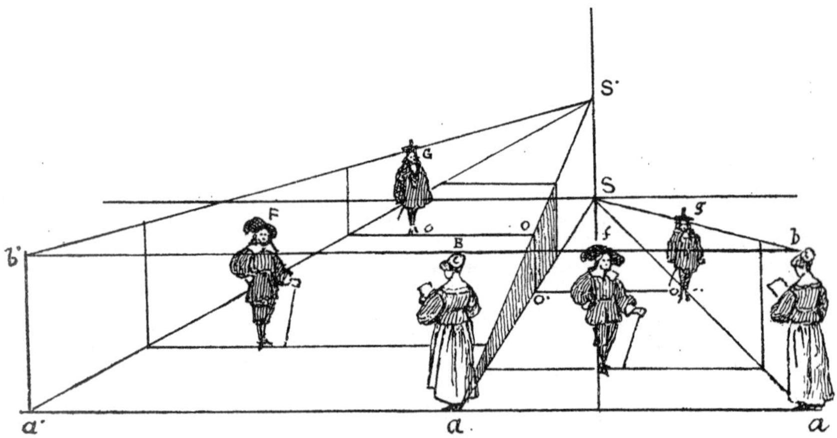

FIG. 96.

The three figures to the right marked *f*, *g*, *b* (Fig. 96) are on level ground, and we measure them by the vanishing scale *a*S, *b*S. Those to the left, which are repetitions of them, are on an inclined plane, the vanishing point of which is S·; by the side of this plane we have placed another vanishing scale *a*·S·, *b*·S·, by which we measure the figures on that incline in the same way as on the level plane. It will be seen that if a horizontal line is drawn from the foot of one of these figures, say G, to point O on the edge of the incline, then dropped vertically to *o*·, then again carried on to *o*·· where the other figure *g* is, we find it is the same height and also that the other vanishing scale is the same width at that distance, so that we can work from either one or the other. In the event of the rising ground being uneven we can make use of the scale on the level plane.

XLI

How to Find the Distance of a Given Figure or Point from the Base Line

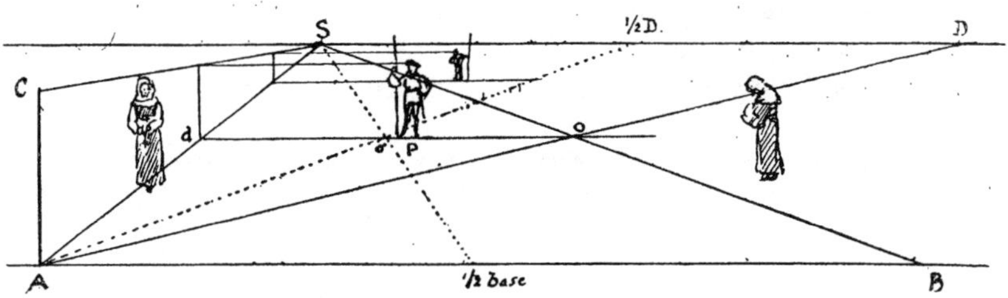

Fig. 97.

Let P be the given figure. Form scale ACS, S being the point of sight and D the distance. Draw horizontal *do* through P. From A draw diagonal AD to distance point, cutting *do* in *o*, through *o* draw SB to base, and we now have a square A*do*B on the perspective plane; and as figure P is standing on the far side of that square it must be the distance AB, which is one side of it, from the base line—or picture plane. For figures very far away it might be necessary to make use of half-distance.

XLII

How to Measure the Height of Figures on Uneven Ground

In previous problems we have drawn figures on level planes, which is easy enough. We have now to represent some above and some below the perspective plane.

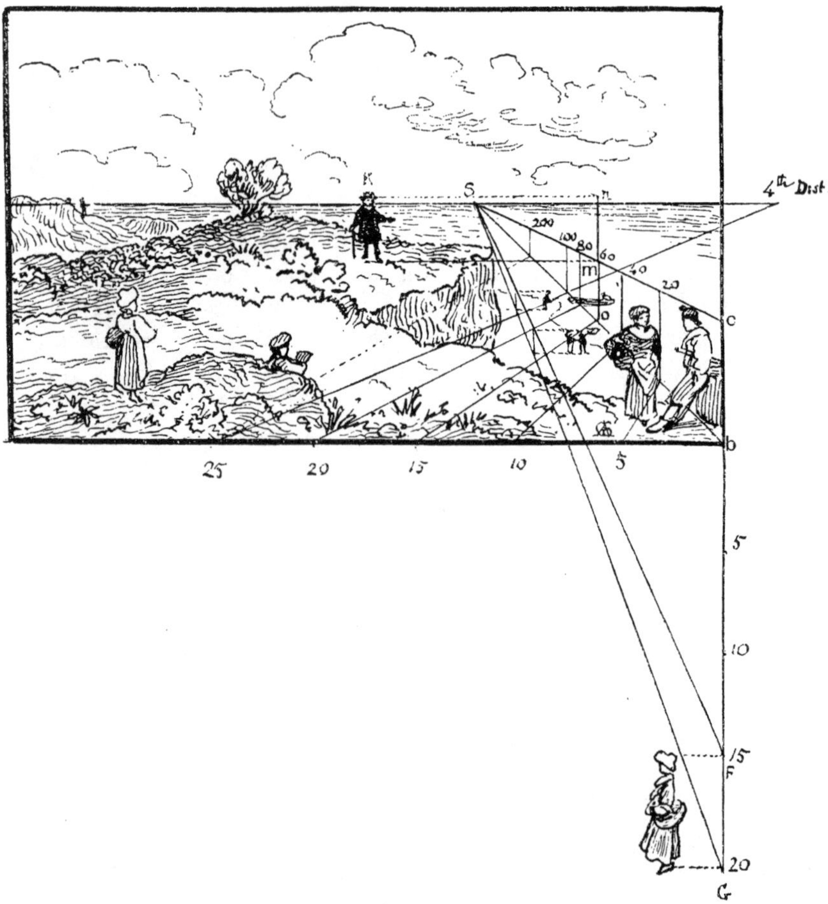

Fig. 98.

Form scale *b*S, *c*S; mark off distances 20 feet, 40 feet, &c. Suppose figure K to be 60 feet off. From point at his feet draw horizontal to meet vertical O*n*, which is 60 feet distant. At the point *m* where this line meets the vertical, measure height *mn* equal to width of scale at that distance, transfer this to K, and you have the required height of the figure in black.

For the figures under the cliff 20 feet below the perspective plane, form scale FS, GS, making it the same width as the other, namely 5 feet, and proceed in the usual way to find the height of the figures on the sands, which are here supposed to be nearly on a level with the sea, of course making allowance for different heights and various other things.

XLIII

Further Illustration of the Size of Figures at Different Distances and on Uneven Ground

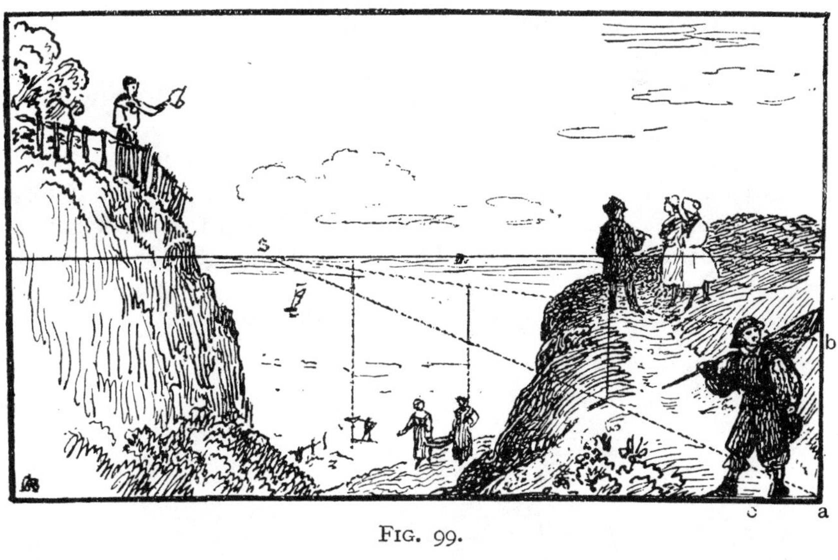

Fig. 99.

Let *ab* be the height of a figure, say 6 feet. First form scale *a*s, *b*s, the lower line of which, *a*s, is on a level with the base or on the perspective plane. The figure marked C is close to base, the group of three is farther off (24 feet), and 6 feet higher up, so we measure the height on the vanishing scale and also above it. The two girls carrying fish are still farther off, and about 12 feet below. To tell how far a figure is away, refer its measurements to the vanishing scale (see Fig. 96).

XLIV

Figures on a Descending Plane

In this case (Fig. 100) the same rule applies as in the previous problem, but as the road on the left is going down hill, the vanishing point of the inclined plane is below the horizon at point S·; AS, BS is the vanishing scale on the level plane; and A·S·, B·S·, that on the incline.

Fig. 101. This is an outline of above figure to show the working more plainly.

Note the wall to the left marked W and the manner in which it appears to drop at certain intervals, its base corresponding with the inclined plane, but the upper lines of each division being made level are drawn to the point of sight, or to their vanishing point on the horizon; it is important to observe this, as it aids greatly in drawing a road going down hill.

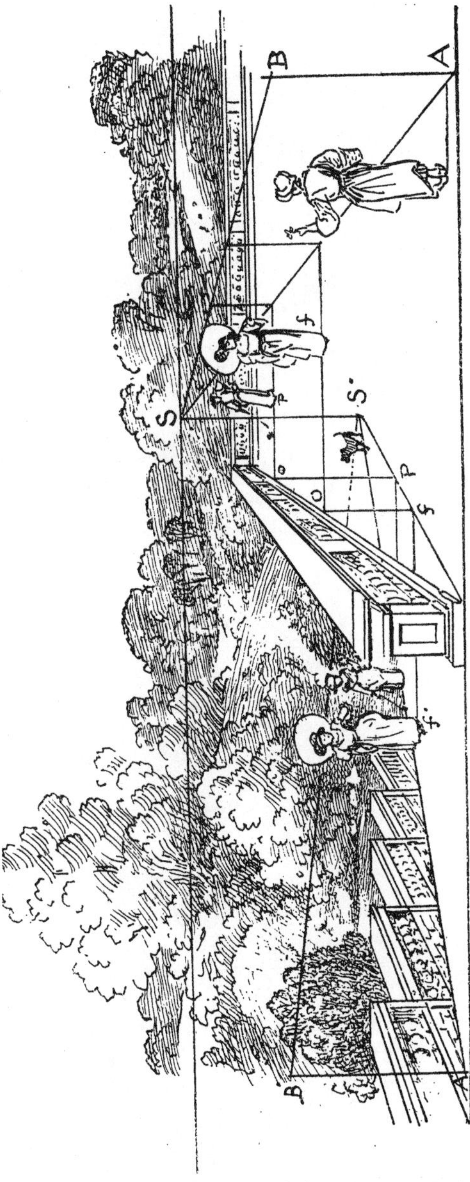

Fig. 100.

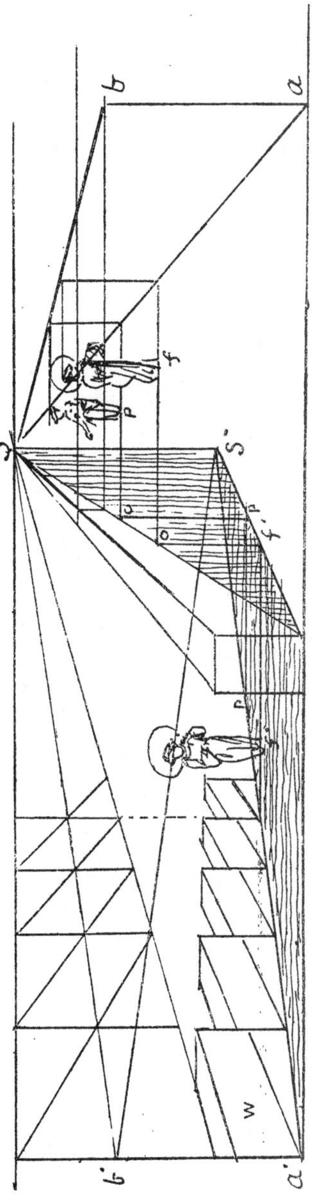

Fig. 101.

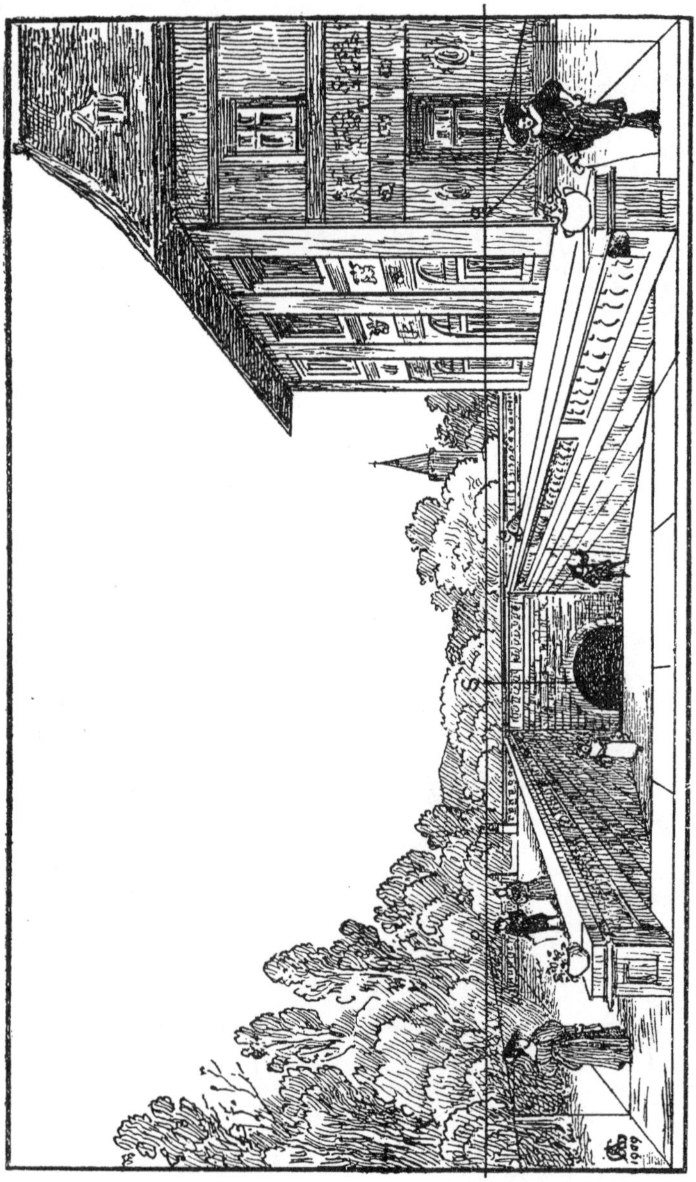

Fig. 102.

XLV

Further Illustration of the Descending Plane

In the centre of this picture (Fig. 102) we suppose the road to be descending till it reaches a tunnel which goes under a road or leads to a river (like one leading out of the Strand near Somerset House). It is drawn on the same principle as the foregoing figure. Of course to see the road the spectator must get pretty near to it, otherwise it will be out of sight. Also a level plane must be shown, as by its contrast to the other we perceive that the latter is going down hill.

XLVI

Further Illustration of Uneven Ground

An extended view drawn from a height of about 30 feet from a road that descends about 45 feet.

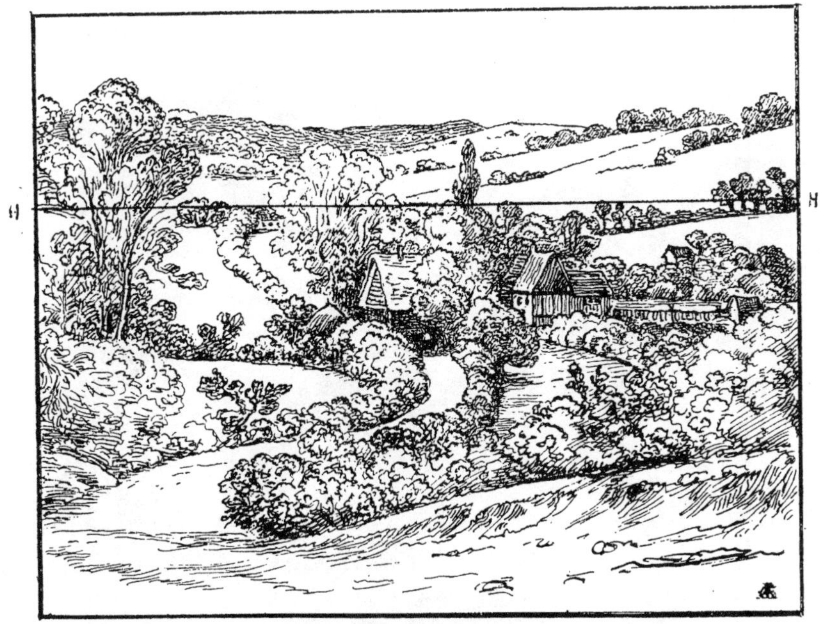

Fig. 103. Farningham.

In drawing a landscape such as Fig. 103 we have to bear in mind the height of the horizon, which being exactly opposite the eye, shows us at once which objects are below and which are above us, and to draw them accordingly, especially roofs, buildings, walls, hedges, &c.; also it is well to sketch in the different fields figures of men and cattle, as from the size of these we can judge of the rest.

XLVII

The Picture Standing on the Ground

Let K represent a frame placed vertically and at a given distance in front of us. If stood on the ground our foreground will touch

K

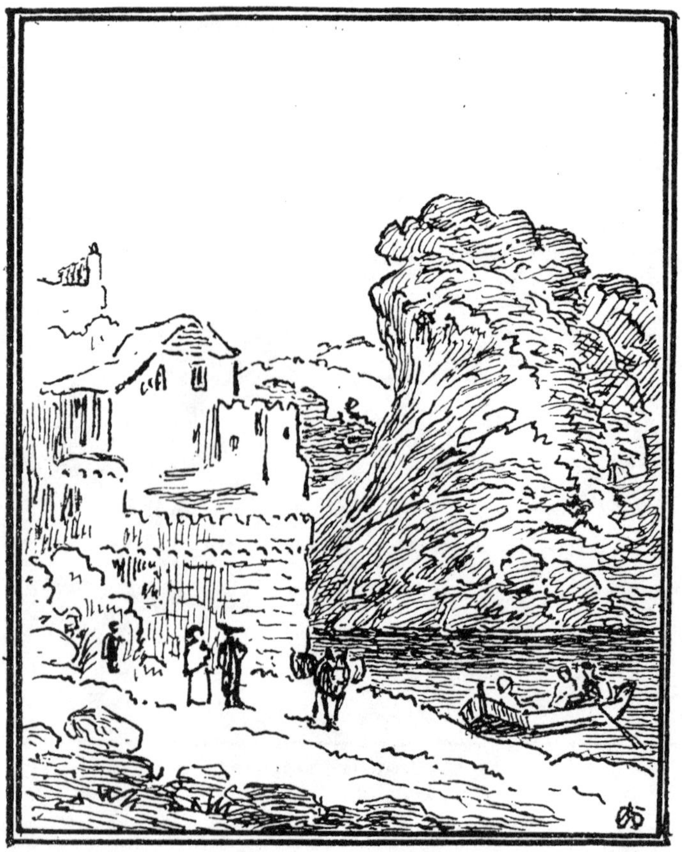

Fig. 104. Toledo

the base line of the picture, and we can fix up a standard of measurement both on the base and on the side as in this sketch, taking 6 feet as about the height of the figures.

XLVIII

THE PICTURE ON A HEIGHT

If we are looking at a scene from a height, that is from a terrace, or a window, or a cliff, then the near foreground, unless it be the terrace, window-sill, &c., would not come into the picture, and we could not see the near figures at A, and the nearest to come into view would be those at B, so that a view from a window, &c., would be as it were without a foreground. Note that the figures at B would be (according to this sketch) 30 feet from the picture plane and about 18 feet below the base line.

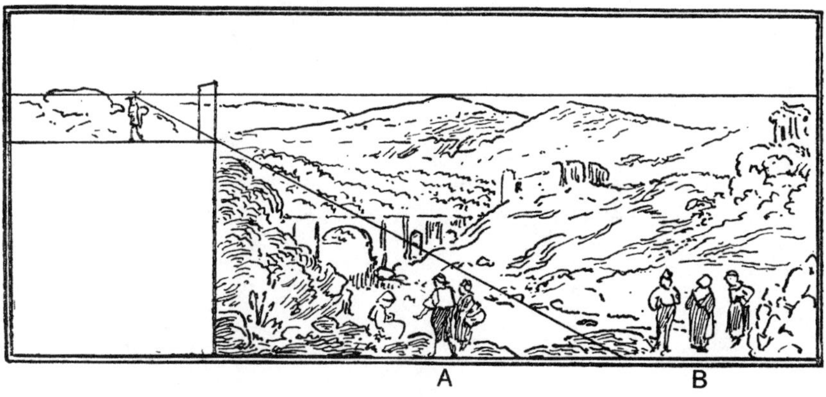

FIG. 105.

BOOK THIRD

XLIX

Angular Perspective

Hitherto we have spoken only of parallel perspective, which is comparatively easy, and in our first figure we placed the cube with one of its sides either touching or parallel to the transparent plane. We now place it so that one angle only (*ab*), touches the picture.

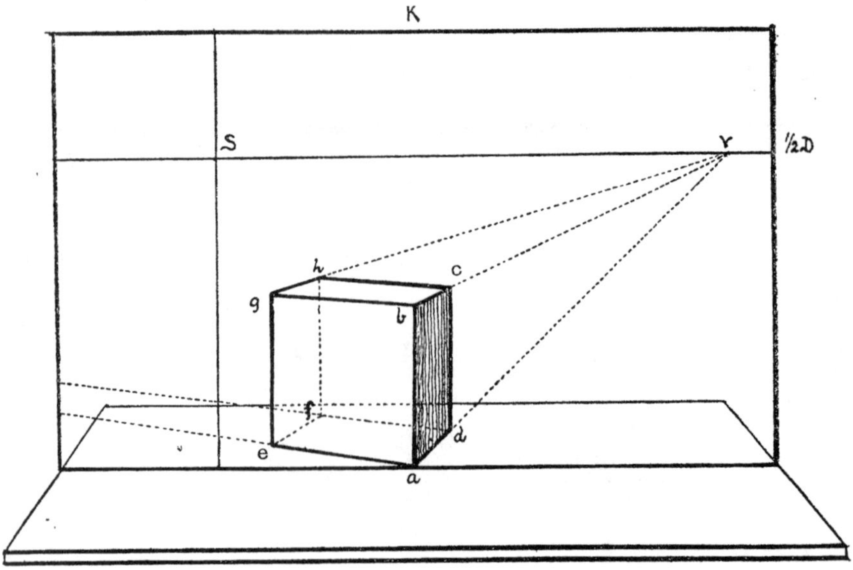

Fig. 106.

Its sides are no longer drawn to the point of sight as in Fig. 7, nor its diagonal to the point of distance, but to some other points on the horizon, although the same rule holds good as regards their parallelism ; as for instance, in the case of *bc* and *ad*, which, if produced, would meet at v, a point on the horizon called a vanishing point. In this figure only one vanishing point is seen, which is to the right of the point of sight S, whilst the other is some distance to the left, and outside the picture. If the cube is correctly drawn, it will be found that the lines *ae*, *bg*, &c., if produced, will meet on the horizon at this other vanishing point. This far-away vanishing point is one of the inconveniences of oblique or angular perspective, and therefore it will be a considerable gain to the draughtsman if we can dispense with it. This can be easily done, as in the above figure, and here our geometry will come to our assistance, as I shall show presently.

L

How to put a Given Point into Perspective

Let us place the given point P on a geometrical plane, to show how far it is from the base line, and indeed in the exact position we wish it to be in the picture. The geometrical plane is sup-

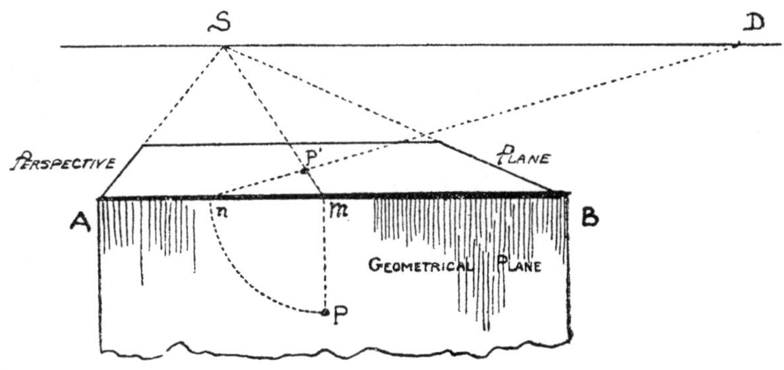

FIG. 107.

posed to face us, to hang down, as it were, from the base line AB, like the side of a table, the top of which represents the perspective plane. It is to that perspective plane that we now have to transfer the point P.

From P raise perpendicular P*m* till it touches the base line at *m*. With centre *m* and radius *m*P describe arc P*n* so that *mn* is now the same length as *m*P. As point P is opposite point *m*, so must it be in the perspective, therefore we draw a line at right angles to the base, that is to the point of sight, and somewhere on this line will be found the required point P·. We now have to find how far from *m* must that point be. It must be the length of *mn*, which is the same as *m*P. We therefore from *n* draw *n*D to the point of distance, which being at an angle of 45°, or half a right angle, makes *m*P· the perspective length of *mn* by its intersection with *m*S, and thus gives us the point P·, which is the perspective of the original point.

LI

A Perspective Point being given, Find its Position on the Geometrical Plane

To do this we simply reverse the foregoing problem. Thus let P be the given perspective point. From point of sight S draw a line through P till it cuts AB at *m*. From distance D draw

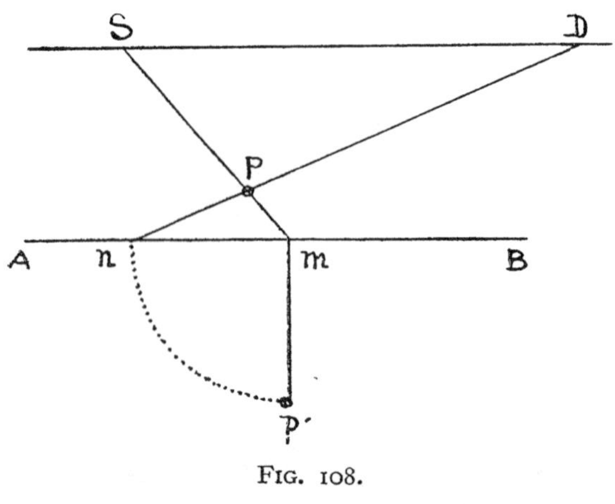

Fig. 108.

another line through P till it cuts the base at *n*. From *m* drop perpendicular, and then with centre *m* and radius *mn* describe arc, and where it cuts that perpendicular is the required point P·. We often have to make use of this problem.

LII

How to put a Given Line into Perspective

This is simply a question of putting two points into perspective, instead of one, or like doing the previous problem twice over, for the two points represent the two extremities of the line. Thus

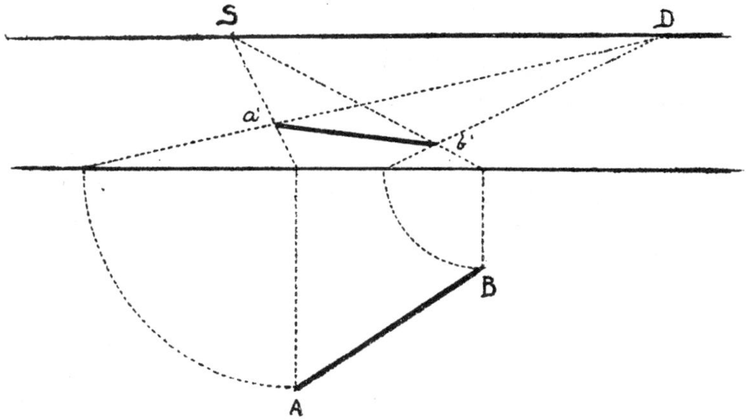

Fig. 109.

we have to find the perspective of A and B, namely $a'b'$. Join those points, and we have the line required.

If one end touches the base, as at A (Fig. 110), then we have

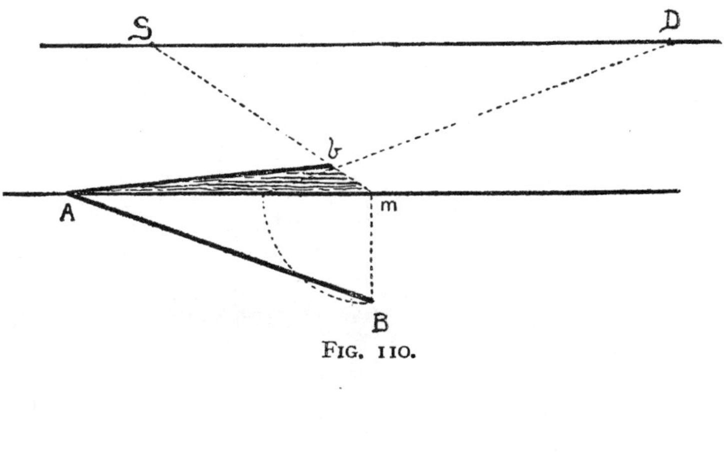

Fig. 110.

but to find one point, namely *b*. We also find the perspective of the angle *m*AB, namely the shaded triangle *m*A*b*. Note also that the perspective triangle equals the geometrical triangle.

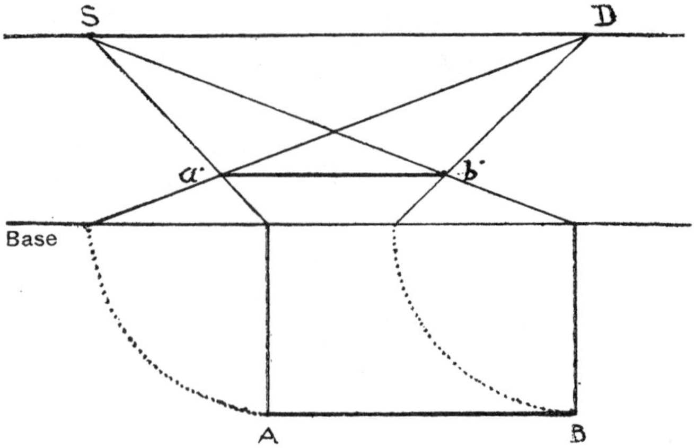

FIG. 111.

When the line required is parallel to the base line of the picture, then the perspective of it is also parallel to that base (see Rule 3).

LIII

To Find the Length of a Given Perspective Line

A perspective line AB being given, find its actual length and the angle at which it is placed.

This is simply the reverse of the previous problem. Let AB be the given line. From distance D through A draw DC, and from S, point of sight, through A draw SO. Drop OP at right angles to base, making it equal to OC. Join PB, and line PB is the actual length of AB.

This problem is useful in finding the position of any given line or point on the perspective plane.

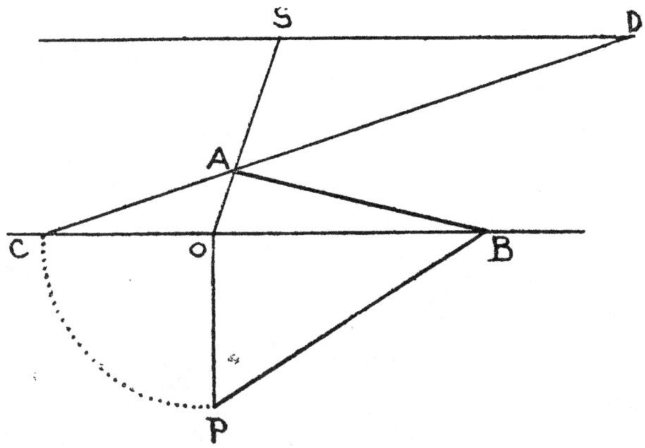

FIG. 112.

LIV

TO FIND THESE POINTS WHEN THE DISTANCE-POINT IS INACCESSIBLE

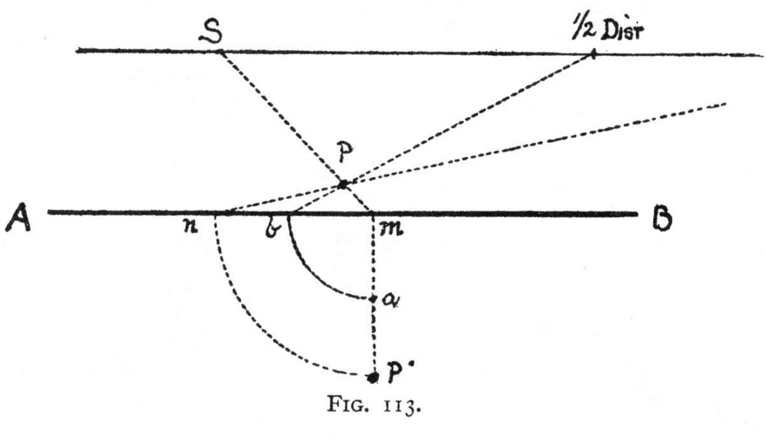

FIG. 113.

If the distance-point is a long way out of the picture, then the same result can be obtained by using the half distance and half base, as already shown.

From *a*, half of *m*P·, draw quadrant *ab*, from *b* (half base), draw line from *b* to half Dist., which intersects S*m* at P, precisely the same point as would be obtained by using the whole distance.

LV

How to put a Given Triangle or other Rectilineal Figure into Perspective

Here we simply put three points into perspective to obtain the given triangle A, or five points to obtain the five-sided figure at B. So can we deal with any number of figures placed at any angle.

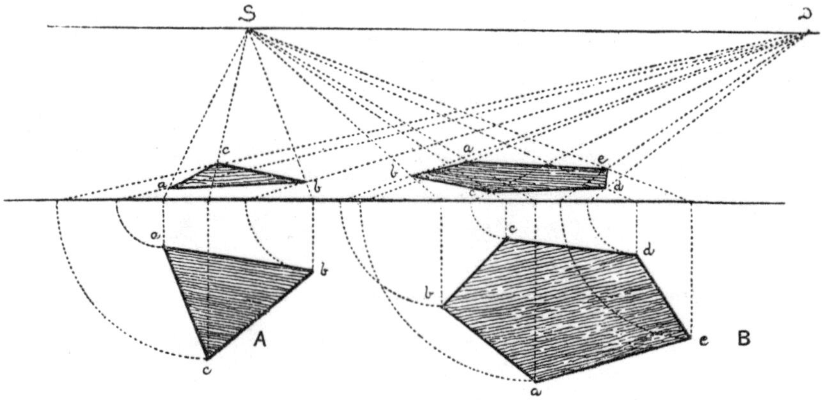

FIG. 114.

Both the above figures are placed in the same diagram, showing how any number can be drawn by means of the same point of sight and the same point of distance, which makes them belong to the same picture.

It is to be noted that the figures appear reversed in the perspective. That is, in the geometrical triangle the base at *ab* is uppermost, whereas in the perspective *ab* is lowermost, yet both are nearest to the ground line.

LVI

How to put a Given Square into Angular Perspective

Let ABCD (Fig. 115) be the given square on the geometrical plane, where we can place it as near or as far from the base and

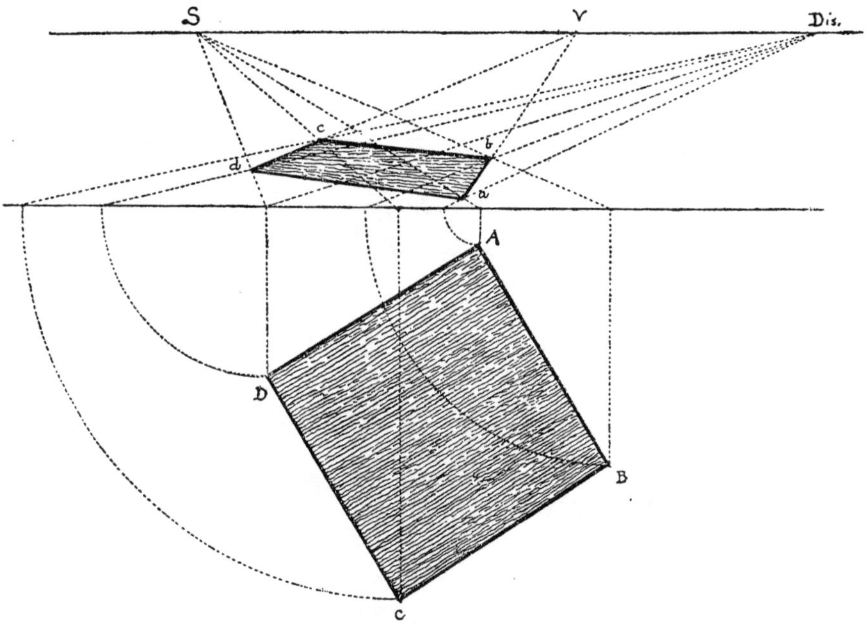

Fig. 115.

at any angle that we wish. We then proceed to find its perspective on the picture by finding the perspective of the four points ABCD as already shown. Note that the two sides of the perspective square *dc* and *ab* being produced, meet at point V on the horizon, which is their vanishing point, but to find the point on the horizon where sides *bc* and *ad* meet, we should have to go a long way to the left of the figure, which by this method is not necessary.

LVII

Of Measuring Points

We now have to find certain points by which to measure those vanishing or retreating lines which are no longer at right angles to the picture plane, as in parallel perspective, and have to be measured in a different way, and here geometry comes to our assistance.

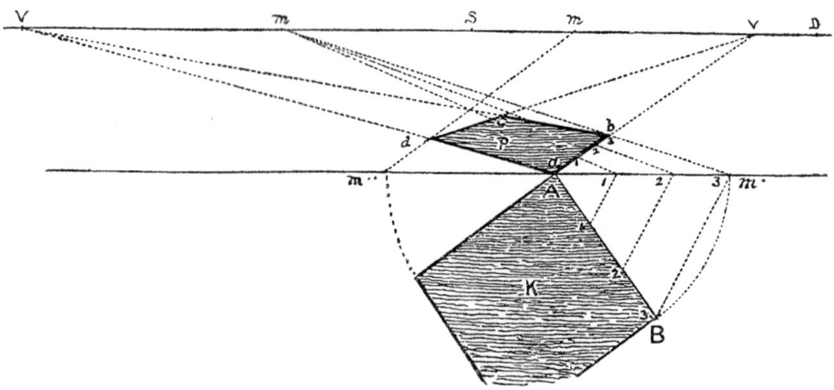

Fig. 116.

Note that the perspective square P equals the geometrical square K, so that side AB of the one equals side *ab* of the other. With centre A and radius AB describe arc B*m*· till it cuts the base line at *m*·. Now AB = A*m*·, and if we join B*m*· then triangle BA*m*· is an isosceles triangle. So likewise if we join *m*·*b* in the perspective figure will *m*·A*b* be the same isosceles triangle in perspective. Continue line *m*·*b* till it cuts the horizon in *m*, which point will be the measuring point for the vanishing line A*b*V. For if in an isosceles triangle we draw lines across it, parallel to its base from one side to the other, we divide both sides in exactly the same quantities and proportions, so that if we measure on the base line of the picture the spaces we require, such as 1, 2, 3, on the length A*m*·, and then from these divisions draw lines to the measuring point, these lines will intersect the vanishing line A*b*V in the lengths and proportions required. To find a measuring point for the lines that go to the other vanishing point, we proceed in the same way. Of course great accuracy is necessary.

Note that the dotted lines 1,1, 2,2, &c., are parallel in the perspective, as in the geometrical figure. In the former the lines are drawn to the same point *m* on the horizon.

LVIII

How to Divide any Given Straight Line into Equal or Proportionate Parts

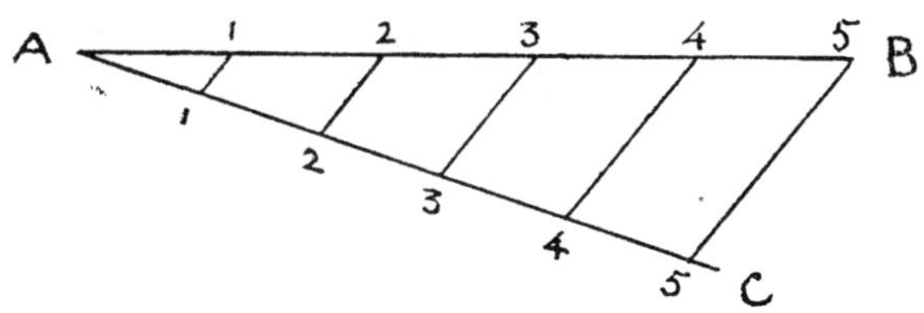

Fig. 117.

Let AB (Fig. 117) be the given straight line that we wish to divide into five equal parts. Draw AC at any convenient angle, and measure off five equal parts with the compasses thereon, as 1, 2, 3, 4, 5. From 5C draw line to 5B. Now from each division on AC draw lines 4,4, 3,3, &c., parallel to 5,5. Then AB will be divided into the required number of equal parts.

LIX

How to Divide a Diagonal Vanishing Line into any Number of Equal or Proportional Parts

In a previous figure (Fig. 116) we have shown how to find a measuring point when the exact measure of a vanishing line is required, but if it suffices merely to divide a line into a given number of equal parts, then the following simple method can be adopted.

We wish to divide *ab* into five equal parts. From *a*, measure off on the ground line the five equal spaces required. From 5, the point to which these measures extend (as they are taken

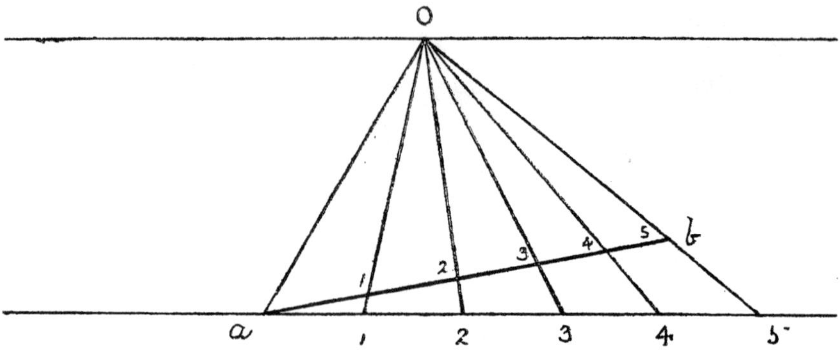

FIG. 118.

at random), draw a line through *b* till it cuts the horizon at O. Then proceed to draw lines from each division on the base to point O, and they will intersect and divide *ab* into the required number of equal parts.

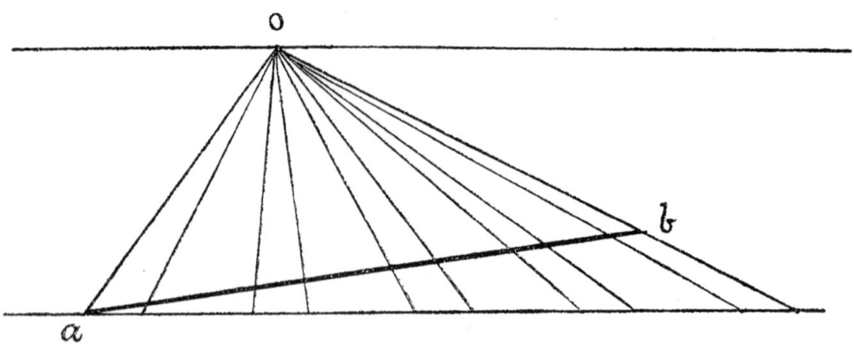

FIG. 119.

The same method applies to a given line to be divided into various proportions, as shown in this lower figure.

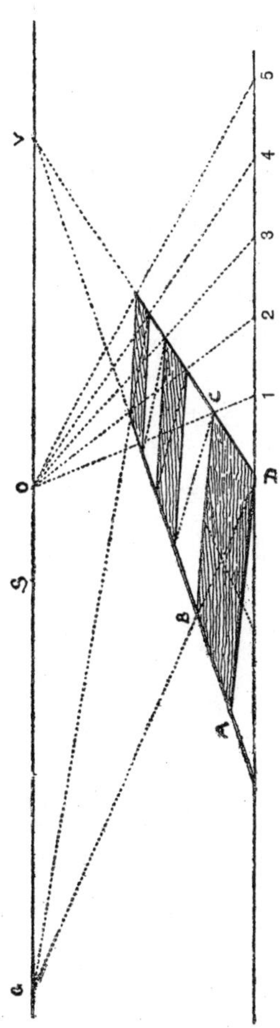

FIG. 120.

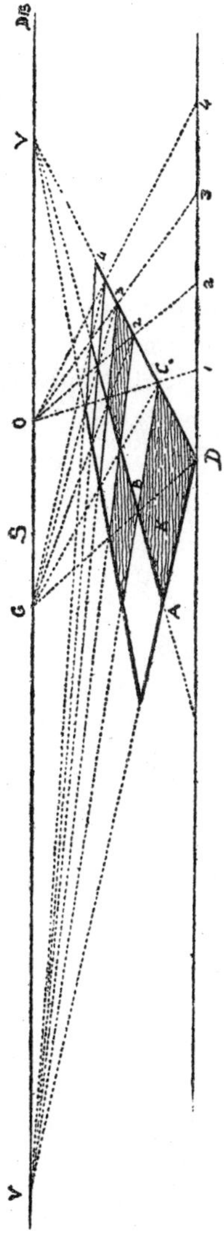

FIG. 121.

LX

Further Use of the Measuring Point O

One square in oblique or angular perspective being given, draw any number of other squares equal to it by means of this point O and the diagonals.

Let ABCD (Fig. 120) be the given square; produce its sides AB, DC till they meet at point V. From D measure off on base any number of equal spaces of any convenient length, as 1, 2, 3, &c.; from 1, through corner of square C, draw a line to meet the horizon at O, and from O draw lines to the several divisions on base line. These lines will divide the vanishing line DV into the required number of parts equal to DC, the side of the square. Produce the diagonal of the square DB till it cuts the horizon at G. From the divisions on line DV draw diagonals to point G: their intersections with the other vanishing line AV will determine the direction of the cross-lines which form the bases of other squares without the necessity of drawing them to the other vanishing point, which in this case is some distance to the left of the picture. If we produce these cross-lines to the horizon we shall find that they all meet at the other vanishing point, to which of course it is easy to draw them when that point is accessible, as in Fig. 121; but if it is too far out of the picture, then this method enables us to do without it.

Figure 121 corroborates the above by showing the two vanishing points and additional squares. Note the working of the diagonals drawn to point G, in both figures.

LXI

Further Use of the Measuring Point O

Suppose we wish to divide the side of a building, as in Fig. 123, or to draw a balcony, a series of windows, or columns, or what not, or, in other words, any line above the horizon, as AB. Then from A we draw AC parallel to the horizon, and mark thereon

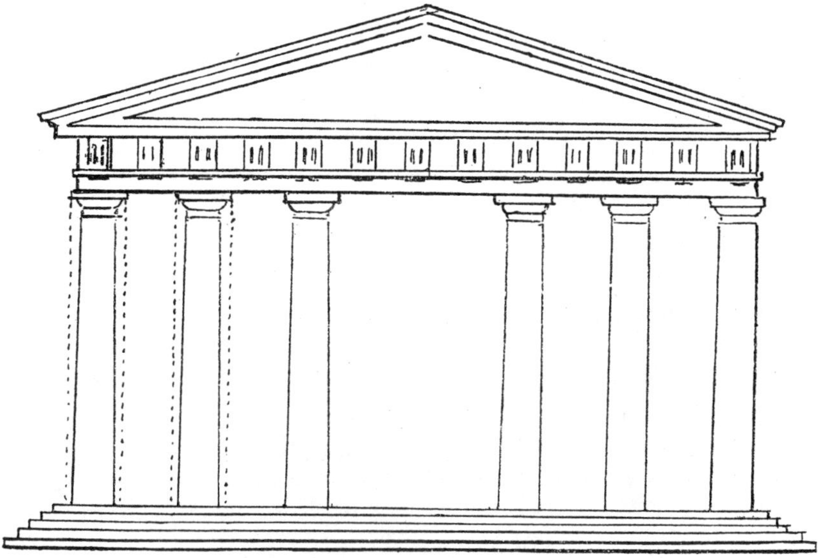

FIG. 122 is a front view of the portico, Fig. 123.

the required divisions 5, 10, 15, &c.: in this case twenty-five (Fig. 122). From C draw a line through B till it cuts the horizon at O. Then proceed to draw the other lines from each division to O, and thus divide the vanishing line AB as required.

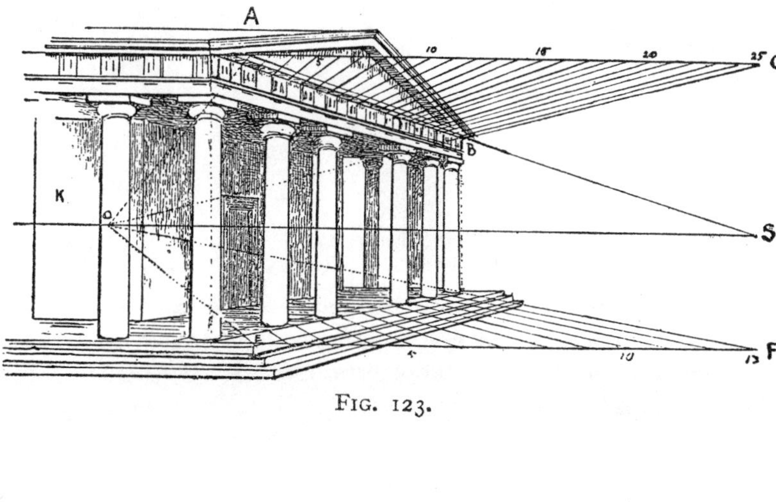

FIG. 123.

In this portico there are thirteen triglyphs with twelve spaces between them, making twenty-five divisions. The required number of parts to draw the columns can be obtained in the same way.

LXII

Another Method of Angular Perspective, being that Adopted in our Art Schools

In the previous method we have drawn our squares by means of a geometrical plan, putting each point into perspective as required, and then by means of the perspective drawing thus obtained, finding our vanishing and measuring points. In this method we proceed in exactly the opposite way, setting out our points first, and drawing the square (or other figure) afterwards.

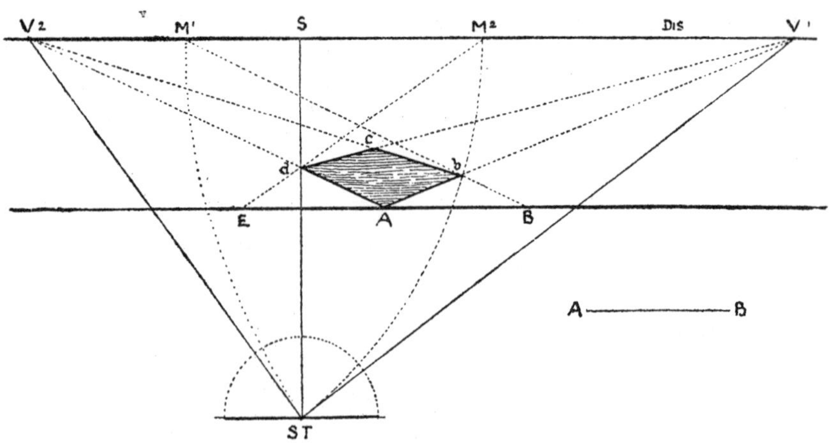

Fig. 124.

Having drawn the horizontal and base lines, and fixed upon the position of the point of sight, we next mark the position of the spectator by dropping a perpendicular, S ST, from that point of sight, making it the same length as the distance we suppose the spectator to be from the picture, and thus we make ST the station-point.

To understand this figure we must first look upon it as a ground-plan or bird's-eye view, the line V^2V^1 or horizon line representing the picture seen edgeways, because of course the station-point cannot be in the picture itself, but a certain distance in front of it. The angle at ST, that is the angle which decides the positions of the two vanishing points V^1, V^2, is always a right angle, and the two remaining angles on that side of the line, called the directing line, are together equal to a right angle or 90°. So that in fixing upon the angle at which the square or other figure is to be placed, we say 'let it be 60° and 30°, or 70° and 20°', &c. Having decided upon the station-point and the angle at which the square is to be placed, draw TV^1 and TV^2, till they cut the horizon at V^1 and V^2. These are the two vanishing points to which the sides of the figure are respectively drawn. But we still want the measuring points for these two vanishing lines. We therefore take first, V^1 as centre and V^1T as radius, and describe arc of circle till it cuts the horizon in M^1, which is the measuring point for all lines drawn to V^1. Then with radius V^2T describe arc from centre V^2 till it cuts the horizon in M^2, which is the measuring point for all vanishing lines drawn to V^2. We have now set out our points. Let us proceed to draw the square A*bcd*. From A, the nearest angle (in this instance touching the base line), measure on each side of it the equal lengths AB and AE, which represent the width or side of the square. Draw EM^2 and BM^1 from the two measuring points, which give us, by their intersections with the vanishing lines AV^1 and AV^2, the perspective lengths of the sides of the square A*bcd*. Join *b* and V^1 and dV^2, which intersect each other at C, then A*dcb* is the square required.

This method, which is easy when you know it, has certain drawbacks, the chief one being that if we require a long-distance point, and a small angle, such as 10° on one side, and 80° on the other, then the size of the diagram becomes so large that it has to be carried out on the floor of the studio with long strings, &c., which is a very clumsy and unscientific way of setting to work. The architects in such cases make use of the centrolinead, a clever mechanical contrivance for getting over the difficulty of the far-off vanishing point, but by the method I have shown you, and shall further illustrate, you will find that you can dispense with all this trouble, and do all your perspective either inside the picture or on a very small margin outside it.

Perhaps another drawback to this method is that it is not self-evident, as in the former one, and being rather difficult to explain, the student is apt to take it on trust, and not to trouble about the reasons for its construction: but to show that it is equally correct, I will draw the two methods in one figure.

LXIII

Two Methods of Angular Perspective in one Figure

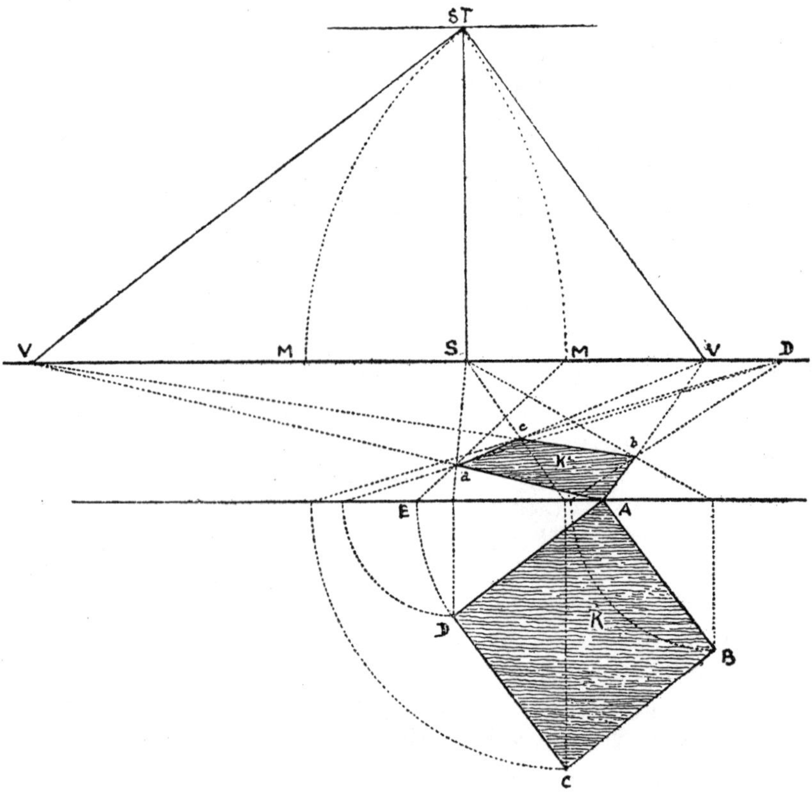

Fig. 125.

It matters little whether the station-point is placed above or below the horizon, as the result is the same. In Fig. 125 it is placed above, as the lower part of the figure is occupied with the geometrical plan of the other method.

In each case we make the square K the same size and at the same angle, its near corner being at A. It must be seen that by whichever method we work out this perspective, the result is the same, so that both are correct: the great advantage of the first or geometrical system being, that we can place the square at any angle, as it is drawn without reference to vanishing points.

We will, however, work out a few figures by the second method.

LXIV

To Draw a Cube, the Points being Given

As in a previous figure (124) we found the various working points of angular perspective, we need now merely transfer them to the horizontal line in this figure, as in this case they will answer our purpose perfectly well.

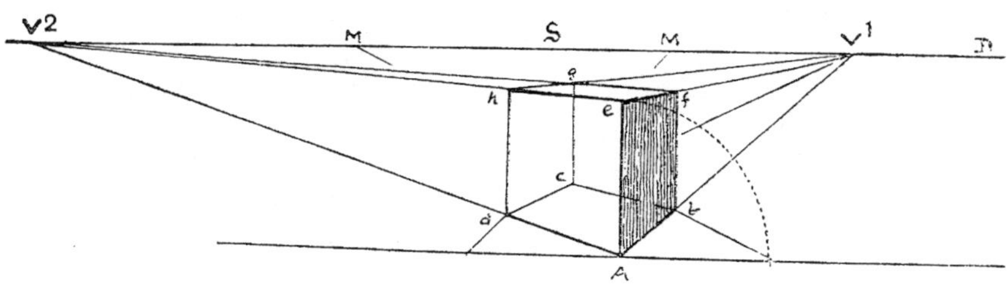

Fig. 126.

Let A be the nearest angle touching the base. Draw AV^1, AV^2. From A, raise vertical A*e*, the height of the cube. From *e* draw ev^1, ev^2, from the other angles raise verticals *bf*, *dh*, *cg*, to meet ev^1, ev^2, fv^2, &c., and the cube is complete.

LXV

Amplification of the Cube Applied to Drawing a Cottage

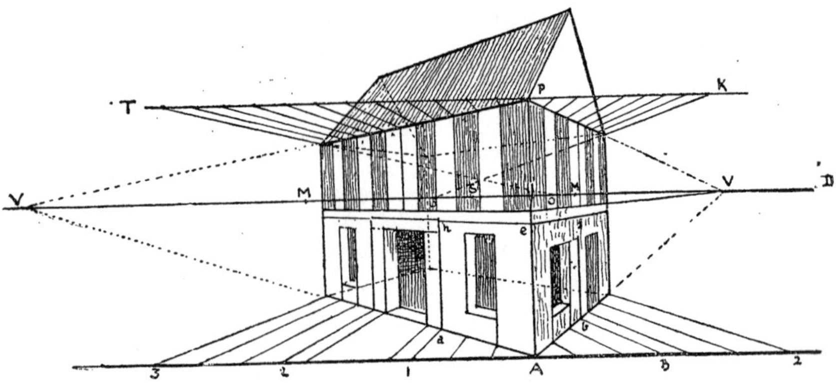

FIG. 127.

Note that we have started this figure with the cube A*dhefb*. We have taken three times AB, its width, for the front of our house, and twice AB for the side, and have made it two cubes high, not counting the roof. Note also the use of the measuring-points in connexion with the measurements on the base line, and the upper measuring line TPK.

LXVI

How to Draw an Interior at an Angle

Here we make use of the same points as in a previous figure, with the addition of the point G, which is the vanishing point of the diagonals of the squares on the floor.

From A draw square A*bcd*, and produce its sides in all directions; again from A, through the opposite angle of the square C, draw a diagonal till it cuts the horizon at G. From G draw diagonals

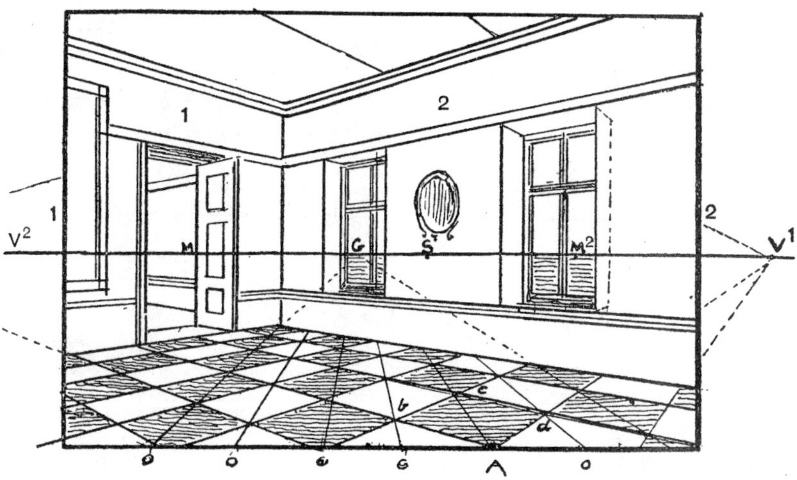

FIG. 128.

through *b* and *d*, cutting the base at *o*, *o*, make spaces *o*, *o*, equal to A*o* all along the base, and from them draw diagonals to G; through the points where these diagonals intersect the vanishing lines drawn in the direction of A*b*, *dc* and A*d*, *bc*, draw lines to the other vanishing point V^1, thus completing the squares, and so cover the floor with them; they will then serve to measure width of door, windows, &c. Of course horizontal lines on wall 1 are drawn to V^1, and those on wall 2 to V^2.

In order to see this drawing properly, the eye should be placed about 3 inches from it, and opposite the point of sight; it will then stand out like a stereoscopic picture, and appear as actual space, but otherwise the perspective seems deformed, and the angles exaggerated. To make this drawing look right from a reasonable distance, the point of distance should be at least twice as far off as it is here, and this would mean altering all the other points and sending them a long way out of the picture; this is why artists use those long strings referred to above. I would however, advise them to make their perspective drawing on a small scale, and then square it up to the size of the canvas.

LXVII

How to Correct Distorted Perspective by Doubling the Line of Distance

Here we have the same interior as the foregoing, but drawn with double the distance, so that the perspective is not so violent and the objects are truer in proportion to each other.

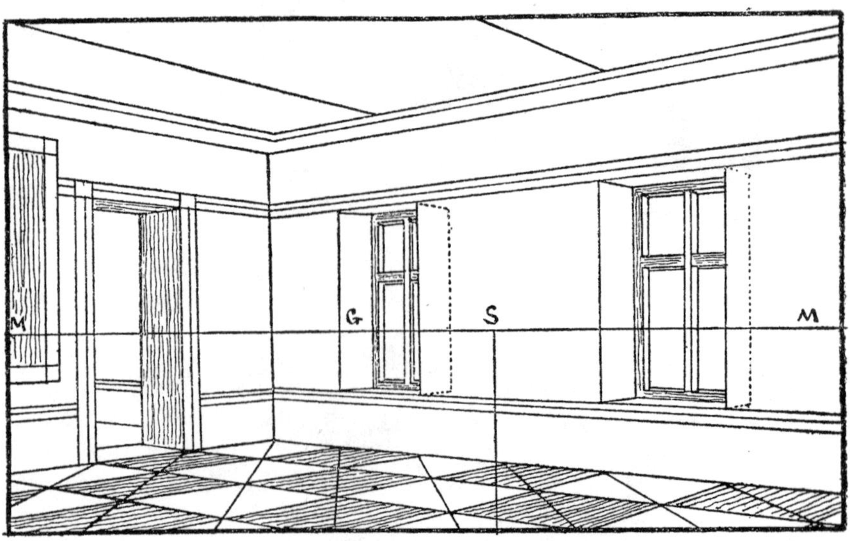

Fig. 129.

To redraw the whole figure double the size, including the station-point, would require a very large diagram, that we could not get into this book without a folding plate, but it comes to the same thing if we double the distances between the various points. Thus, if from S to G in the small diagram is 1 inch, in the larger one make it 2 inches. If from S to M^2 is 2 inches, in the larger make it 4, and so on.

Or this form may be used: make AB twice the length of AC (Fig. 130), or in any other proportion required. On AC mark the points as in the drawing you wish to enlarge. Make AB the length that you wish to enlarge to, draw CB, and then from each division on AC draw lines parallel to CB, and AB will be divided in the same proportions, as I have already shown (Fig. 117).

There is no doubt that it is easier to work direct from the vanishing points themselves, especially in complicated archi-

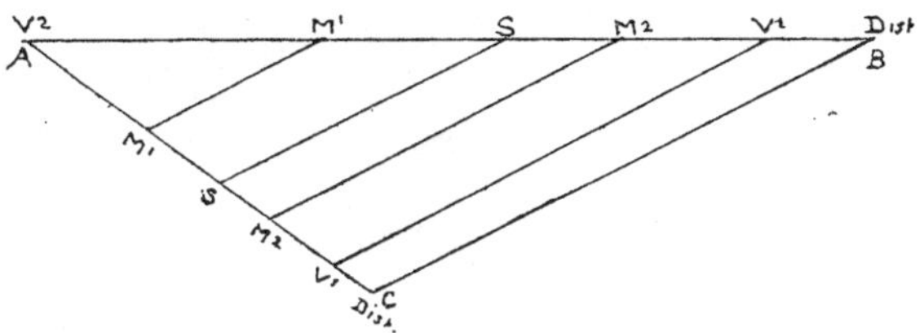

FIG. 130.

tectural work, but at the same time I will now show you how we can dispense with, at all events, one of them, and that the farthest away.

LXVIII

How to Draw a Cube on a Given Square, using only One Vanishing Point

ABCD is the given square (Fig. 131). At A raise vertical A*a* equal to side of square AB', from *a* draw *ab* to the vanishing point. Raise B*b*. Produce VD to E to touch the base line. From E raise vertical EF, making it equal to A*a*. From F draw FV. Raise D*d* and C*c*, their heights being determined by the line FV. Join *da* and the cube is complete. It will be seen that the verticals raised at each corner of the square are equal perspectively, as they are drawn between parallels which start from equal heights, namely, from EF and A*a* to the same point V, the vanishing point. Any other line, such as oo·, can be directed to the inaccessible vanishing point in the same way as *ad*, &c.

Note. This is only one of many original figures and problems in this book which have been called up by the wish to facilitate the work of the artist, and as it were by necessity.

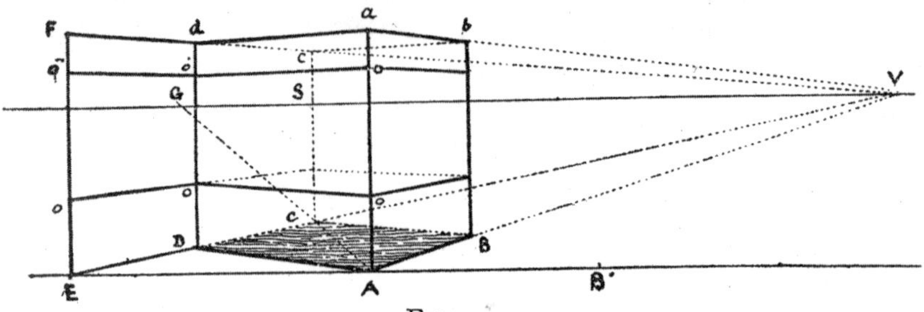

FIG. 131.

LXIX

A COURTYARD OR CLOISTER DRAWN WITH ONE VANISHING POINT

In this figure I have first drawn the pavement by means of the diagonals GA, G*o*, G*o*, &c., and the vanishing point V, the square at A being given. From A draw diagonal through opposite corner till it cuts the horizon at G. From this same point G draw

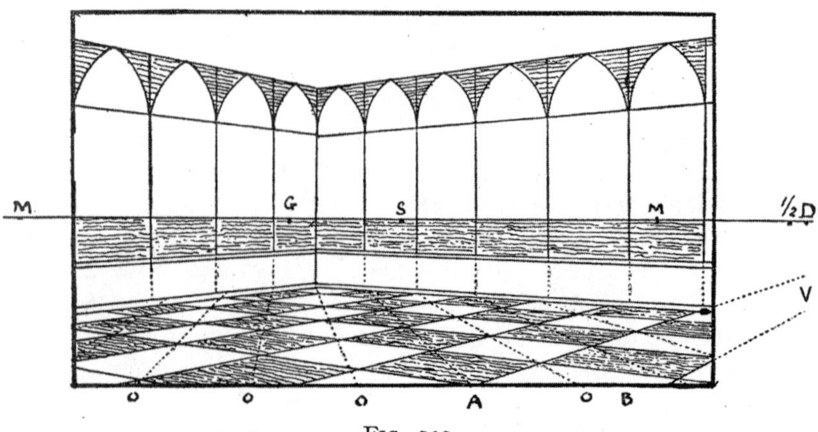

FIG. 132.

lines through the other corners of the square till they cut the ground line at *o*, *o*. Take this measurement A*o* and mark it along the base right and left of A, and the lines drawn from these points *o* to point G will give the diagonals of all the squares on the pavement. Produce sides of square A, and where these lines are intersected by the diagonals G*o* draw lines from the vanishing point V to base. These will give us the outlines of the squares lying between them and also guiding points that will enable us to draw as many more as we please. These again will give us our measurements for the widths of the arches, &c., or between the columns. Having fixed the height of wall or dado, we make use of V point to draw the sides of the building, and by means of proportionate measurement complete the rest, as in Fig. 128.

LXX

How to Draw Lines which shall Meet at a Distant Point, by Means of Diagonals

This is in a great measure a repetition of the foregoing figure, and therefore needs no further explanation.

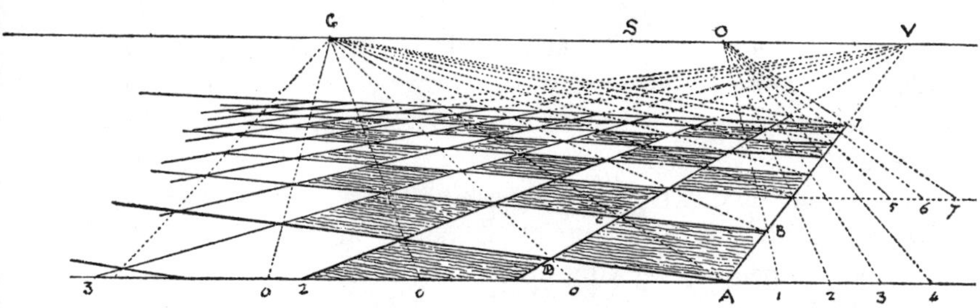

FIG. 133.

I must, however, point out the importance of the point G. In angular perspective it in a measure takes the place of the point of distance in parallel perspective, since it is the vanishing point of diagonals at 45° drawn between parallels such as AV, DV, drawn to a vanishing point V. The method of dividing line AV into a number of parts equal to AB, the side of the square, is also shown in a previous figure (Fig. 120).

LXXI

How to Divide a Square Placed at an Angle into a Given Number of Small Squares

ABCD is the given square, and only one vanishing point is accessible. Let us divide it into sixteen small squares. Produce side CD to base at E. Divide EA into four equal parts. From each division draw lines to vanishing point V. Draw diagonals BD

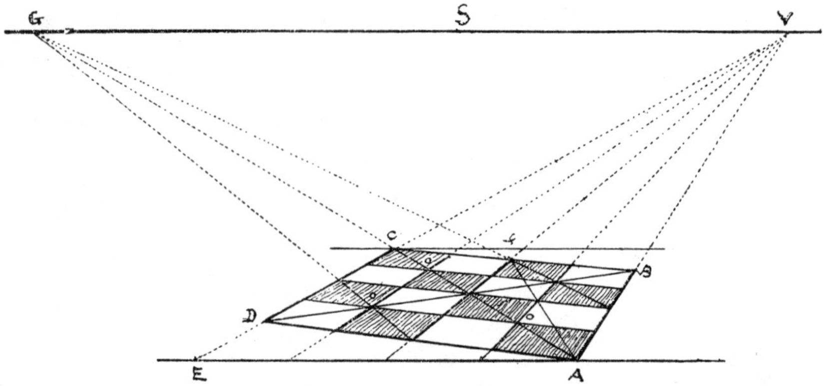

FIG. 134.

and AC, and produce the latter till it cuts the horizon in G. Draw the three cross-lines through the intersections made by the diagonals and the lines drawn to V, and thus divide the square into sixteen.

This is to some extent the reverse of the previous problem. It also shows how the long vanishing point can be dispensed with, and the perspective drawing brought within the picture.

LXXII

Further Example of how to Divide a Given Oblique Square into a Given Number of Equal Squares, say Twenty-five

Having drawn the square ABCD, which is enclosed, as will be seen, in a dotted square in parallel perspective, I divide the line

EA into five equal parts instead of four (Fig. 135), and have made use of the device for that purpose by measuring off the required number on line EF, &c. Fig. 136 is introduced here simply to show that the square can be divided into any number of smaller squares. Nor need the figure be necessarily a square; it is just

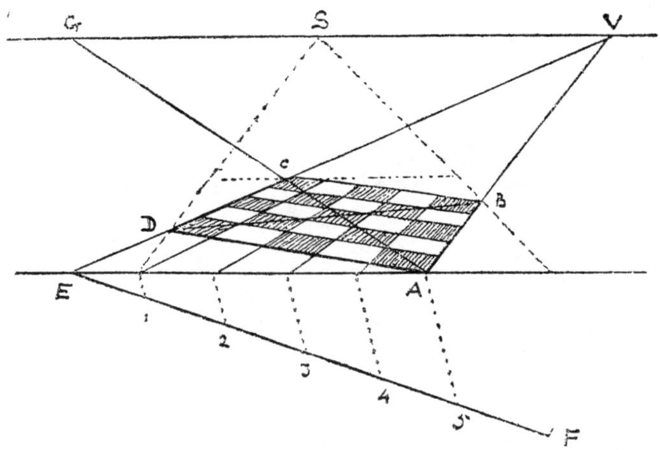

FIG. 135.

as easy to make it an oblong, as ABEF (Fig. 136); for although we begin with a square we can extend it in any direction we please, as here shown.

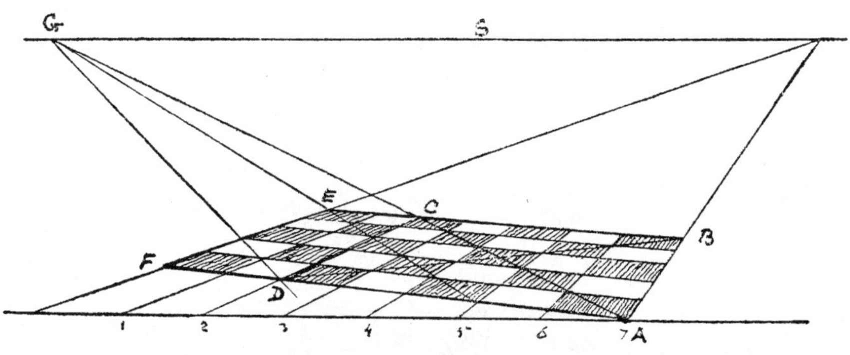

FIG. 136.

LXXIII

Of Parallels and Diagonals

To find the centre of a square or other rectangular figure we have but to draw its two diagonals, and their intersection will give us the centre of the figure (see 137 A). We do the same

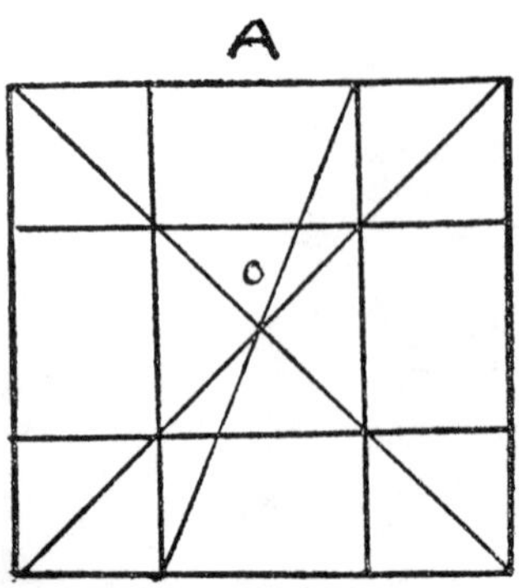

Fig. 137 A.

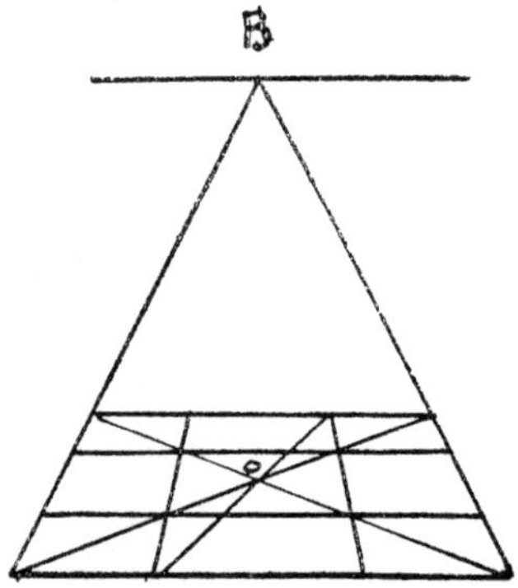

Fig. 137 B.

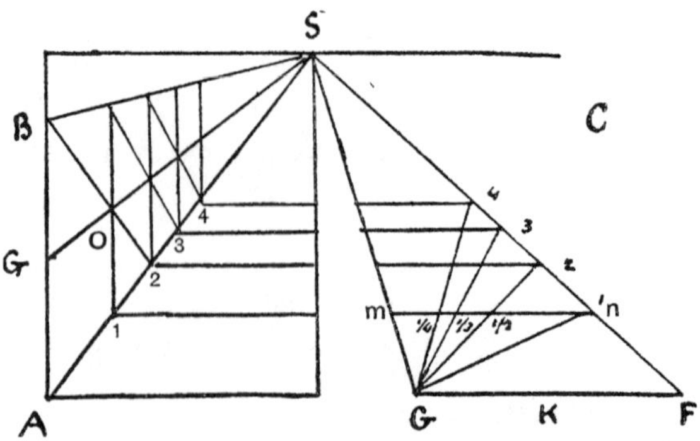

Fig. 137 C.

with perspective figures, as at B. In Fig. C is shown how a diagonal, drawn from one angle of a square B through the centre O of the opposite side of the square, will enable us to find a second square lying between the same parallels, then a third, a fourth, and so on. At figure K lying on the ground, I have divided the farther side of the square *mn* into $\frac{1}{4}$, $\frac{1}{3}$, $\frac{1}{2}$. If I draw a diagonal from G (at the base) through the half of this line I cut off on FS the lengths or sides of two squares; if through the quarter I cut off the length of four squares on the vanishing line FS, and so on. In Fig. 137 D is shown how easily any number of objects at any equal distances apart, such as posts, trees, columns, &c., can be drawn by means of diagonals between parallels, guided by a central line GS.

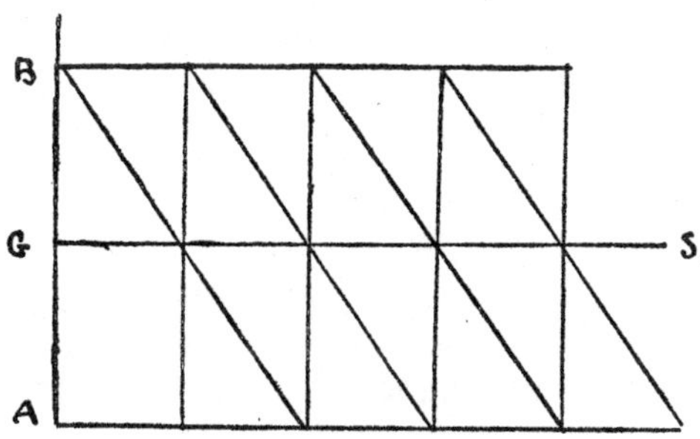

FIG. 137 D.

LXXIV

THE SQUARE, THE OBLONG, AND THEIR DIAGONALS

Having found the centre of a square or oblong, such as Figs. 138 and 139, if we draw a third line through that centre at a given angle and then at each of its extremities draw perpendiculars AB, DC, we divide that square or oblong into three parts, the two outer portions being equal to each other, and the centre one either

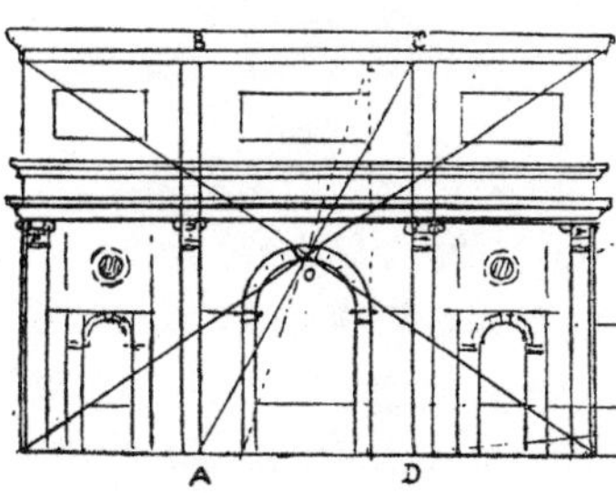

FIG. 138.

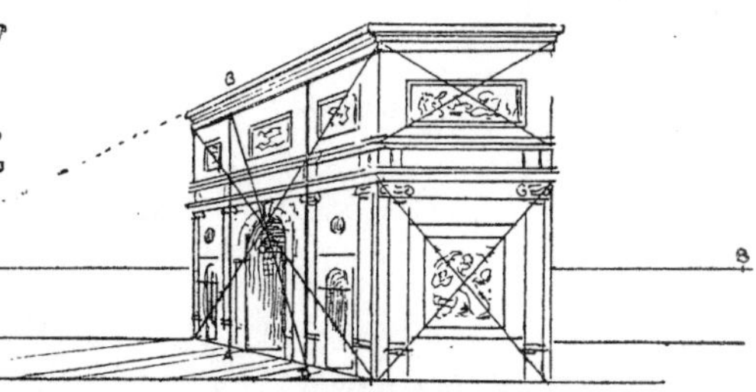

FIG. 139.

larger or smaller as desired; as, for instance, in the triumphal arch we make the centre portion larger than the two outer sides. When certain architectural details and spaces are to be put into perspective, a scale such as that in Fig. 123 will be found of great convenience; but if only a ready division of the principal proportions is required, then these diagonals will be found of the greatest use.

LXXV

Showing the Use of the Square and Diagonals in Drawing Doorways, Windows, and other Architectural Features

This example is from Serlio's *Architecture* (1663), showing what excellent proportion can be obtained by the square and

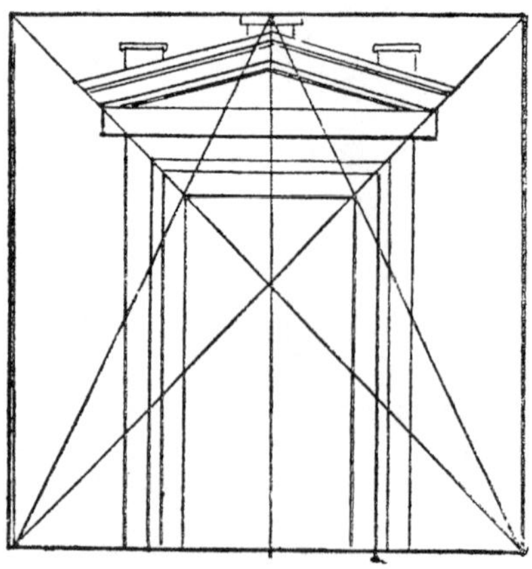

Fig. 140.

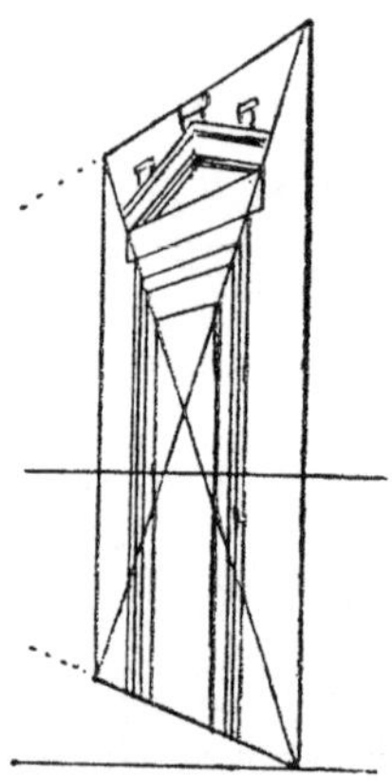

Fig. 141.

diagonals. The width of the door is one-third of the base of square, the height two-thirds. As a further illustration we have drawn the same figure in perspective.

LXXVI

How to Measure Depths by Diagonals

If we take any length on the base of a square, say from A to *g*, and from *g* raise a perpendicular till it cuts the diagonal AB in O, then from O draw horizontal O*g*·, we form a square A*g*O*g*·, and

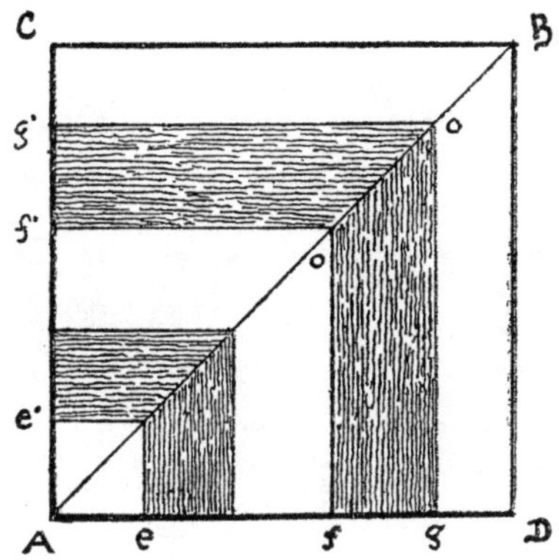

Fig. 142.

thus measure on one side of the square the distance or depth A*g*·. So can we measure any other length, such as *fg*, in like manner.

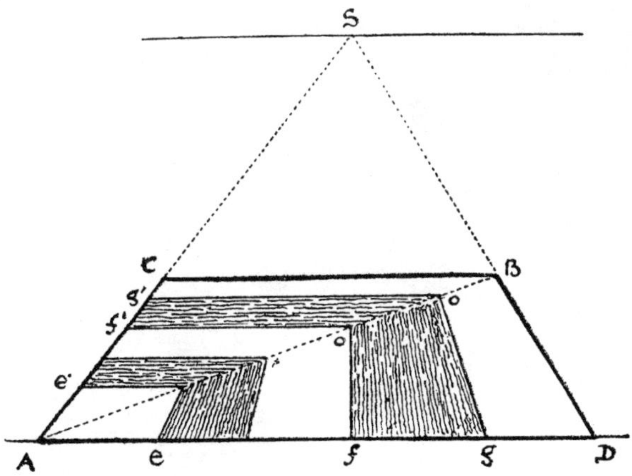

Fig. 143.

To do this in perspective we pursue precisely the same method, as shown in this figure (143).

To measure a length A*g* on the side of square AC, we draw a line from *g* to the point of sight *s*, and where it crosses diagonal AB at O we draw horizontal O*g*, and thus find the required depth A*g* in the picture.

LXXVII

How to Measure Distances by the Square and Diagonal

It may sometimes be convenient to have a ready method by which to measure the width and length of objects standing against the wall of a gallery, without referring to distance-points, &c.

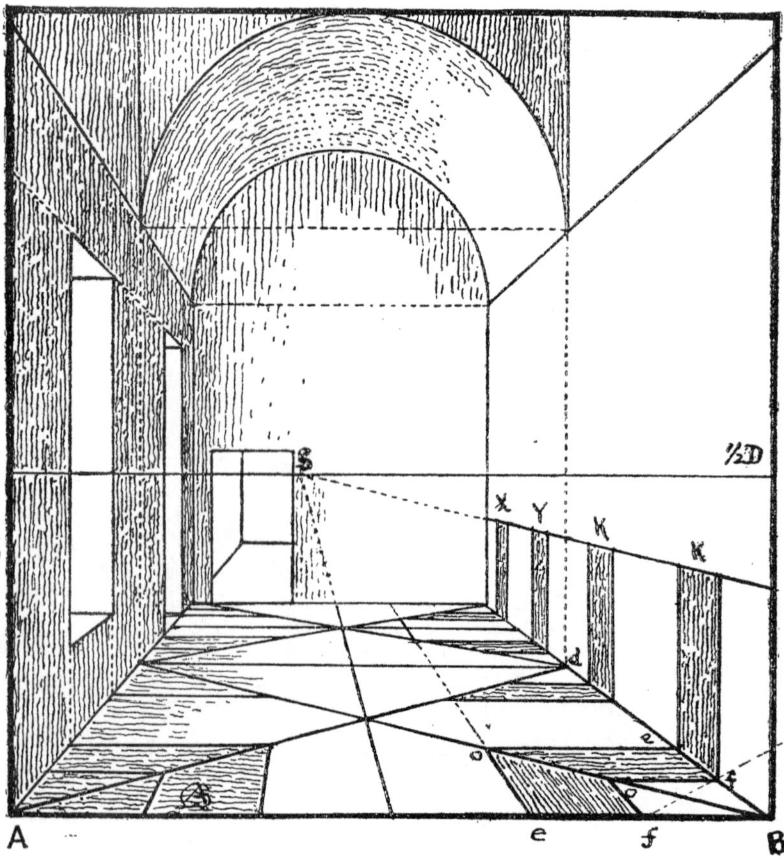

Fig. 144.

In Fig. 144 the floor is divided into two large squares with their diagonals. Suppose we wish to draw a fireplace or a piece of furniture K, we measure its base *ef* on AB, as far from B as we wish it to be in the picture; draw *eo* and *fo* to point of sight, and proceed as in the previous figure by drawing parallels from *oo*, &c.

Let it be observed that the great advantage of this method is, that we can use it to measure such distant objects as XY just as easily as those near to us.

There is, however, a still further advantage arising from it, and that is that it introduces us to a new and simpler method of perspective, to which I have already referrèd, and it will, I hope, be found of infinite use to the artist.

Note.—As we have founded many of these figures on a given square in angular perspective, it is as well to have a ready and certain means of drawing that square without the elaborate setting out of a geometrical plan, as in the first method, or the more cumbersome and extended system of the second method. I shall therefore show you another method equally correct, but much simpler than either, which I have invented for our use, and which indeed forms one of the chief features of this book.

LXXVIII

How by Means of the Square and Diagonal we can Determine the Position of Points in Space

Apart from the aid that perspective affords the draughtsman, there is a further value in it, in that it teaches us almost a new science, which we might call the mystery of aspect, and how it is that the objects around us take so many different forms, or rather appearances, although they themselves remain the same. And also that it enables us, with, I think, great pleasure to ourselves, to fathom space, to work out difficult problems by simple reasoning, and to exercise those inventive and critical faculties which give strength and enjoyment to mental life.

And now, after this brief excursion into philosophy, let us come down to the simple question of the perspective of a point.

Here, for instance, are two aspects of the same thing: the geometrical square A, which is facing us, and the perspective

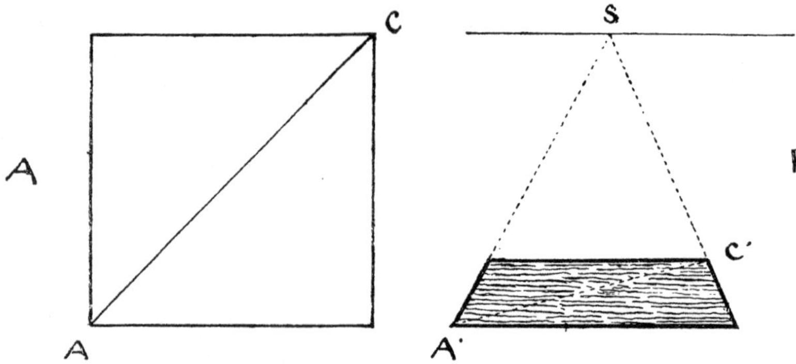

FIG. 145.

square B, which we suppose to lie flat on the table, or rather on the perspective plane. Line A·C· is the perspective of line AC. On the geometrical square we can make what measurements we

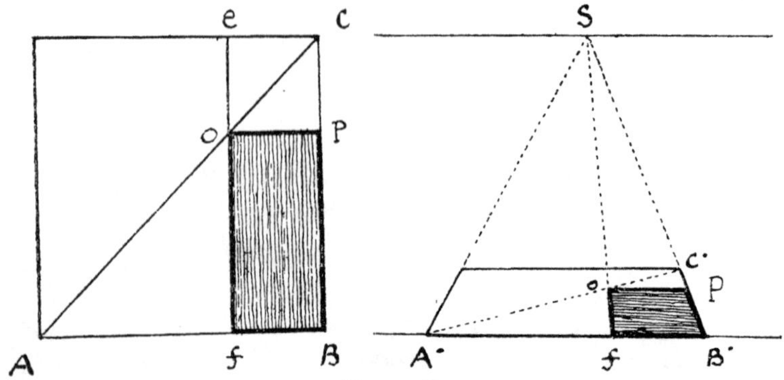

FIG. 146.

please with the compasses, but on the perspective square B· the only line we can actually measure is the base line. In both figures this base line is the same length. Suppose we want to find the perspective of point P (Fig. 146), we make use of the diagonal CA. From P in the geometrical square draw PO to meet the diagonal in O; through O draw perpendicular *fe*; transfer length *f*B, so found, to the base of the perspective square; from *f* draw *f*S to point of sight; where it cuts the diagonal in O, draw horizontal OP·, which gives us the point required. In the same way we can find the perspective of any number of points on any side of the square.

LXXIX

Perspective of a Point Placed in any Position within the Square

Let the point P be the one we wish to put into perspective. We have but to repeat the process of the previous problem, making use of our measurements on the base, the diagonals, &c.

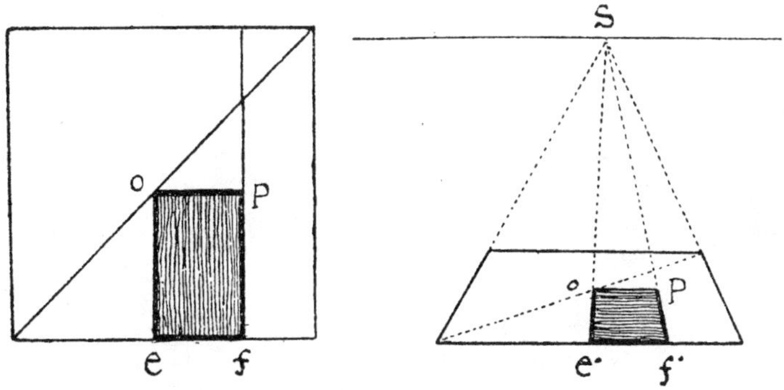

Fig. 147.

Indeed these figures are so plain and evident that further description of them is hardly necessary, so I will here give two drawings of triangles which explain themselves. To put a triangle into perspective we have but to find three points, such as *f*EP, Fig. 148 A, and then transfer these points to the perspective square 148 B, as there shown, and form the perspective triangle; but these figures explain themselves. Any other triangle or rectilineal

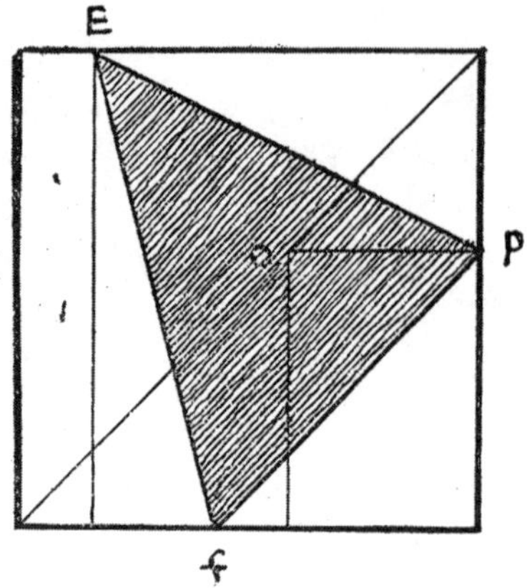

FIG. 148 A.

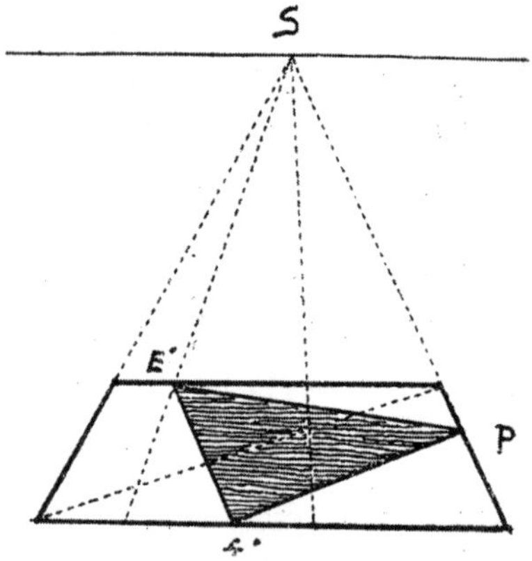

FIG. 148 B.

figure can be worked out in the same way, which is not only the simplest method, but it carries its mathematical proof with it.

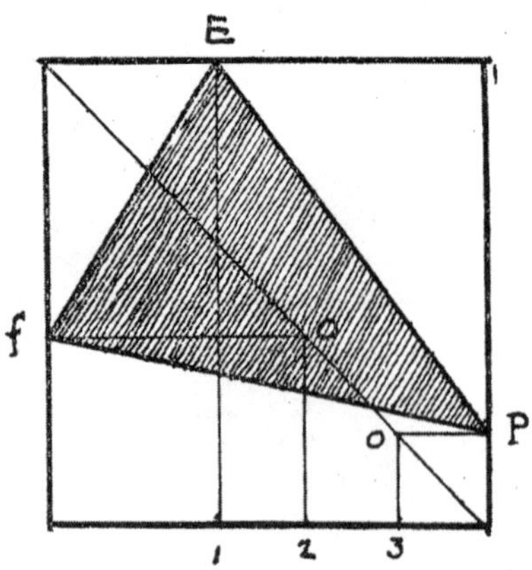

FIG. 149 A.

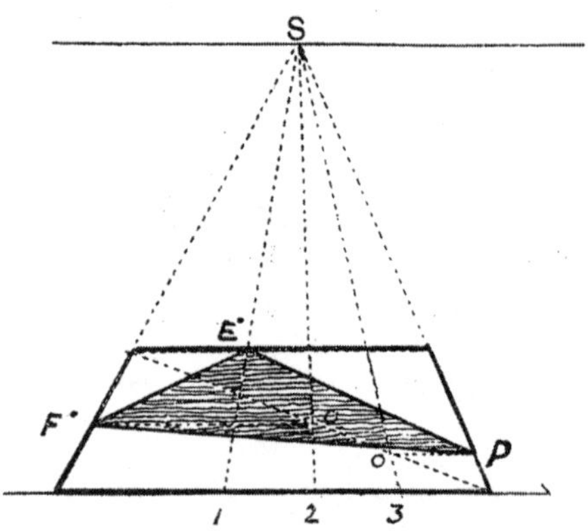

FIG. 149 B.

LXXX

Perspective of a Square Placed at an Angle

New Method

As we have drawn a triangle in a square so can we draw an oblique square in a parallel square. In Figure 150 A we have drawn the oblique square GEP*n*. We find the points on the base A*m*, as in the previous figures, which enable us to construct the oblique perspective square *n*·G·E·P· in the parallel perspective square Fig. 150 B. But it is not necessary to construct the

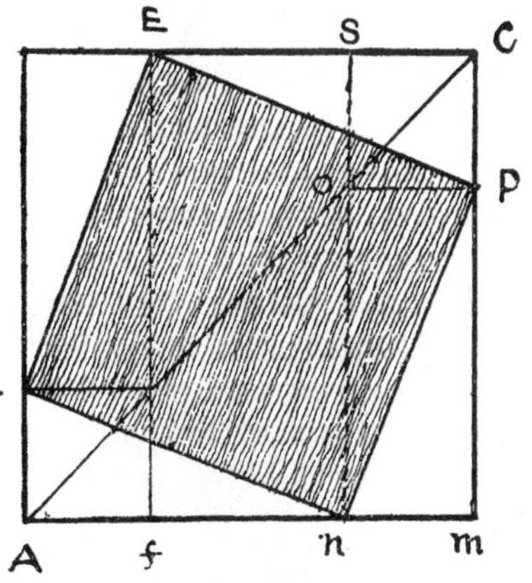

Fig. 150 A.

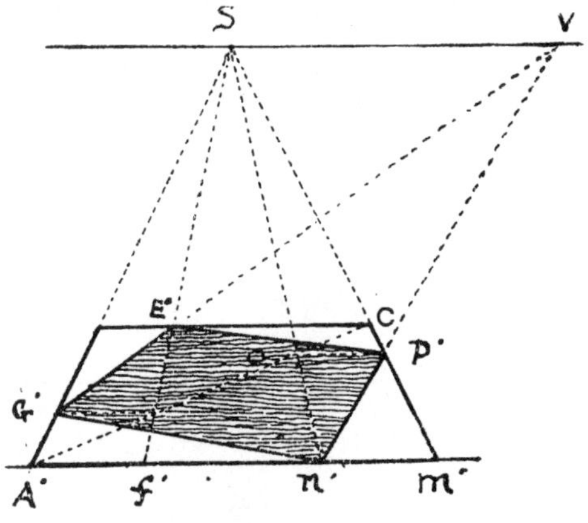

Fig. 150 B.

geometrical figure, as I will show presently. It is here introduced to explain the method.

Fig. 150 B. To test the accuracy of the above, produce sides G·E· and *n*·P· of perspective square till they touch the horizon, where they will meet at V, their vanishing point, and again produce the other sides *n*·G· and P·E· till they meet on the horizon at the other vanishing point, which they must do if the figure is correctly drawn.

In any parallel square construct an oblique square from

a given point—given the parallel square at Fig. 150 B, and given point *n*· on base. Make A·*f*· equal to *n*·*m*·, draw *f*·S and *n*·S to point of sight. Where these lines cut the diagonal AC draw horizontals to P· and G·, and so find the four points G·E·P·*n*· through which to draw the square.

LXXXI

On a Given Line Placed at an Angle to the Base Draw a Square in Angular Perspective, the Point of Sight, and Distance, being given.

Let AB be the given line, S the point of sight, and D the distance (Fig. 151, 1). Through A draw SC from point of sight to

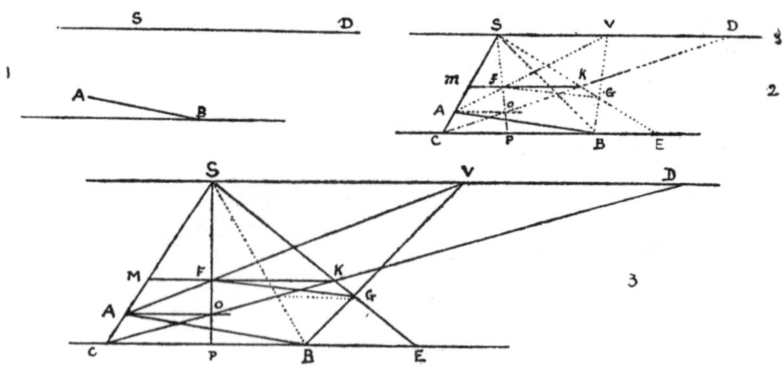

Fig. 151.

base (Fig. 151, 2 and 3). From C draw CD to point of distance. Draw A*o* parallel to base till it cuts CD at *o*, through *o* draw SP, from B mark off BE equal to CP. From E draw ES intersecting CD at K, from K draw KM, thus completing the outer parallel square. Through F, where PS intersects MK, draw AV till it cuts the horizon in V, its vanishing point. From V draw VB cutting side KE of outer square in G, and we have the four points

AFGB, which are the four angles of the square required. Join FG, and the figure is complete.

Any other side of the square might be given, such as AF. First through A and F draw SC, SP, then draw A*o*, then through *o* draw CD. From C draw base of parallel square CE, and at M through F draw MK cutting diagonal at K, which gives top of square. Now through K draw SE, giving KE the remaining side thereof, produce AF to V, from V draw VB. Join FG, GB, and BA, and the square required is complete.

The student can try the remaining two sides, and he will find they work out in a similar way.

LXXXII

How to Draw Solid Figures at any Angle by the New Method

As we can draw planes by this method so can we draw solids, as shown in these figures. The heights of the corners of the

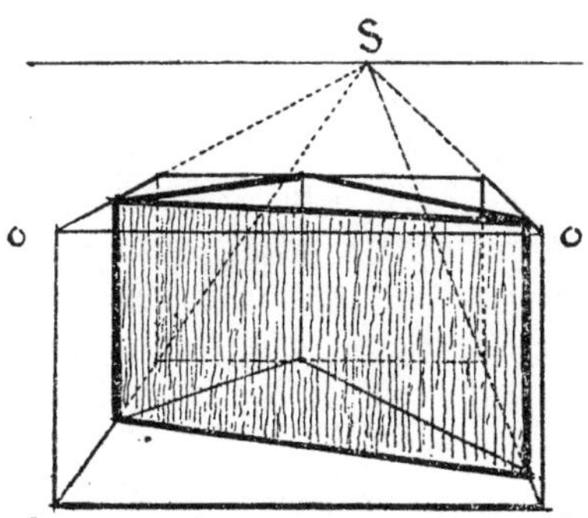

Fig. 152.

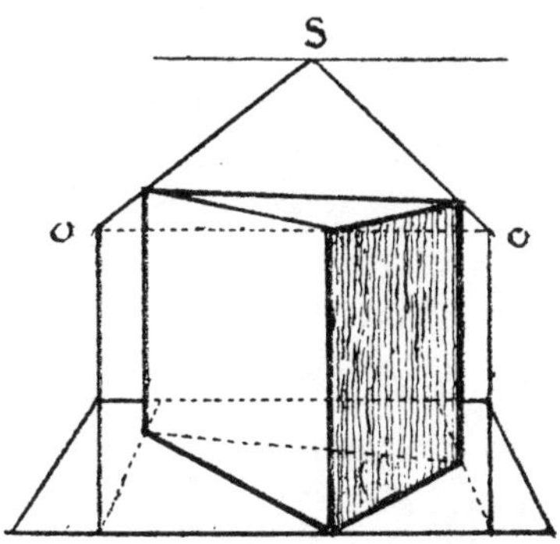

Fig. 153.

triangles are obtained by means of the vanishing scales AS, OS, which have already been explained.

In the same manner we can draw a cubic figure (Fig. 154)—a box, for instance—at any required angle. In this case, besides the scale AS, OS, we have made use of the vanishing lines DV, BV, to corroborate the scale, but they can be dispensed with in these simple objects, or we can use a scale on each side of the figure as *a·o·*S, should both vanishing points be inaccessible. Let it be

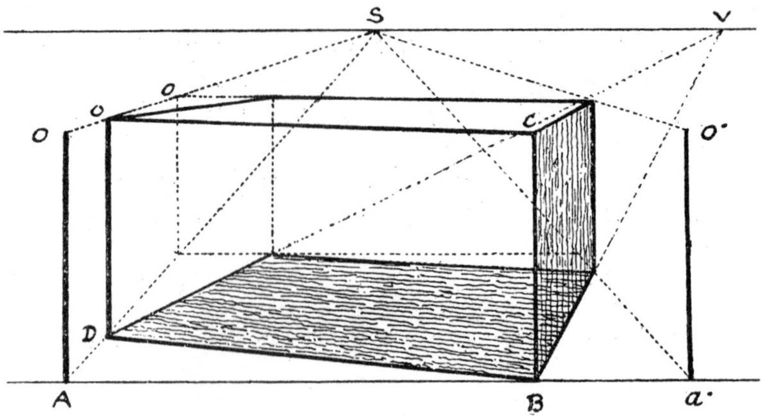

FIG. 154.

noted that in the scale AOS, AO is made equal to BC, the height of the box.

By a similar process we draw these two figures, one on the square, the other on the circle.

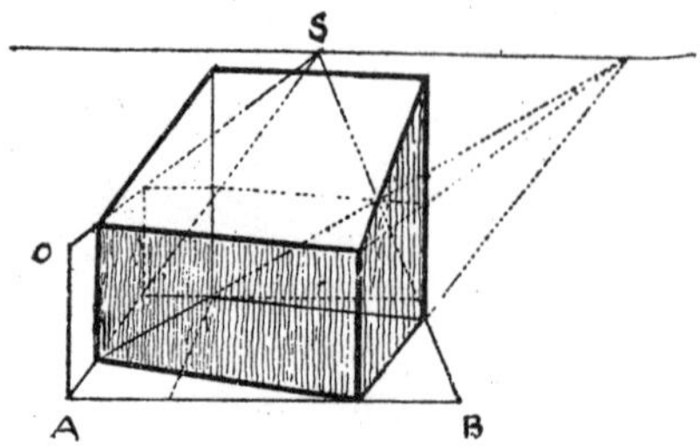

FIG. 155.

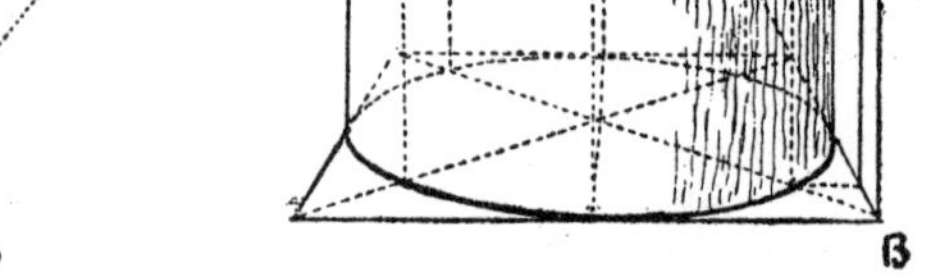

FIG. 156.

LXXXIII

Points in Space

The chief use of these figures is to show how by means of diagonals, horizontals, and perpendiculars almost any figure in space can be set down. Lines at any slope and at any angle can be drawn by this descriptive geometry.

The student can examine these figures for himself, and will understand their working from what has gone before. Here (Fig. 157) in the geometrical square we have a vertical plane

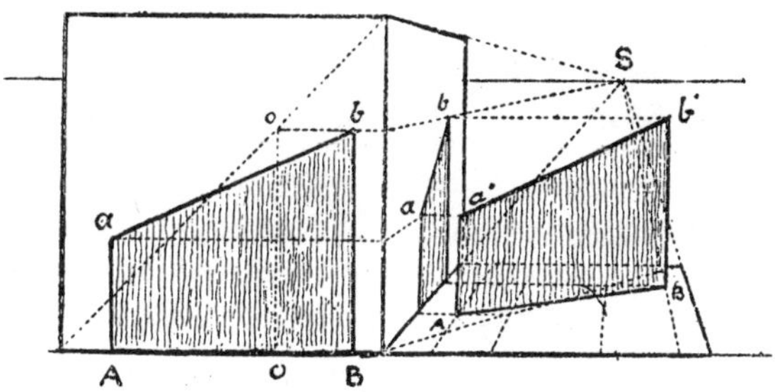

Fig. 157.

A*ab*B standing on its base AB. We wish to place a projection of this figure at a certain distance and at a given angle in space. First of all we transfer it to the side of the cube, where it is seen in perspective, whilst at its side is another perspective square lying flat, on which we have to stand our figure. By means of the diagonal of this flat square, horizontals from figure on side of cube, and lines drawn from point of sight (as already explained), we obtain the direction of base line AB, and also by means of lines *aa*· and *bb*· we obtain the two points in space *a*·*b*·. Join A*a*·, *a*·*b*· and B*b*·, and we have the projection required, and which may be said to possess the third dimension.

In this other case (Fig. 158) we have a wedge-shaped figure standing on a triangle placed on the ground, as in the previous figure, its three corners being the same height. In the vertical geometrical square we have a ground-plan of the figure, from which we draw lines to diagonal and to base, and notify by numerals 1, 3,

2, 1, 3; these we transfer to base of the horizontal perspective square, and then construct shaded triangle 1, 2, 3, and raise to the height required as shown at 1·, 2·, 3·. Although we may not want to make use of these special figures, they show us how we could work out almost any form or object suspended in space.

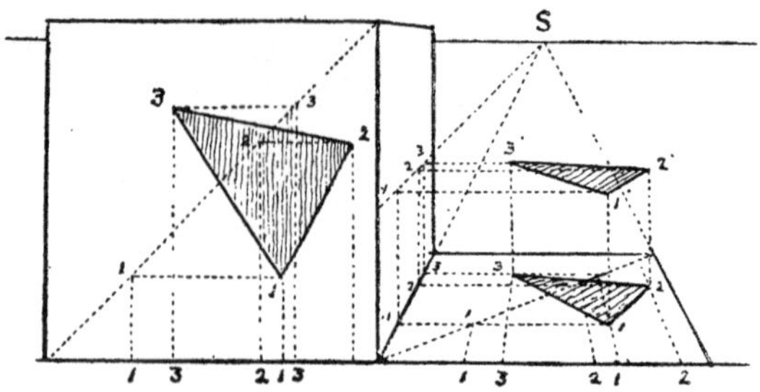

FIG. 158.

LXXXIV

The Square and Diagonal Applied to Cubes and Solids Drawn Therein

As we have made use of the square and diagonal to draw figures at various angles so can we make use of cubes either in parallel or angular perspective to draw other solid figures within

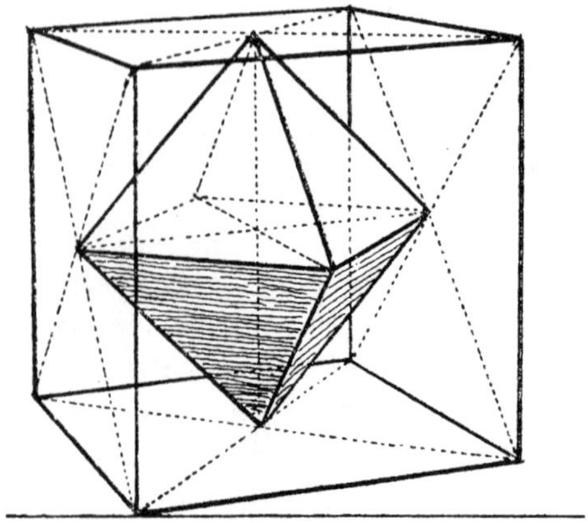

FIG. 159.

them, as shown in these drawings, for this is simply an amplification of that method. Indeed we might invent many more such things. But subjects for perspective treatment will constantly present themselves to the artist or draughtsman in the course of his experience, and while I endeavour to show him how to grapple with any new difficulty or subject that may arise, it is impossible to set down all of them in this book.

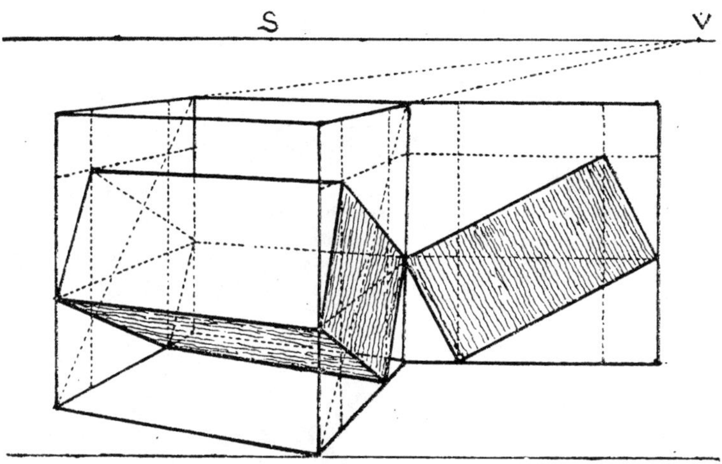

FIG. 160.

LXXXV

To Draw an Oblique Square in Another Oblique Square without Using Vanishing Points

It is not often that both vanishing points are inaccessible, still it is well to know how to proceed when this is the case. We first draw the square ABCD inside the parallel square, as in previous figures. To draw the smaller square K we simply draw a smaller parallel square *h h h h*, and within that, guided by the intersections of the diagonals therewith, we obtain the four points through which to draw square K. To raise a solid figure on these squares we can make use of the vanishing scales as shown on each side of the figure, thus obtaining the upper square 1 2 3 4, then by means of the diagonal 1 3 and 2 4 and verticals raised from each corner of square K to meet them we obtain the smaller upper square corresponding to K.

It might be said that all this can be done by using the two vanishing points in the usual way. In the first place, if they were as far off as required for this figure we could not get them into a page unless it were three or four times the width of this

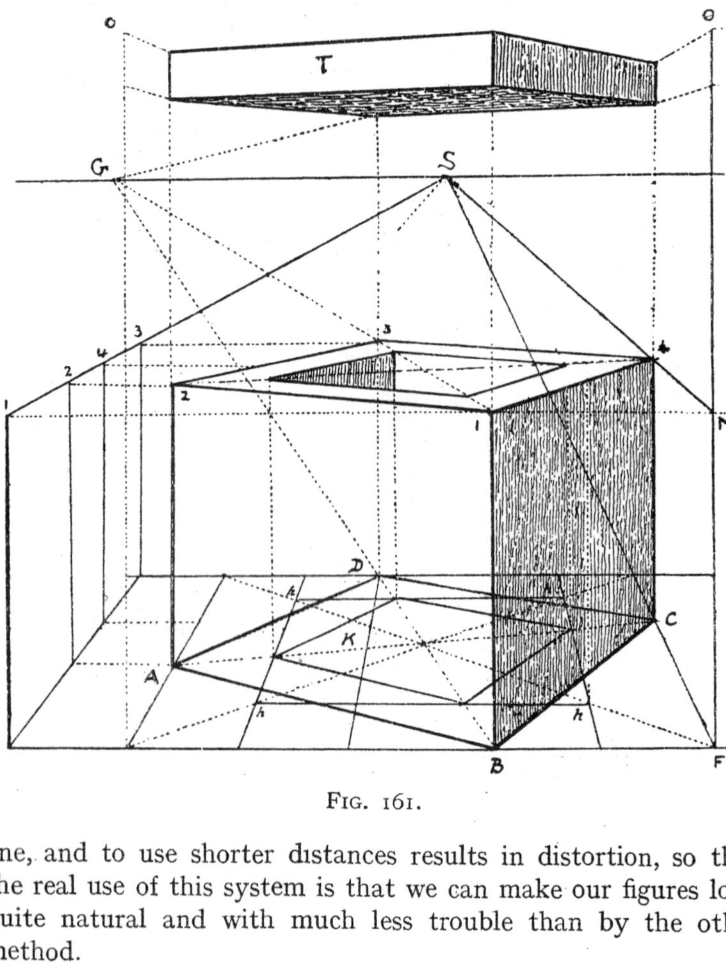

FIG. 161.

one, and to use shorter distances results in distortion, so that the real use of this system is that we can make our figures look quite natural and with much less trouble than by the other method.

LXXXVI

Showing How a Pedestal can be Drawn by the New Method

This is a repetition of the previous problem, or rather the application of it to architecture, although when there are

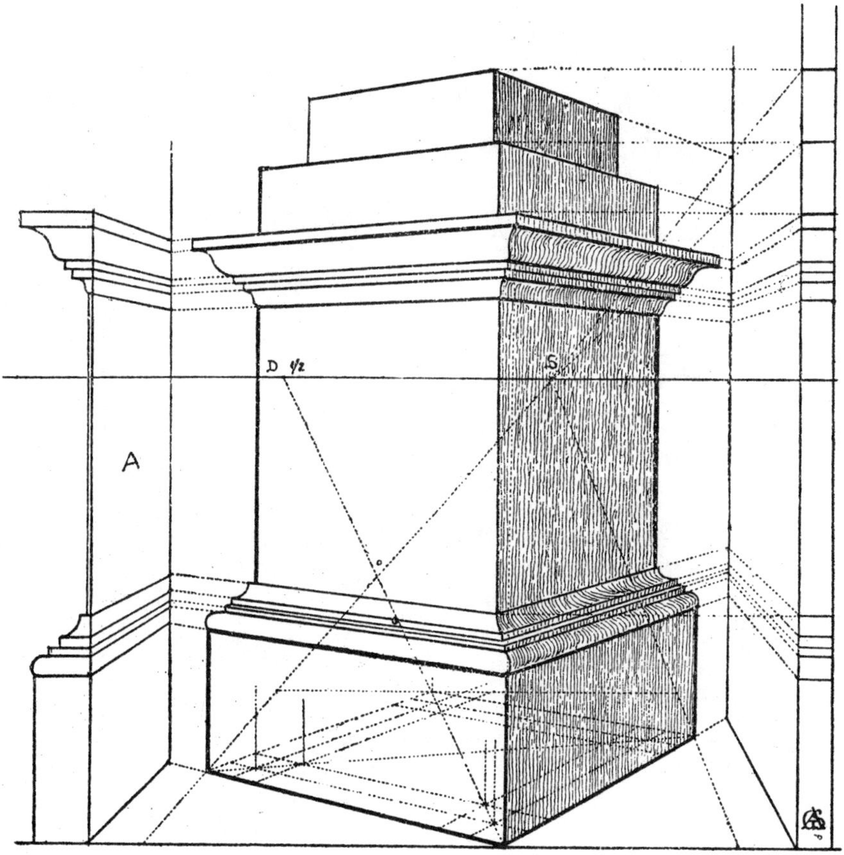

Fig. 162.

many details it may be more convenient to use vanishing points or the centrolinead.

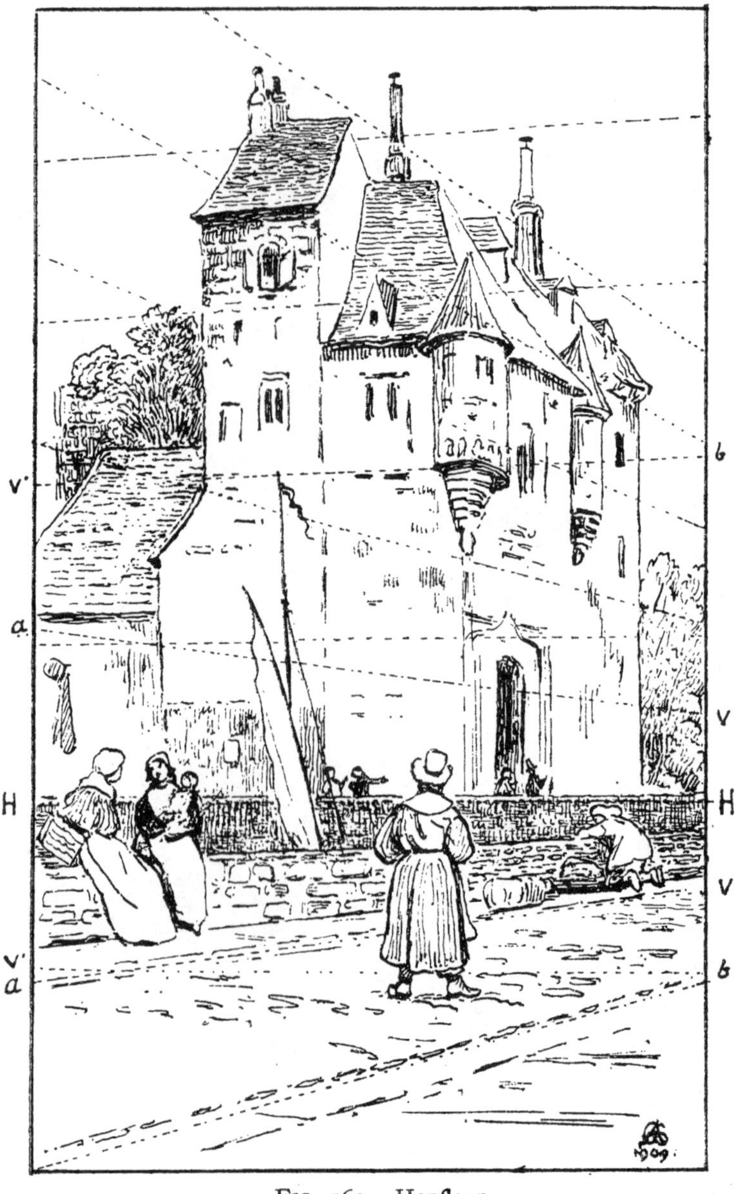

FIG. 163. Honfleur.

LXXXVII

Scale on Each Side of the Picture

As one of my objects in writing this book is to facilitate the working of our perspective, partly for the comfort of the artist, and partly that he may have no excuse for neglecting it, I will here show you how you may, by a very simple means, secure the general correctness of your perspective when sketching or painting out of doors.

Let us take this example from a sketch made at Honfleur (Fig. 163), and in which my eye was my only guide, but it stands the test of the rule. First of all note that line HH, drawn from one side of the picture to the other, is the horizontal line ; below that is a wall and a pavement marked *a*V, also going from one side of the picture to the other, and being lower down at *a* than at V it runs up as it were to meet the horizon at some distant point. In order to form our scale I take first the length of H*a*, and measure it above and below the horizon, along the side to our left as many times as required, in this case four or five. I now take the length HV on the right side of the picture and measure it above and below the horizon, as in the other case ; and then from these divisions obtain dotted lines crossing the picture from one side to the other which must all meet at some distant point on the horizon. These act as guiding lines, and are sufficient to give us the direction of any vanishing lines going to the same point. For those that go in the opposite direction we proceed in the same way, as from *b* on the right to V· on the left. They are here put in faintly, so as not to interfere with the drawing. In the sketch of Toledo (Fig. 164) the same thing is shown by double lines on each side to separate the two sets of lines, and to make the principle more evident.

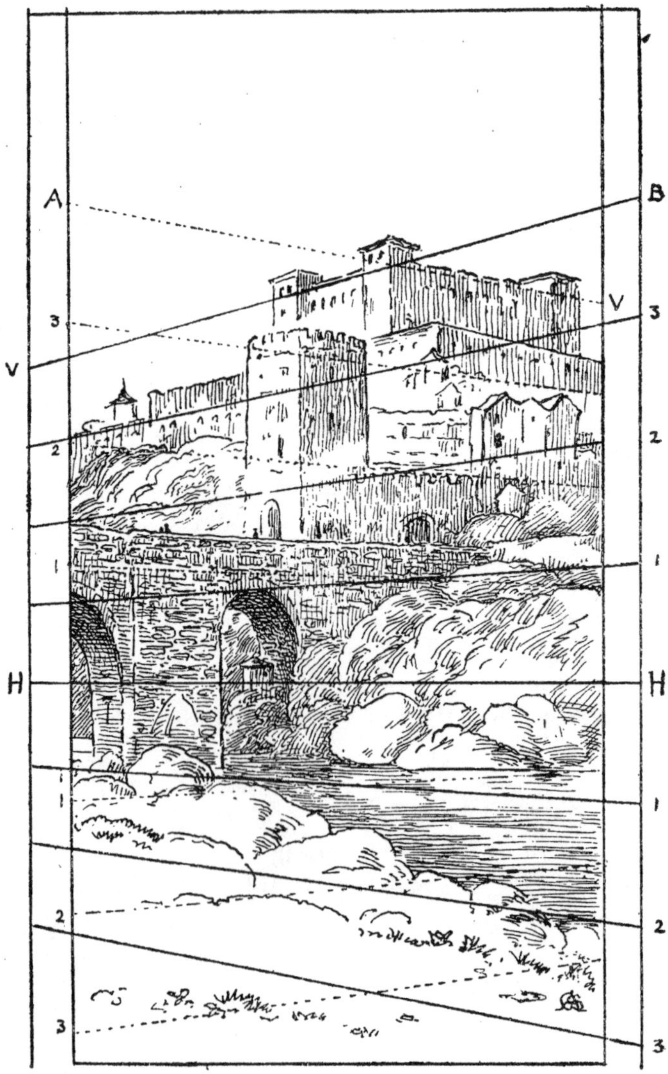

FIG. 164. Toledo.

LXXXVIII

The Circle

If we inscribe a circle in a square we find that it touches that square at four points which are in the middle of each side, as at *a b c d*. It will also intersect the two diagonals at the four points *o* (Fig. 165). If, then, we put this square and its

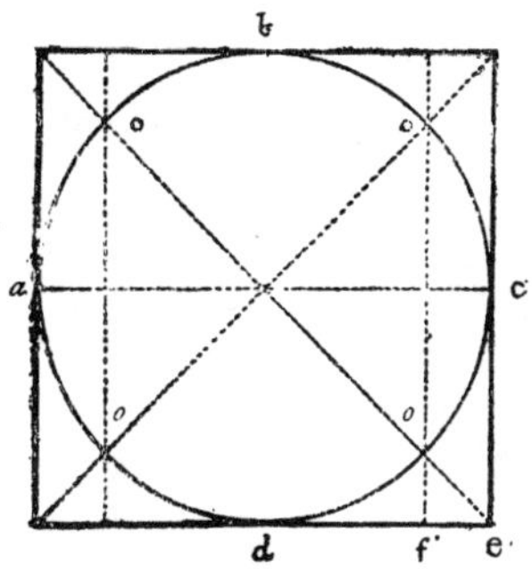

Fig. 165.

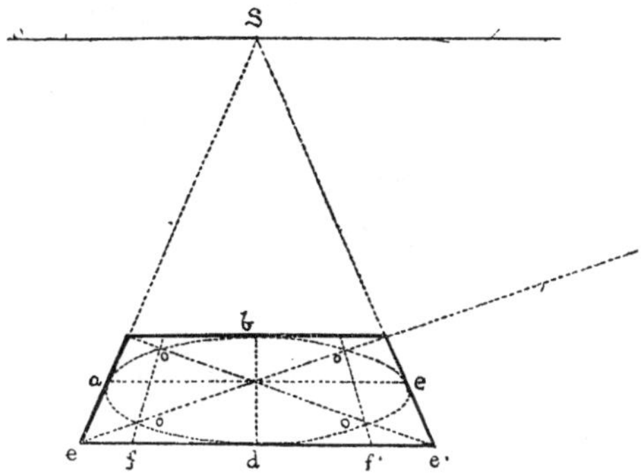

Fig. 166.

diagonals, &c., into perspective we shall have eight guiding points through which to trace the required circle, as shown in Fig. 166, which has the same base as Fig. 165.

LXXXIX

The Circle in Perspective a True Ellipse

Although the circle drawn through certain points must be a freehand drawing, which requires a little practice to make it true, it is sufficient for ordinary purposes and on a small scale, but to be mathematically true it must be an ellipse. We will first draw an ellipse (Fig. 167). Let *ee* be its long, or transverse, diameter, and *db* its short or conjugate diameter. Now take half of the long diameter *e*E, and from point *d* with *c*E for radius mark on *ee* the two points *ff*·, which are the foci of the ellipse. At each focus fix a pin, then make a loop of fine string that does not stretch and of such a length that when drawn out the double thread will reach from *f* to *e*. Now place this double thread round the two pins at the foci *ff'* and distend it with the pencil point until it forms triangle *fdf'*, then push the pencil along and right round the two foci, which being guided by the thread will draw the curve, which is a true ellipse, and will pass through the eight points indicated in our first figure. This will be a sufficient proof that the circle in perspective and the ellipse are identical curves. We must also remember that the ellipse is an oblique projection of a circle, or an oblique section of a cone.

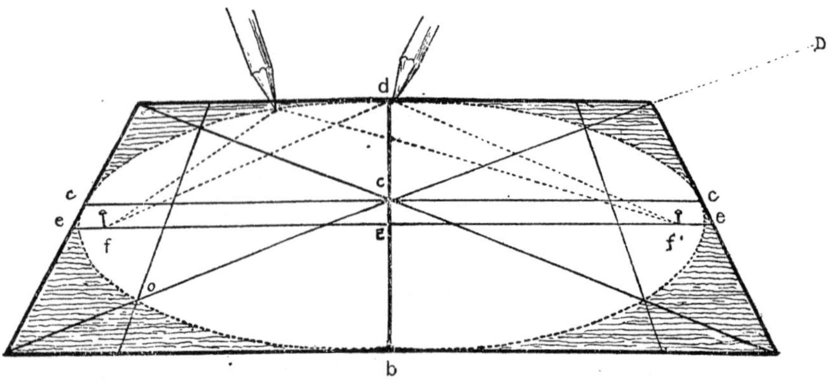

FIG. 167.

The difference between the two figures consists in their centres not being in the same place, that of the perspective circle being at *c*, higher up than *e* the centre of the ellipse. The latter being a geometrical figure, its long diameter is exactly in the centre of the figure, whereas the centre *c* and the diameter of the perspective are at the intersection of the diagonals of the perspective square in which it is inscribed.

XC

FURTHER ILLUSTRATION OF THE ELLIPSE

In order to show that the ellipse drawn by a loop as in the previous figure is also a circle in perspective we must reconstruct around it the square and its eight points by means of which it was drawn in the first instance. We start with nothing but the ellipse itself. We have to find the points of sight and distance, the base, &c. Let us start with base AB, a horizontal tangent to the curve extending beyond it on either side. From A and B draw two other tangents so that they shall touch the curve at points such as TT· a little above the transverse diameter and on a level with each other. Produce these tangents till they meet at point S, which will be the point of sight. Through this point draw horizontal line H. Now draw tangent CD parallel to AB.

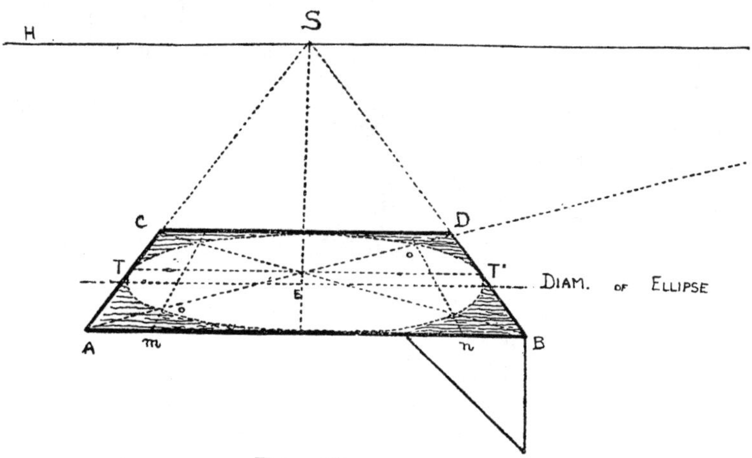

FIG. 168.

Draw diagonal AD till it cuts the horizon at the point of distance, this will cut through diameter of circle at its centre, and so proceed to find the eight points through which the perspective circle passes, when it will be found that they all lie on the ellipse we have drawn with the loop, showing that the two curves are identical although their centres are distinct.

XCI

How to Draw a Circle in Perspective Without a Geometrical Plan

Divide base AB into four equal parts. At B drop perpendicular B*n*, making B*n* equal to B*m*, or one-fourth of base. Join *mn* and transfer this measurement to each side of *d* on base line; that is, make *df* and *df*· equal to *mn*. Draw *f*S and *f*·S, and the intersections of these lines with the diagonals of square will give us the four points *o o o o*.

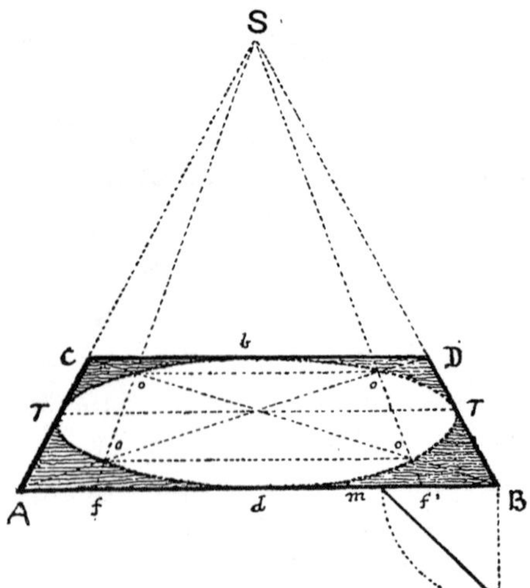

Fig. 169.

The reason of this is that *ff*· is the measurement on the base AB of another square *o o o o* which is exactly half of the outer square. For if we inscribe a circle in a square and then inscribe a second square in that circle, this second square will be exactly half the area of the larger one; for its side will be equal to half the diagonal of the larger square, as can be seen by studying the following figures. In Fig. 170, for instance, the side of small square K is half the diagonal of large square *o*.

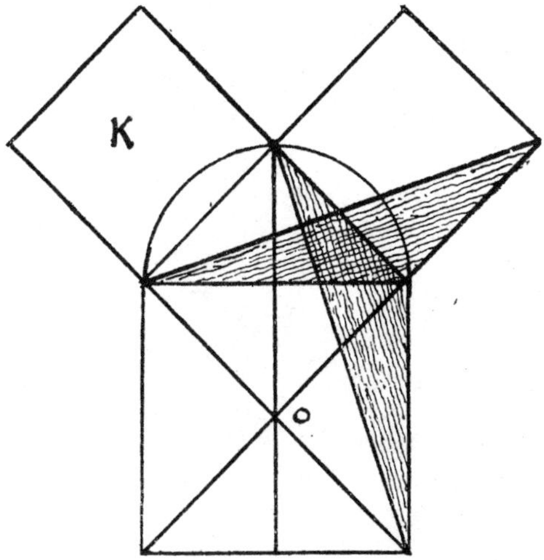

FIG. 170.

In Fig. 171, CB represents half of diagonal EB of the outer square in which the circle is inscribed. By taking a fourth

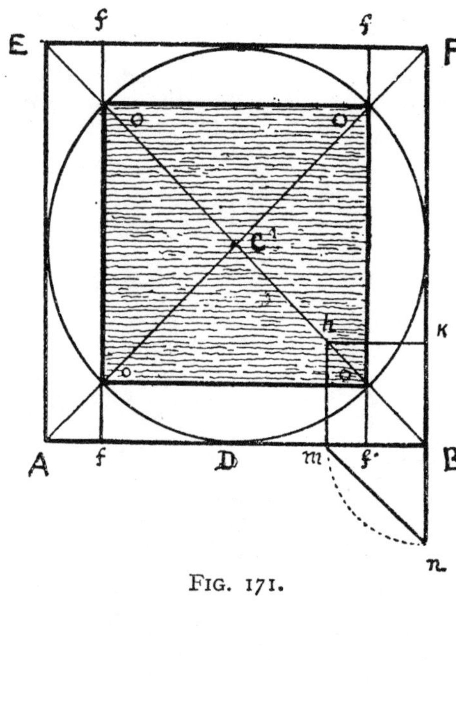

FIG. 171.

of the base *m*B and drawing perpendicular *mh* we cut CB at *h* in two equal parts, C*h*, *h*B. It will be seen that *h*B is equal to *mn*, one-quarter of the diagonal, so if we measure *mn* on each side of D we get *ff'* equal to CB, or half the diagonal. By drawing *ff*, *f'f* passing through the diagonals we get the four points *o o o o* through which to draw the smaller square. Without referring to geometry we can see at a glance by Fig. 172, where we have simply turned the square *o o o o* on its centre so that its

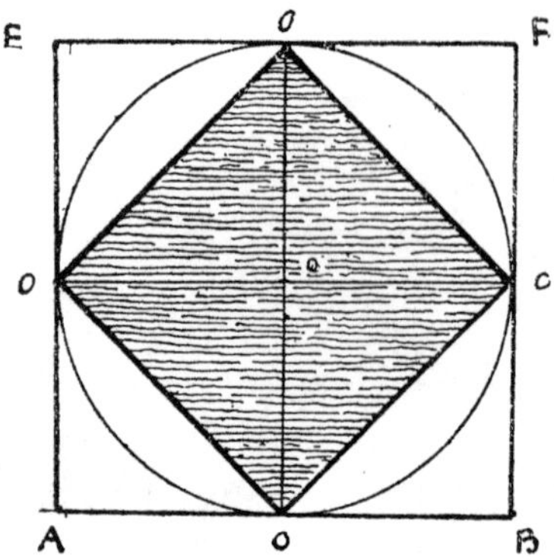

FIG. 172.

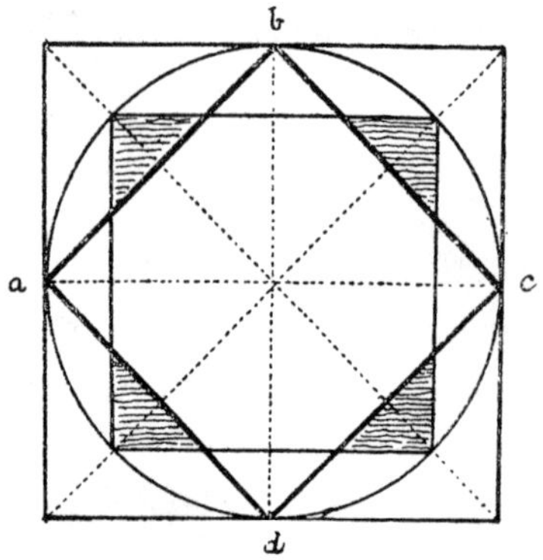

FIG. 173.

angles touch the sides of the outer square, that it is exactly half of square ABEF, since each quarter of it, such as E*o*C*o*, is bisected by its diagonal *oo*.

XCII

How to Draw a Circle in Angular Perspective

Let ABCD be the oblique square. Produce VA till it cuts the base line at G.

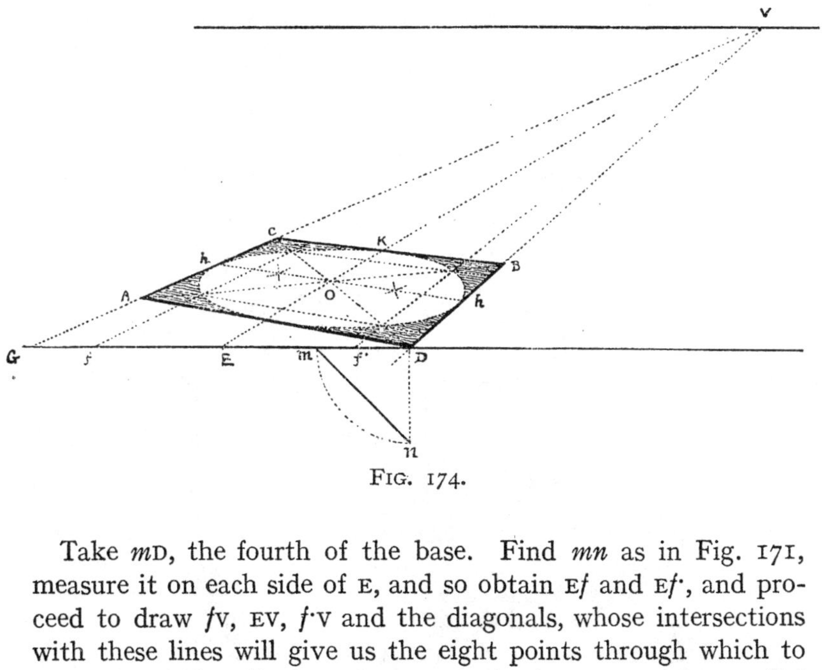

Fig. 174.

Take *m*D, the fourth of the base. Find *mn* as in Fig. 171, measure it on each side of E, and so obtain E*f* and E*f*·, and proceed to draw *f*V, EV, *f*·V and the diagonals, whose intersections with these lines will give us the eight points through which to draw the circle. In fact the process is the same as in parallel perspective, only instead of making our divisions on the actual base AD of the square, we make them on GD, the base line.

To obtain the central line *hh* passing through O, we can make use of diagonals of the half squares; that is, if the other vanishing point is inaccessible, as in this case.

XCIII

How to Draw a Circle in Perspective more Correctly, by Using Sixteen Guiding Points

First draw square ABCD. From o, the middle of the base,

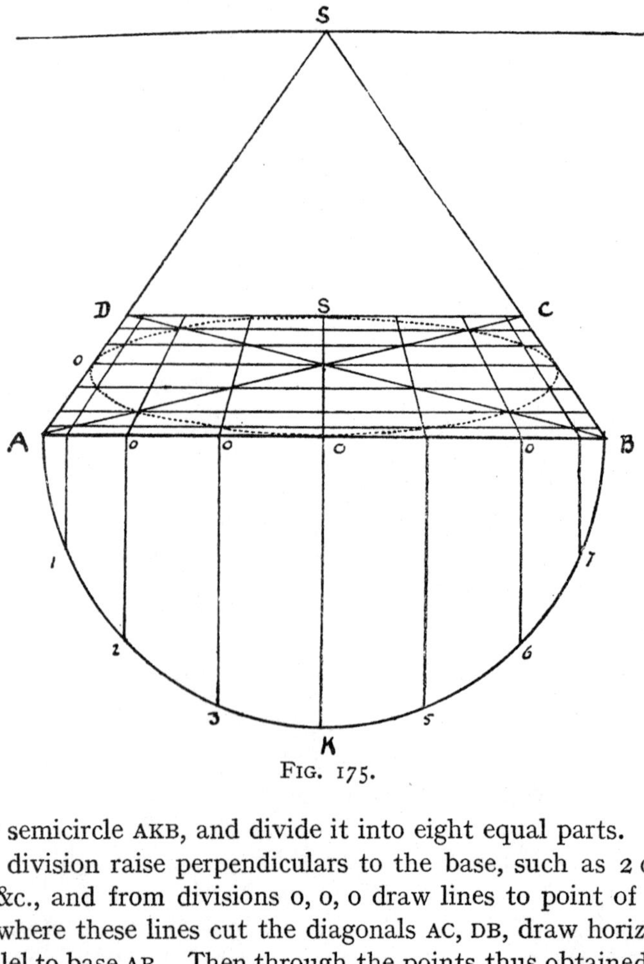

Fig. 175.

draw semicircle AKB, and divide it into eight equal parts. From each division raise perpendiculars to the base, such as 2 o, 3 o, 5 o, &c., and from divisions o, o, o draw lines to point of sight, and where these lines cut the diagonals AC, DB, draw horizontals parallel to base AB. Then through the points thus obtained draw the circle as shown in this figure, which also shows us how the circumference of a circle in perspective may be divided into any number of equal parts.

XCIV

How to Divide a Perspective Circle into any Number of Equal Parts

This is simply a repetition of the previous figure as far as its construction is concerned, only in this case we have divided the semicircle into twelve parts and the perspective into twenty-four.

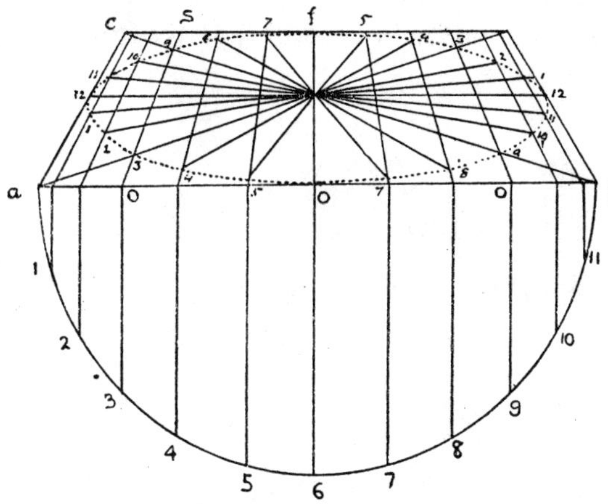

Fig. 176.

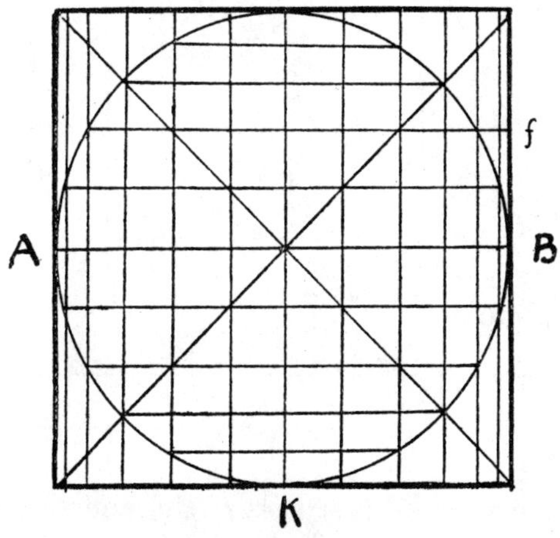

Fig. 177.

We have raised perpendiculars from the divisions on the semicircle, and proceeded as before to draw lines to the point of sight, and have thus by their intersections with the circumference already drawn in perspective divided it into the required number of equal parts, to which from the centre we have drawn the radii. This will show us how to draw traceries in Gothic windows, columns in a circle, cart-wheels, &c.

The geometrical figure (177) will explain the construction of the perspective one by showing how the divisions are obtained on the line AB, which represents base of square, from the divisions on the semicircle AKB.

XCV

How to Draw Concentric Circles

First draw a square with its diagonals (Fig. 178), and from its centre O inscribe a circle; in this circle inscribe a square,

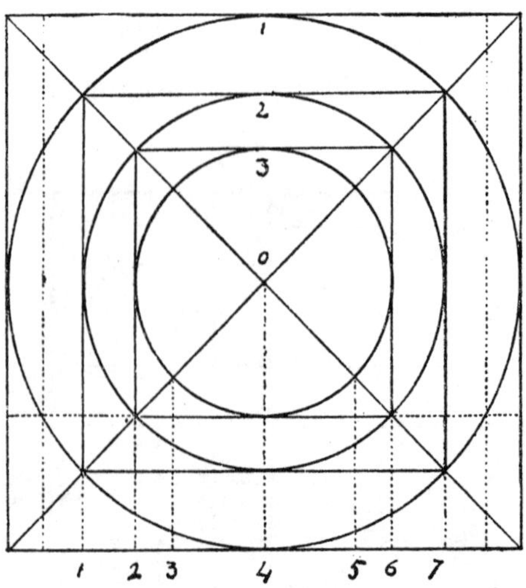

Fig. 178.

and in this again inscribe a second circle, and so on. Through their intersections with the diagonals draw lines to base, and number them 1, 2, 3, 4, &c.; transfer these measurements to the base of the perspective square (Fig. 179), and proceed to construct the circles as before, drawing lines from each point on the base to the point of sight, and drawing the curves through the inter-sections of these lines with the diagonals.

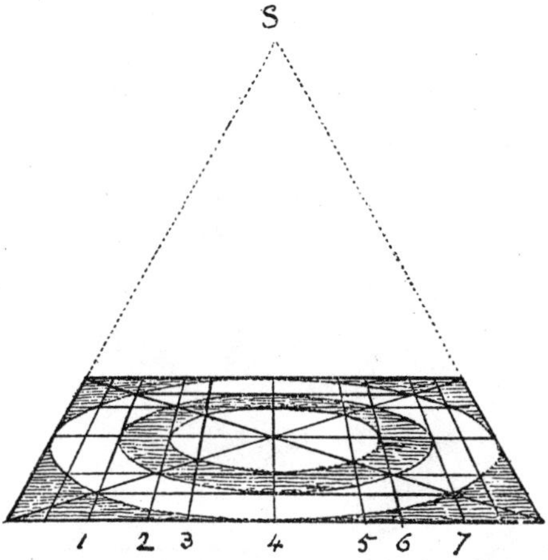

FIG. 179.

Should it be required to make the circles at equal distances, as for steps for instance, then the geometrical plan should be made accordingly.

Or we may adopt the method shown at Fig. 180, by taking quarter base of both outer and inner square, and finding the measurement *mn* on each side of C, &c.

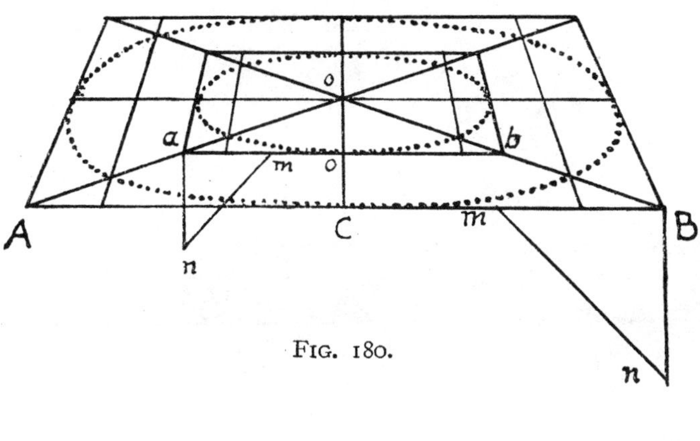

FIG. 180.

XCVI

The Angle of the Diameter of the Circle in Angular and Parallel Perspective

The circle, whether in angular or parallel perspective, is always an ellipse. In angular perspective the angle of the circle's diameter varies in accordance with the angle of the square in which it is placed, as in Fig. 181, *cc* is the diameter of the circle and *ee* the

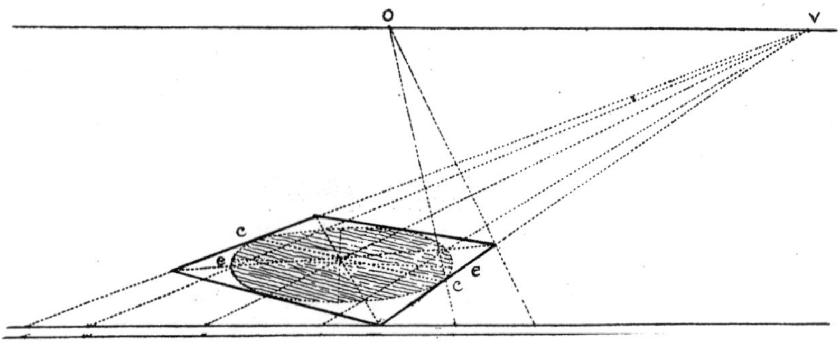

Fig. 181.

diameter of the ellipse. In parallel perspective the diameter of the circle always remains horizontal, although the long diameter of the ellipse varies in inclination according to the distance it is from the point of sight, as shown in Fig. 182, in which the third circle is much elongated and distorted, owing to its being outside the angle of vision.

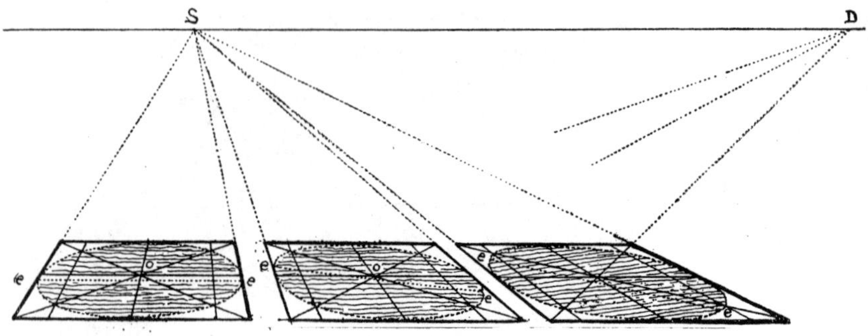

Fig. 182.

XCVII

How to Correct Disproportion in the Width of Columns

The disproportion in the width of columns in Fig. 183 arises from the point of distance being too near the point of sight, or, in other words, taking too wide an angle of vision. It will be seen that column 3 is much wider than column 1.

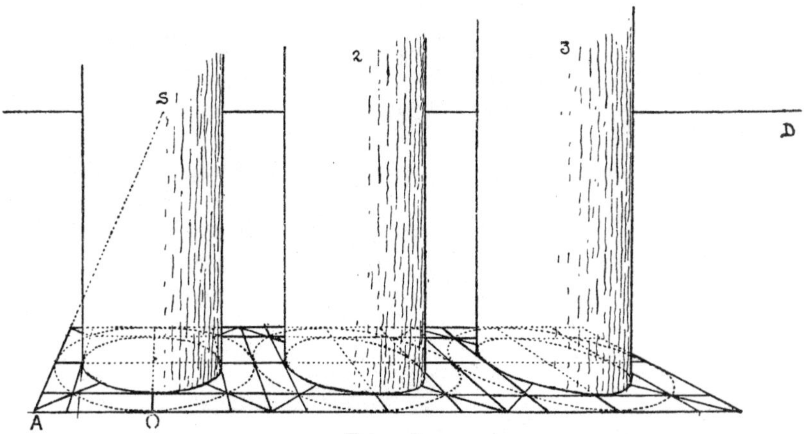

Fig. 183.

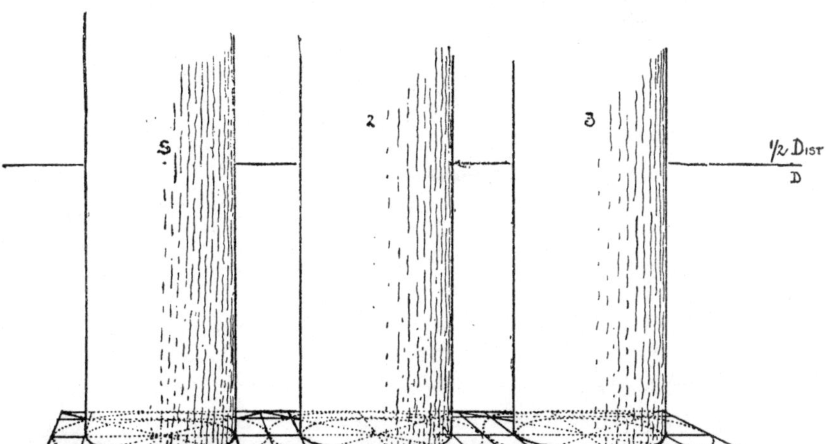

Fig. 184.

In our second figure (184) is shown how this defect is remedied, by doubling the distance, or by counting the same distance as half, which is easily effected by drawing the diagonal from O to ½D, instead of from A, as in the other figure, O being at half base. Here the squares lie much more level, and the columns are nearly the same width, showing the advantage of a long distance.

XCVIII

How to Draw a Circle over a Circle or a Cylinder

First construct square and circle ABE, then draw square CDF with its diagonals. Then find the various points O, and from

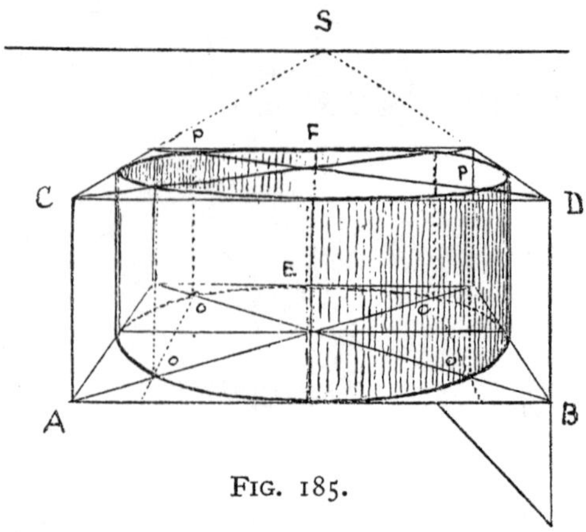

FIG. 185.

these raise perpendiculars to meet the diagonals of the upper square at points P, which, with the other points will be sufficient guides to draw the circle required. This can be applied to towers, columns, &c. The size of the circles can be varied so that the upper portion of a cylinder or column shall be smaller than the lower.

XCIX

To Draw a Circle Below a Given Circle

Construct the upper square and circle as before, then by means of the vanishing scale POV, which should be made the depth required, drop perpendiculars from the various points marked

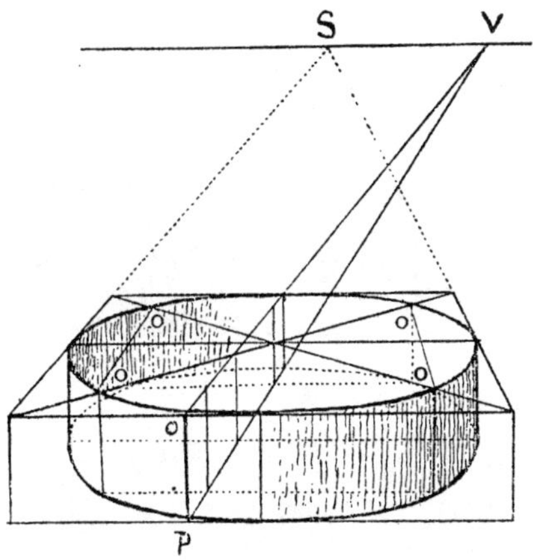

Fig. 186.

O, obtained by the diagonals, making them the right depth by referring them to the vanishing scale, as shown in this figure. This can be used for drawing garden fountains, basins, and various architectural objects.

C

Application of Previous Problem

That is, to draw a circle above a circle. In Fig. 187 can be

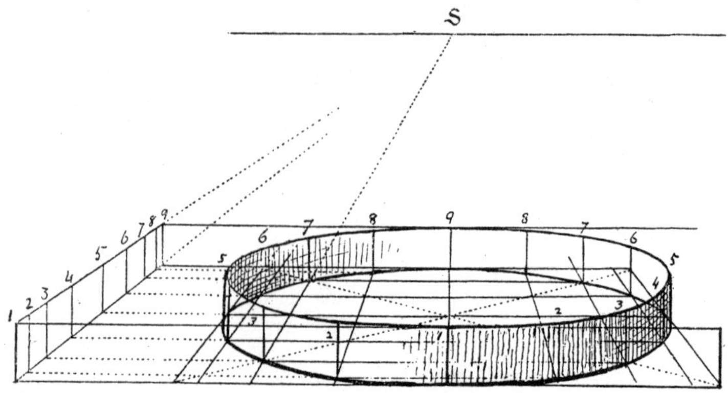

Fig. 187.

seen how by means of the vanishing scale at the side we obtain the height of the verticals 1, 2, 3, 4, &c., which determine the

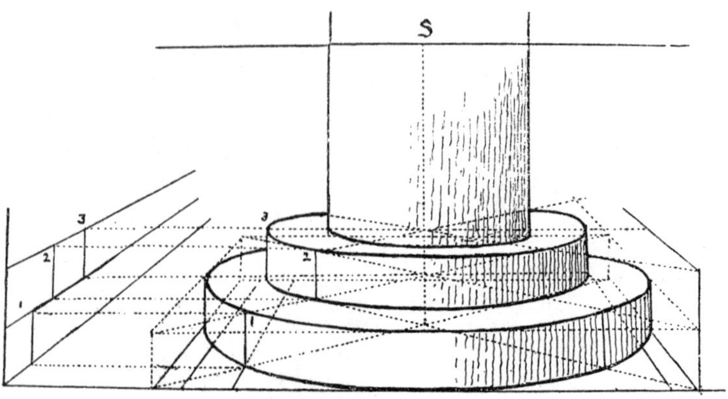

Fig. 188.

direction of the upper circle; and in this second figure, how we resort to the same means to draw circular steps.

CI

Doric Columns

It is as well for the art student to study the different orders of architecture, whether architect or not, as he frequently has to

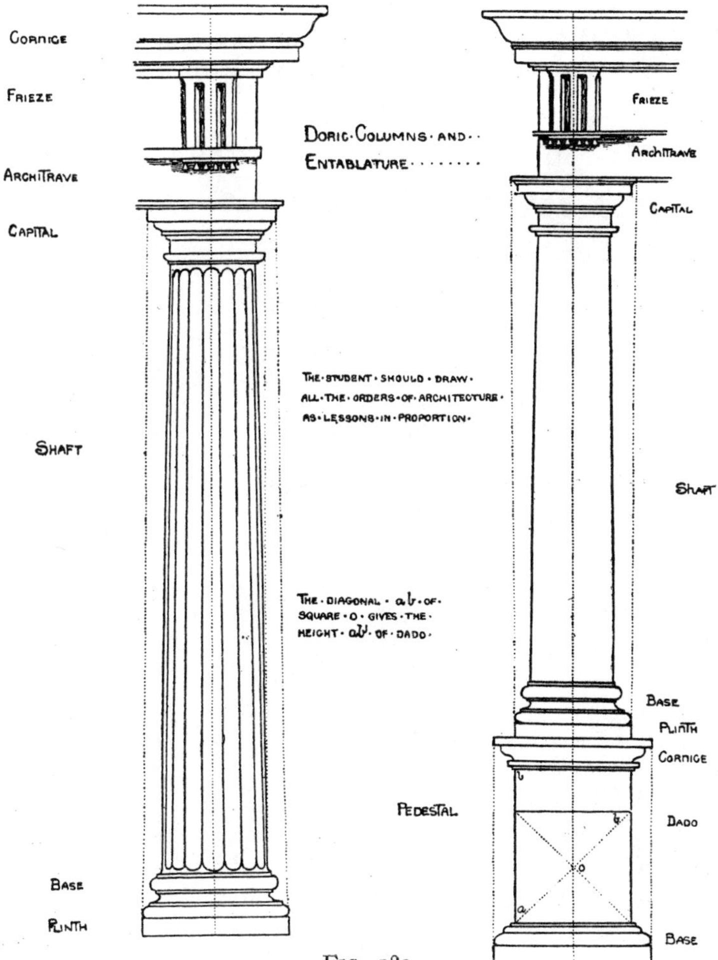

Fig. 189.

introduce them into his pictures, and at least must know their proportions, and how columns diminish from base to capital, as shown in this illustration.

CII

To Draw Semicircles Standing upon a Circle at any Angle

Given the circle ACBH, on diagonal AB draw semicircle AKB, and on the same line AB draw rectangle AEFB, its height being deter-

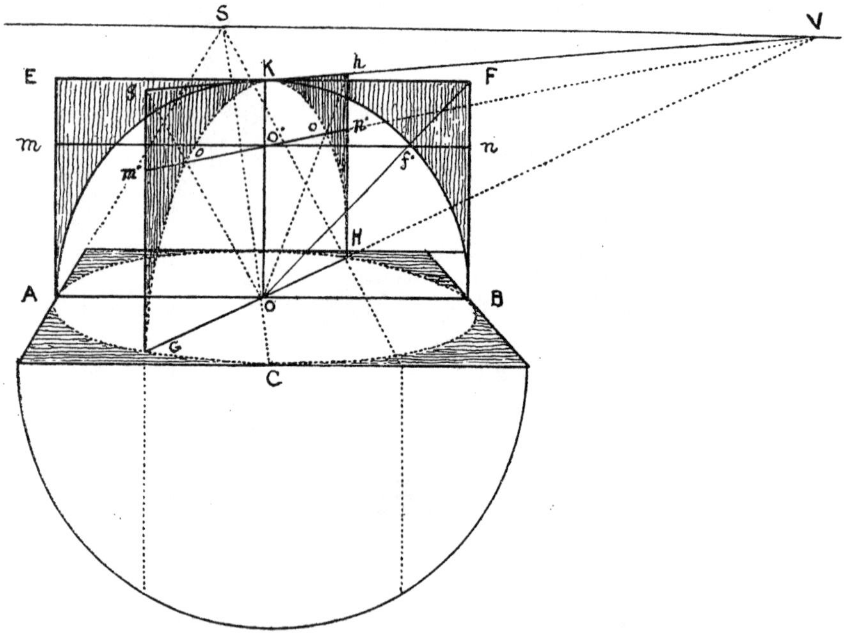

Fig. 190.

mined by radius OK of semicircle. From centre O draw OF to corner of rectangle. Through *f*·, where that line intersects the semicircle, draw *mn* parallel to AB. This will give intersection O· on the vertical OK, through which all such horizontals as *m·n·*, level with *mn*, must pass. Now take any other diameter, such as GH, and thereon raise rectangle G*gh*H, the same height as the other. The manner of doing this is to produce diameter GH to the horizon till it finds its vanishing point at V. From V through

K draw *hg*, and through O· draw *n·m·*. From O draw the two diagonals *og* and *oh*, intersecting *m·n·* at O, O, and thus we have the five points GOKOH through which to draw the required semicircle.

CIII

A Dome Standing on a Cylinder

This figure is a combination of the two preceding it. A cylinder

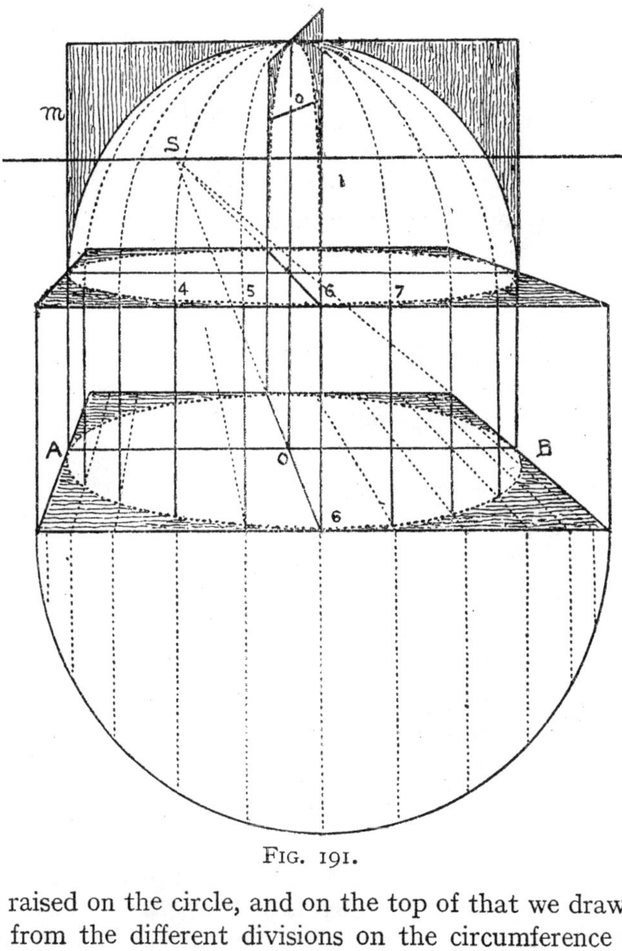

FIG. 191.

is first raised on the circle, and on the top of that we draw semicircles from the different divisions on the circumference of the upper circle. This, however, only represents a small half-globular object. To draw the dome of a cathedral, or other building high above us, is another matter. From outside, where we can get to a distance, it is not difficult, but from within it will tax all our knowledge of perspective to give it effect.

We shall go more into this subject when we come to archways and vaulted roofs, &c.

CIV

Section of a Dome or Niche

First draw outline of the niche GFDBA (Fig. 193), then at its base draw square and circle GOA, S being the point of sight, and divide the circumference of the circle into the required number of parts. Then draw semicircle FOB, and over that another semicircle EOC. The manner of drawing them is shown in Fig. 192.

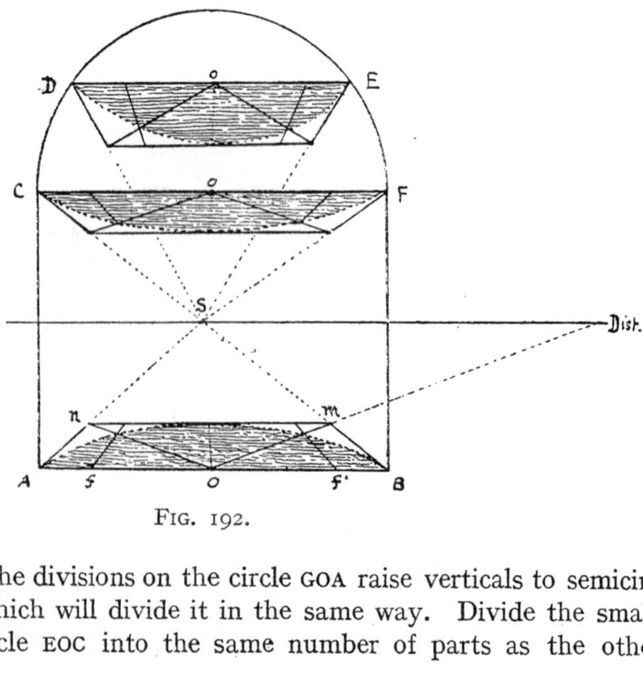

Fig. 192.

From the divisions on the circle GOA raise verticals to semicircle FOB, which will divide it in the same way. Divide the smaller semicircle EOC into the same number of parts as the others, which divisions will serve as guiding points in drawing the curves of the dome that are drawn towards D, but the shading must assist greatly in giving the effect of the recess.

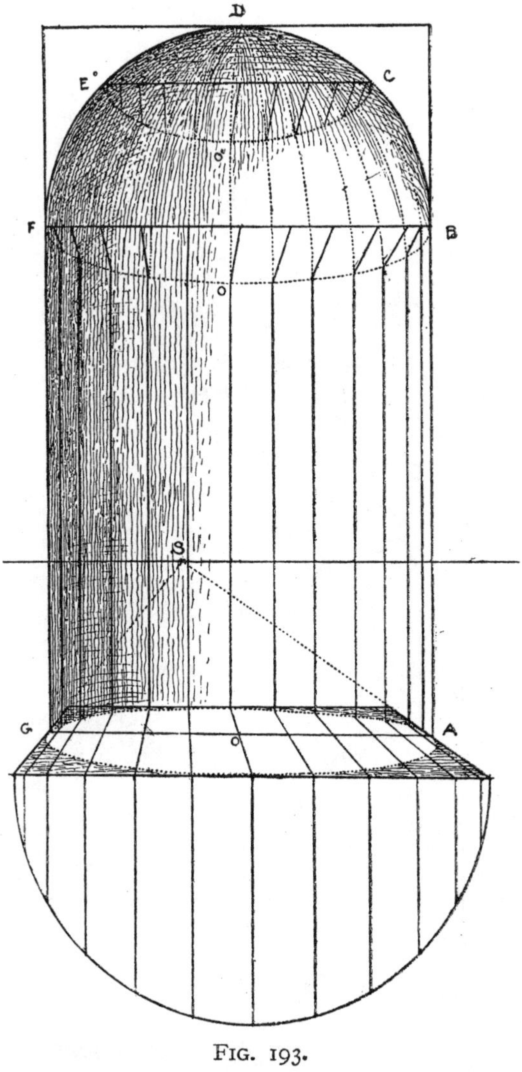

FIG. 193.

In Fig. 192 will be seen how to draw semicircles in perspective. We first draw the half squares by drawing from centres O of their diameters diagonals to distance-point, as OD, which cuts the vanishing line BS at *m*, and gives us the depth of the square, and in this we draw the semicircle in the usual way.

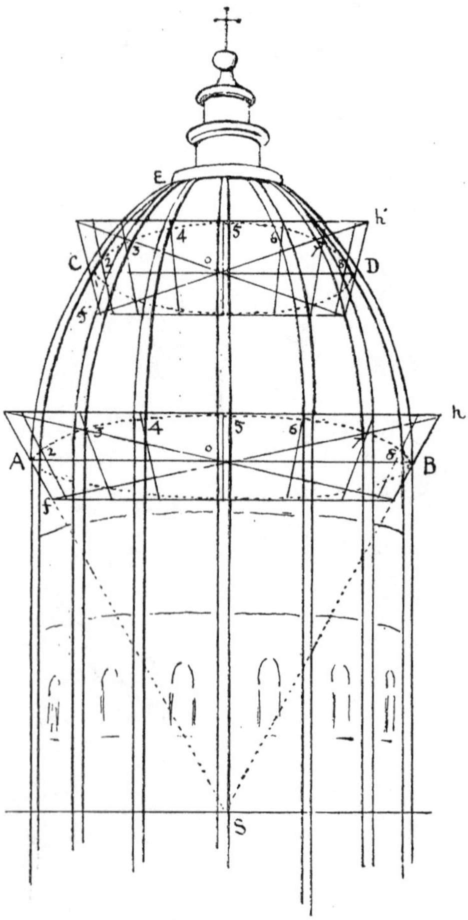

FIG. 194. A Dome.

V

A Dome

First draw a section of the dome ACEDB (Fig. 194) the shape required. Draw AB at its base and CD at some distance above it. Keeping these as central lines, form squares thereon by drawing SA, SB, SC, SD, &c., from point of sight, and determining their lengths by diagonals *fh*, *f·h·* from point of distance, passing through O. Having formed the two squares, draw perspective circles in each, and divide their circumferences into twelve or whatever number of parts are needed. To complete the figure draw from each division in the lower circle curves passing through the corresponding divisions in the upper one, to the apex. But as these are freehand lines, it requires some taste and knowledge to draw them properly, and of course in a large drawing several more squares and circles might be added to aid the draughtsman. The interior of the dome can be drawn in the same way.

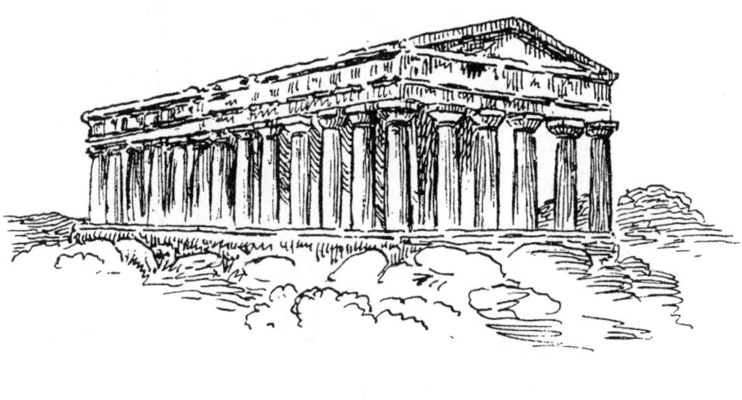

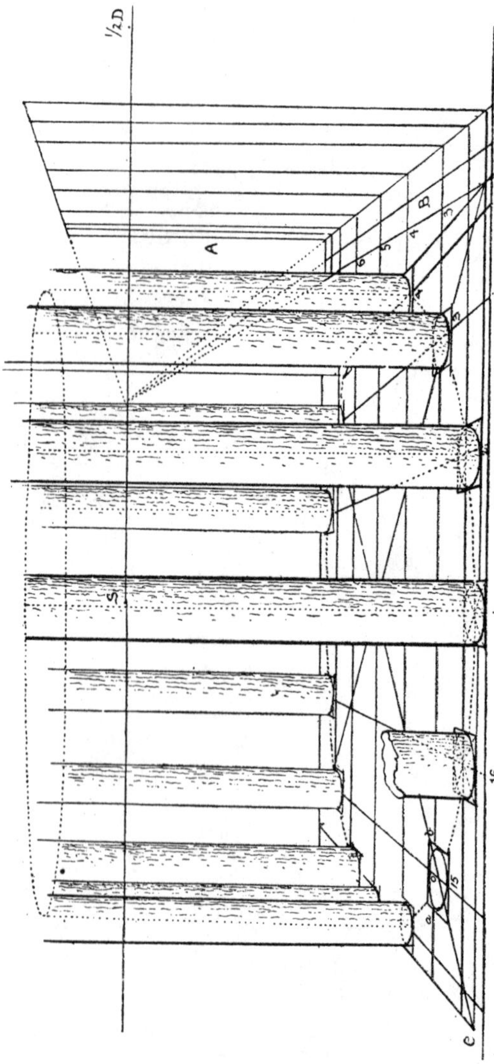

Fig. 195.

CVI

How to Draw Columns Standing in a Circle

In Fig. 195 are sixteen cylinders or columns standing in a circle. First draw the circle on the ground, then divide it into sixteen equal parts, and let each division be the centre of the circle on which to raise the column. The question is how to make each one the right width in accordance with its position, for it is evident that a near column must appear wider than the opposite one. On the right of the figure is the vertical scale A, which gives the heights of the columns, and at its foot is a horizontal scale, or a scale of widths B. Now, according to the line on which the column stands, we find its apparent width marked on the scale. Thus take the small square and circle at 15, without its column, or the broken column at 16; and note that on each side of its centre O I have measured *oa*, *ob*, equal to spaces marked 3 on the same horizontal in the scale B. Through these points *a* and *b* I have drawn lines towards point of sight S. Through their intersections with diagonal *e*, which is directed to point of distance, draw the farther and nearer sides of the square in which to describe the circle and the cylinder or column thereon. I have made all the squares thus obtained in parallel perspective, but they do not represent the bases of columns arranged in circles, which should converge towards the centre, and I believe in some cases are modified in form to suit that design.

CVII

Columns and Capitals

This figure shows the application of the square and diagonal in drawing and placing columns in angular perspective.

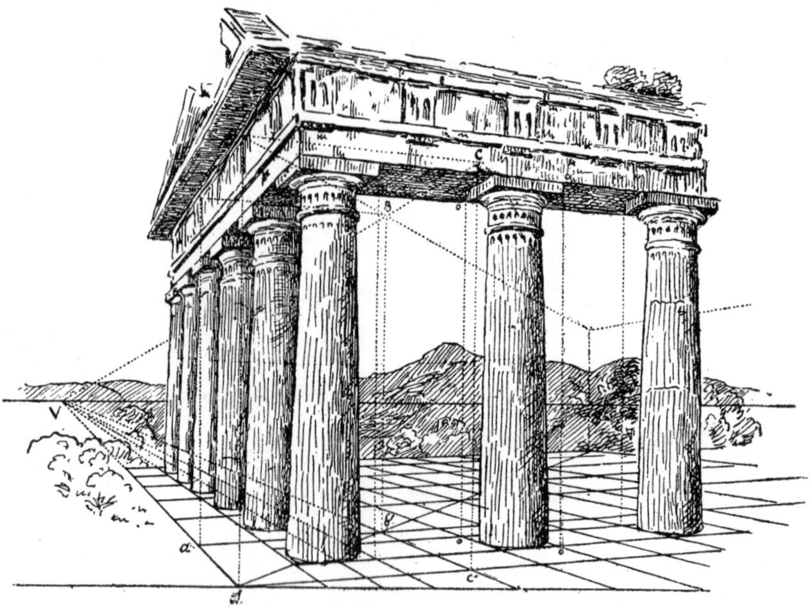

Fig. 196.

CVIII

Method of Perspective Employed by Architects

The architects first draw a plan and elevation of the building to be put into perspective. Having placed the plan at the required angle to the picture plane, they fix upon the point of sight, and the distance from which the drawing is to be viewed. They then draw a line SP at right angles to the picture plane VV·, which represents that distance so that P is the station-point. The eye is generally considered to be the station-point, but when lines are drawn to that point from the ground-plan, the station-point

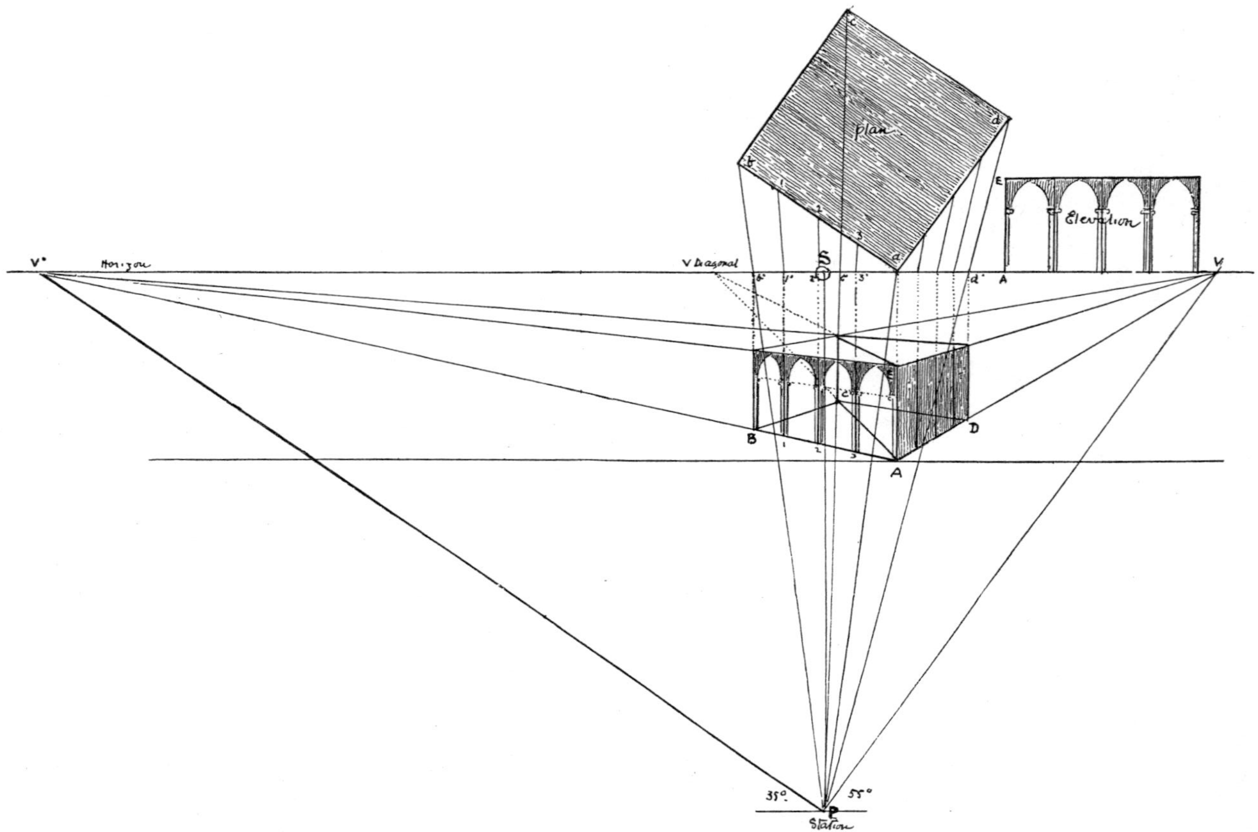

FIG. 197. A method of angular Perspective employed by architects.

is placed on the ground, and is in fact the trace or projection exactly under the point at which the eye is placed. From this station-point P, draw lines PV and PV· parallel to the two sides of the plan *ba* and *ad* (which will be at right angles to each other), and produce them to the horizon, which they will touch at points V and V·. These points thus obtained will be the two vanishing points.

The next operation is to draw lines from the principal points of the plan to the station-point P, such as *b*P, *c*P, *d*P, &c., and where these lines intersect the picture plane (VV· here represents it as well as the horizon), drop perpendiculars *b*·B, *a*A, *d*·D, &c., to meet the vanishing lines AV, AV·, which will determine the points A, B, C, D, 1, 2, 3, &c., and also the perspective lengths of the sides of the figure AB, AD, and the divisions B, 1, 2, &c. Taking the height of the figure AE from the elevation, we measure it on A*a*; as in this instance A touches the ground line, it may be used as a line of heights.

I have here placed the perspective drawing under the ground plan to show the relation between the two, and how the perspective is worked out, but the general practice is to find the required measurements as here shown, to mark them on a straight edge of card or paper, and transfer them to the paper on which the drawing is to be made.

This of course is the simplest form of a plan and elevation. It is easy to see, however, that we could set out an elaborate building in the same way as this figure, but in that case we should not place the drawing underneath the ground-plan, but transfer the measurements to another sheet of paper as mentioned above.

CIX

The Octagon

To draw the geometrical figure of an octagon contained in a square, take half of the diagonal of that square as radius, and

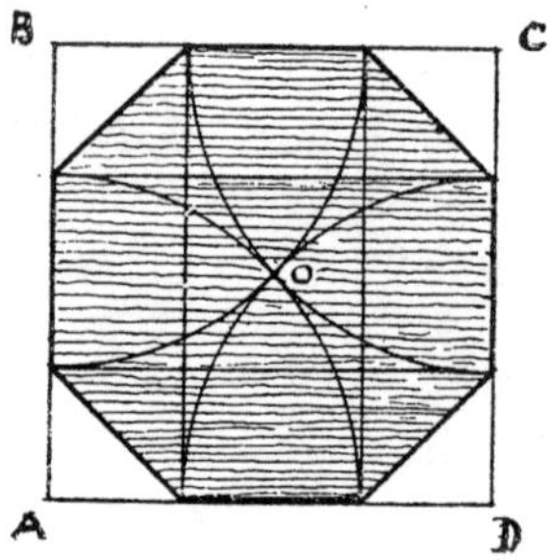

Fig. 198.

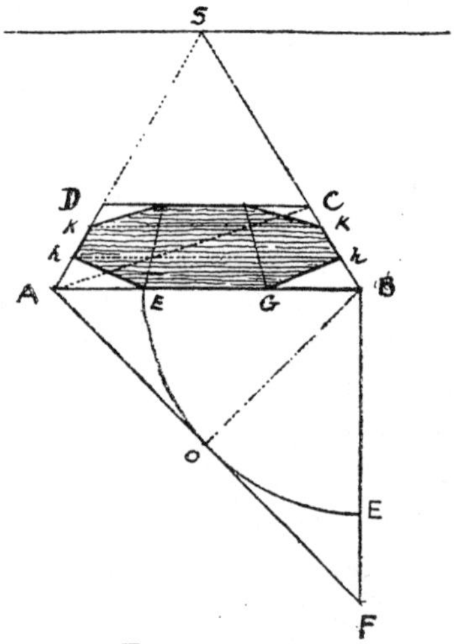

Fig. 199.

from each corner describe a quarter circle. At the eight points where they touch the sides of the square, draw the eight sides of the octagon.

To put this into perspective take the base of the square AB and thereon form the perspective square ABCD. From either extremity of that base (say B) drop perpendicular BF, draw diagonal AF, and then from B with radius BO, half that diagonal, describe arc EOE. This will give us the measurement AE. Make GB equal to AE. Then draw lines from G and E towards S, and by means of the diagonals find the transverse lines KK, *hh*, which will give us the eight points through which to draw the octagon.

CX

How to Draw the Octagon in Angular Perspective

Form square ABCD (new method), produce sides BC and AD to the horizon at V, and produce VA to a' on base. Drop per-

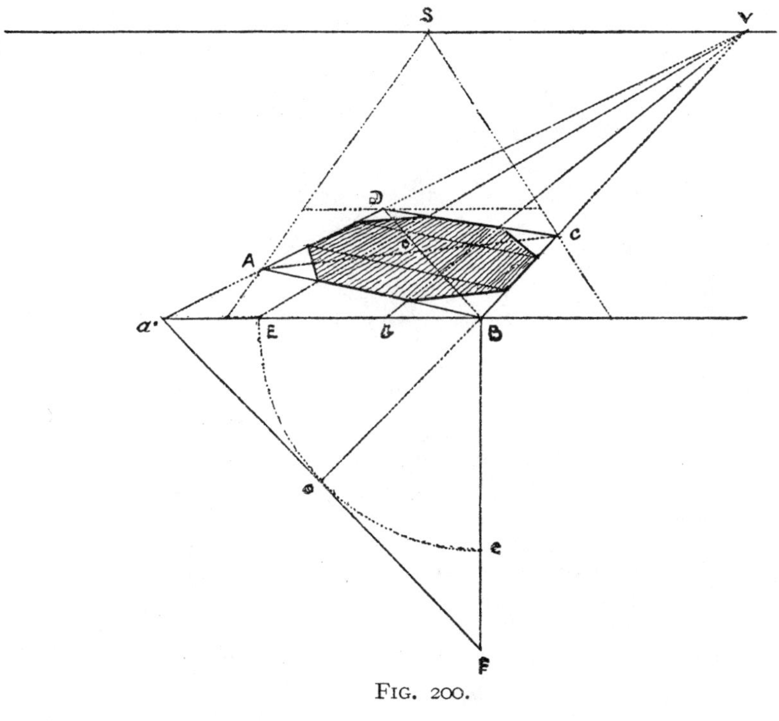

Fig. 200.

pendicular from B to F the same length as a'B, and proceed as in the previous figure to find the eight points on the oblique square through which to draw the octagon.

It will be seen that this operation is very much the same as in parallel perspective, only we make our measurements on the base line a'B as we cannot measure the vanishing line BA otherwise.

CXI

How to Draw an Octagonal Figure in Angular Perspective

In this figure in angular perspective we do precisely the same thing as in the previous problem, taking our measurements on the base line EB instead of on the vanishing line BA. If we wish to raise a figure on this octagon the height of EG we form the vanishing scale EGO, and from the eight points on the ground

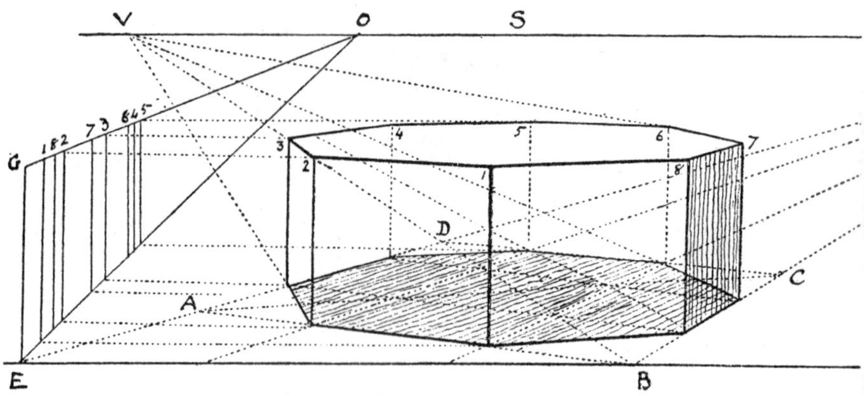

Fig. 201.

draw horizontals to EO and thus find all the points that give us the perspective height of each angle of the octagonal figure.

CXII

How to Draw Concentric Octagons, with Illustration of a Well

The geometrical figure 202 A shows how by means of diagonals AC and BD and the radii 1 2 3, &c., we can obtain smaller octagons inside the larger ones. Note how these are carried out in the second figure (202 B), and their application to this drawing of an octagonal well on an octagonal base.

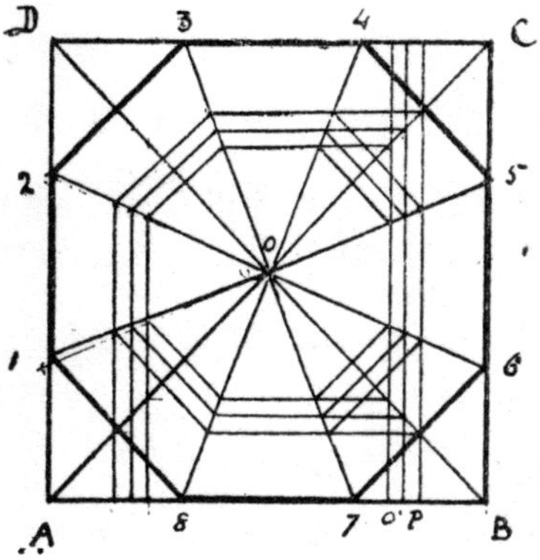

FIG. 202 A.

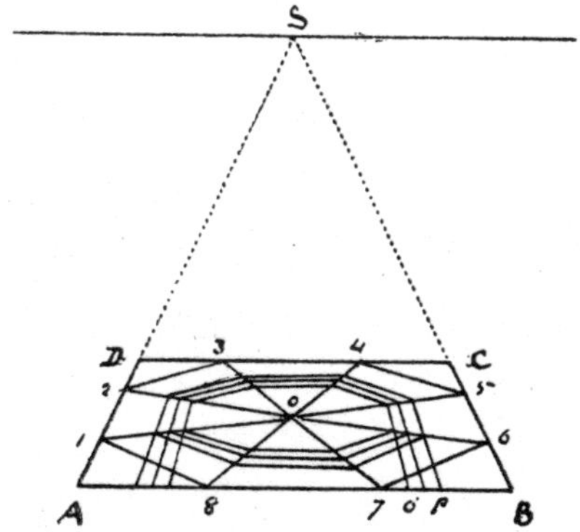

FIG. 202 B.

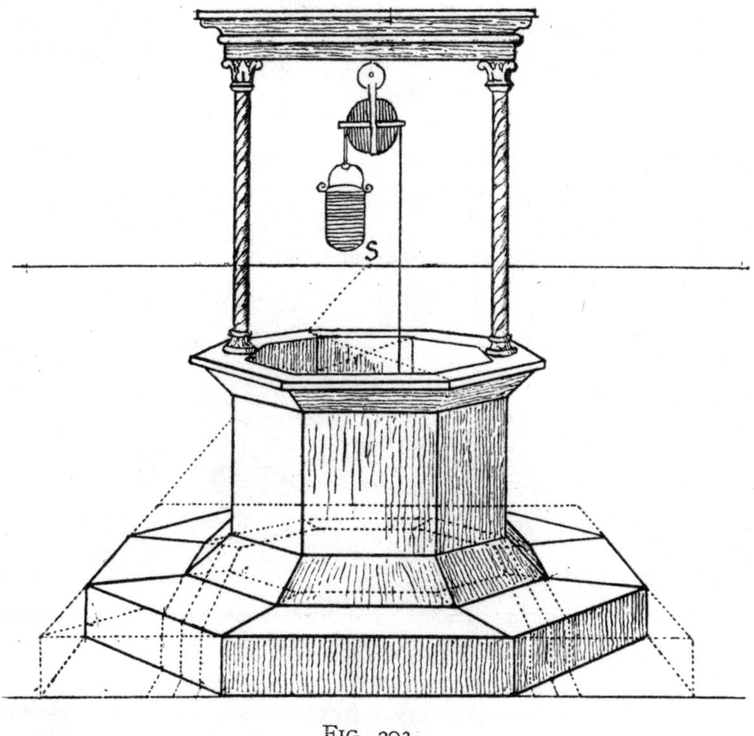

FIG. 203.

CXIII

A Pavement Composed of Octagons and Small Squares

To draw a pavement with octagonal tiles we will begin with an octagon contained in a square *abcd*. Produce diagonal *ac* to V.

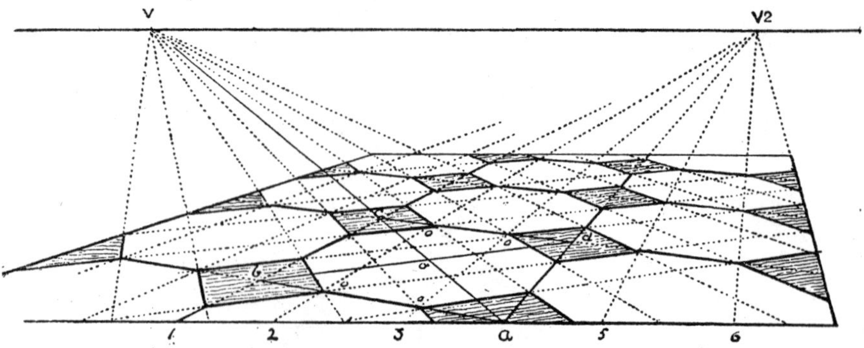

FIG. 204.

This will be the vanishing point for the sides of the small squares directed towards it. The other sides are directed to an inaccessible point out of the picture, but their directions are determined by the lines drawn from divisions on base to V^2 (see back, Fig. 133).

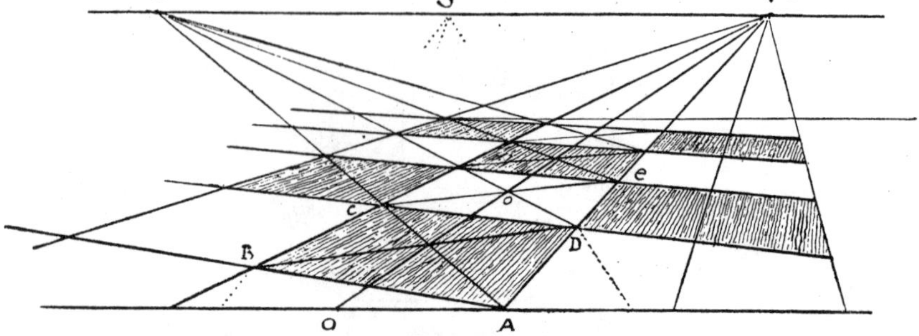

FIG. 205.

I have drawn the lower figure to show how the squares which contain the octagons are obtained by means of the diagonals,

BD, AC, and the central line ov^2. Given the square ABCD. From D draw diagonal to G, then from C through centre *o* draw CE, and so on all the way up the floor until sufficient are obtained. It is easy to see how other squares on each side of these can be produced.

CXIV

The Hexagon

The hexagon is a six-sided figure which, if inscribed in a circle, will have each of its sides equal to the radius of that circle (Fig. 206). If inscribed in a rectangle ABCD, that rectangle will

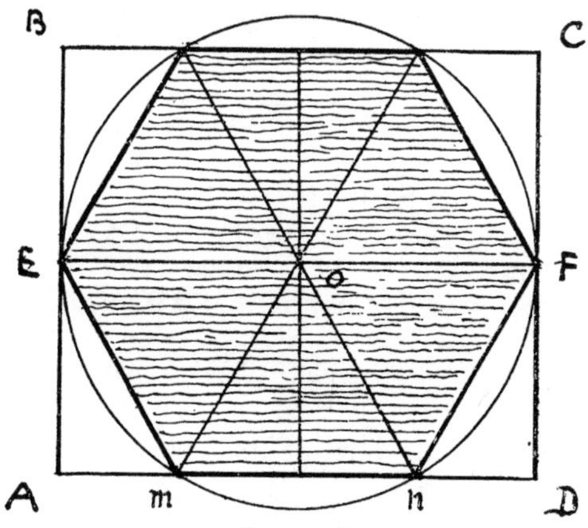

Fig. 206.

be equal in length to two sides of the hexagon or two radii of the circle, as EF, and its width will be twice the height of an equilateral triangle *mon*.

To put the hexagon into perspective, draw base of quadrilateral AD, divide it into four equal parts, and from each division draw lines to point of sight. From *h* drop perpendicular *ho*, and form equilateral triangle *mno*. Take the height *ho* and measure it twice along the base from A to 2. From 2 draw line to point of distance, or from 1 to ½ distance, and so find length of side AB equal to A2. Draw BC, and EF through centre *o*·, and thus we have the six points through which to draw the hexagon.

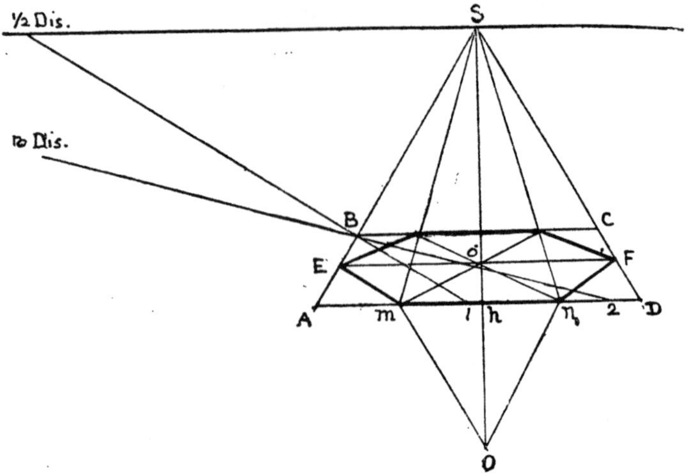

FIG. 207.

CXV

A PAVEMENT COMPOSED OF HEXAGONAL TILES

In drawing pavements, except in the cases of square tiles, it is necessary to make a plan of the required design, as in this figure composed of hexagons. First set out the hexagon as at A, then draw parallels 1 1, 2 2, &c., to mark the horizontal ends of the tiles and the intermediate lines *oo*. Divide the base into the required number of parts, each equal to one side of the hexagon, as 1, 2, 3, 4, &c.; from these draw perpendiculars as shown in the figure, and also the diagonals passing through their intersections. Then mark with a strong line the outlines of the hexagonals, shading some of them; but the figure explains itself.

It is easy to put all these parallels, perpendiculars, and diagonals into perspective, and then to draw the hexagons.

First draw the hexagon on AD as in the previous figure, dividing

AD into four, &c., set off right and left spaces equal to these fourths, and from each division draw lines to point of sight. Produce sides *me*, *nf* till they touch the horizon in points V, V· ; these will be the two vanishing points for all the sides of the tiles that are receding from us. From each division on base draw lines to each of these vanishing points, then draw parallels through their intersections as shown on the figure. Having all these guiding lines it will not be difficult to draw as many hexagons as you please.

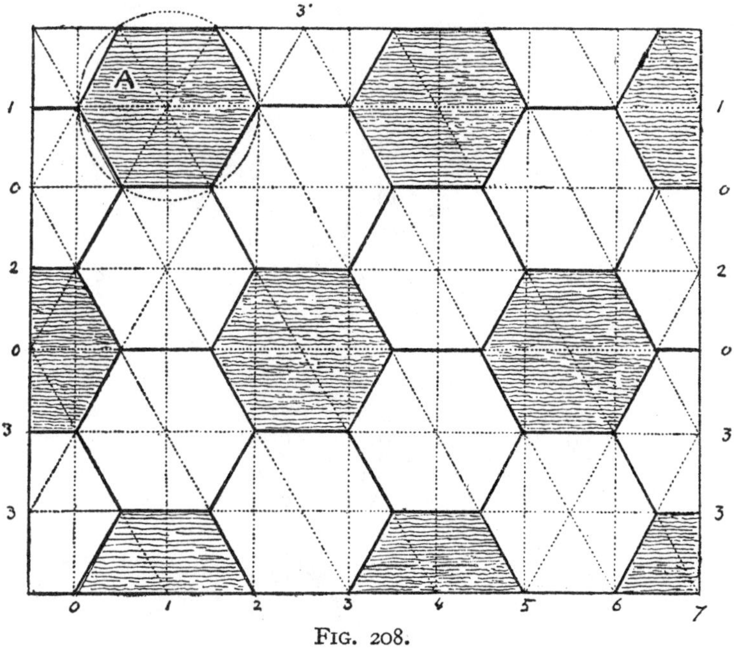

FIG. 208.

Note that the vanishing points should be at equal distances from S, also that the parallelogram in which each tile is contained is oblong, and not square, as already pointed out.

We have also made use of the triangle *omn* to ascertain the length and width of that oblong. Another thing to note is that we have made use of the half distance, which enables us to make our pavement look flat without spreading our lines outside the picture.

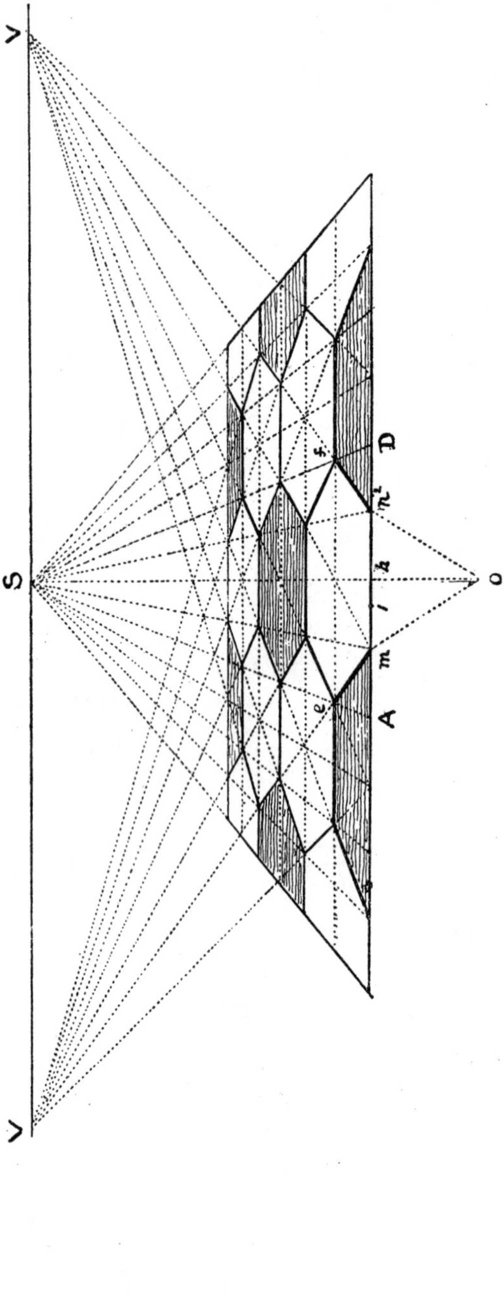

Fig. 209

CXVI

A Pavement of Hexagonal Tiles in Angular Perspective

This is more difficult than the previous figure, as we only make use of one vanishing point; but it shows how much can be done by diagonals, as nearly all this pavement is drawn by their aid. First make a geometrical plan A at the angle required. Then draw its perspective K. Divide line 4*b* into four equal

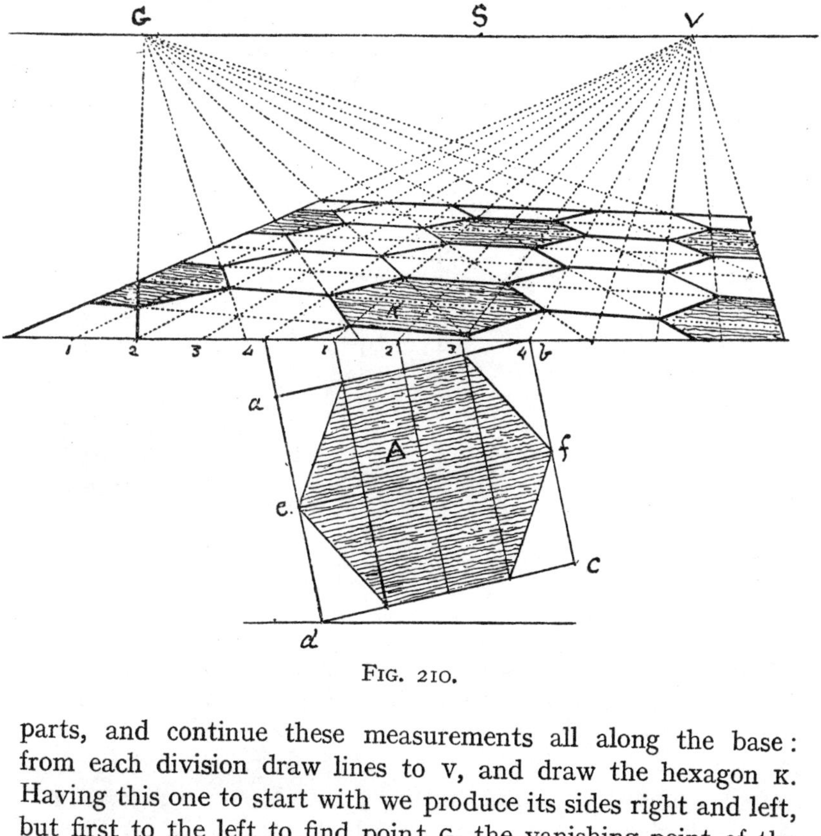

Fig. 210.

parts, and continue these measurements all along the base: from each division draw lines to V, and draw the hexagon K. Having this one to start with we produce its sides right and left, but first to the left to find point G, the vanishing point of the diagonals. Those to the right, if produced far enough, would meet at a distant vanishing point not in the picture. But the student should study this figure for himself, and refer back to Figs. 204 and 205.

CXVII

Further Illustration of the Hexagon

To draw the hexagon in perspective we must first find the rectangle in which it is inscribed, according to the view we take of it. That at A we have already drawn. We will now work

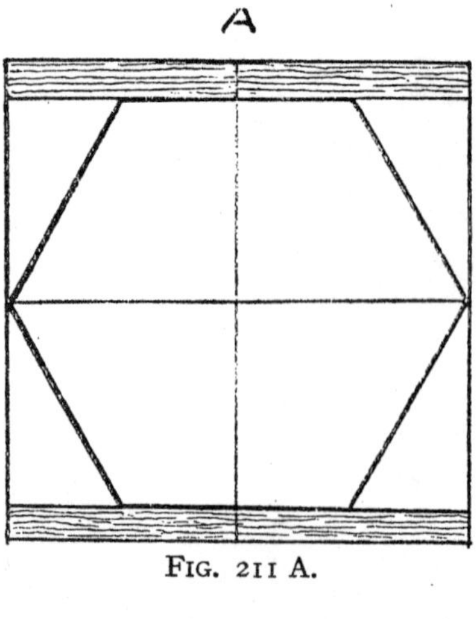

Fig. 211 A.

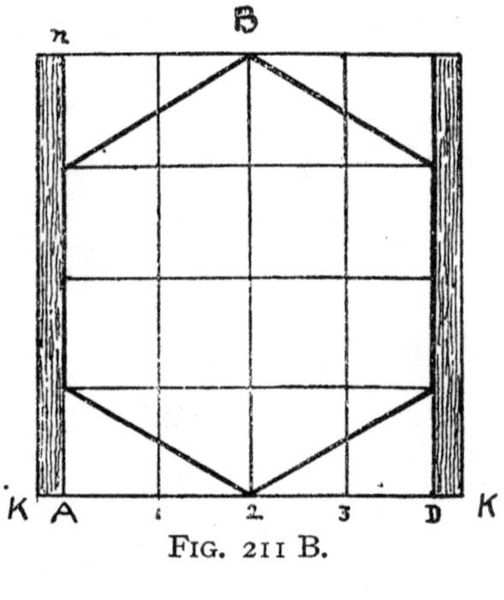

Fig. 211 B.

out that at B. Divide the base AD into four equal parts and transfer those measurements to the perspective figure C, as at AD, measuring other equal spaces along the base. To find the depth A*n* of the rectangle, make DK equal to base of square. Draw KO to distance-point, cutting DO at O, and thus find line LO. Draw diagonal D*n*, and through its intersections with the lines 1, 2, 3, 4 draw lines parallel to the base, and we shall thus have the framework, as it were, by which to draw the pavement.

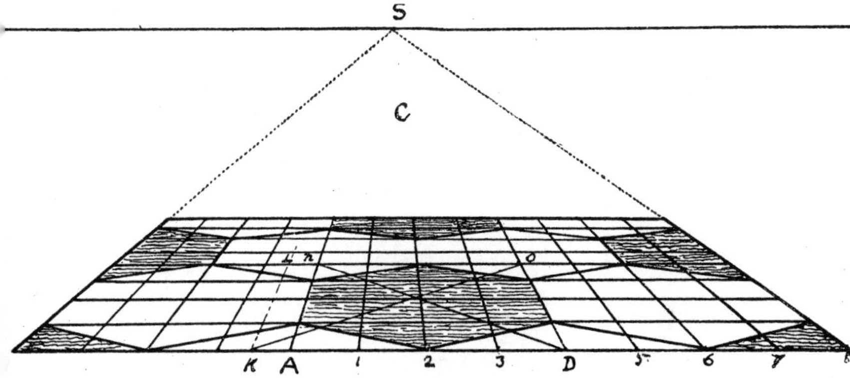

FIG. 212.

CXVIII

ANOTHER VIEW OF THE HEXAGON IN ANGULAR PERSPECTIVE

Given the rectangle ABCD in angular perspective, produce side DA to E on base line. Divide EB into four equal parts, and from

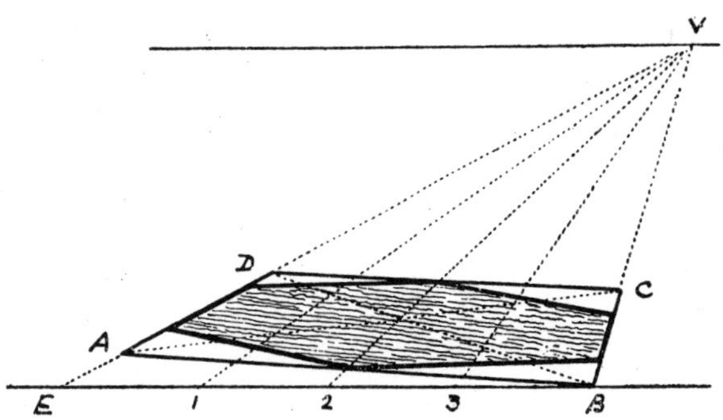

FIG. 213.

each division draw lines to vanishing point, then by means of diagonals, &c., draw the hexagon.

In Fig. 214 we have first drawn a geometrical plan, G, for the sake of clearness, but the one above shows that this is not necessary.

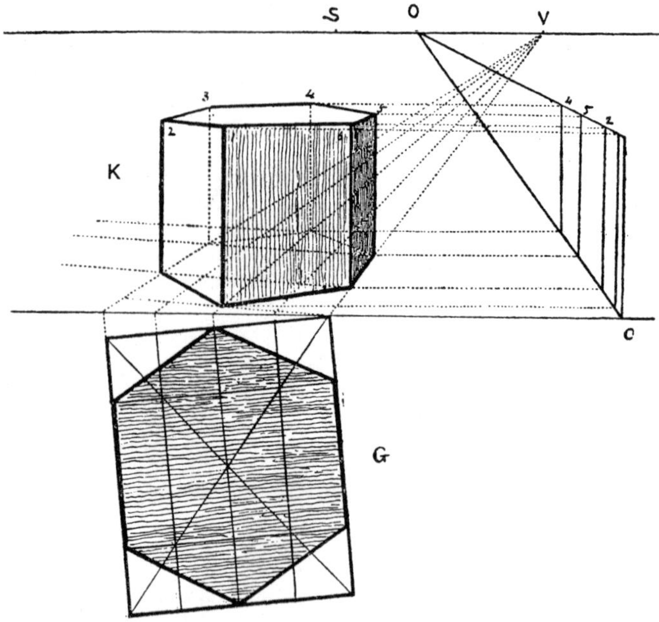

FIG. 214.

To raise the hexagonal figure K we have made use of the vanishing scale O and the vanishing point V. Another method could be used by drawing two hexagons one over the other at the required height.

CXIX

Application of the Hexagon to Drawing a Kiosk

This figure is built up from the hexagon standing on a rectangular base, from which we have raised verticals, &c.

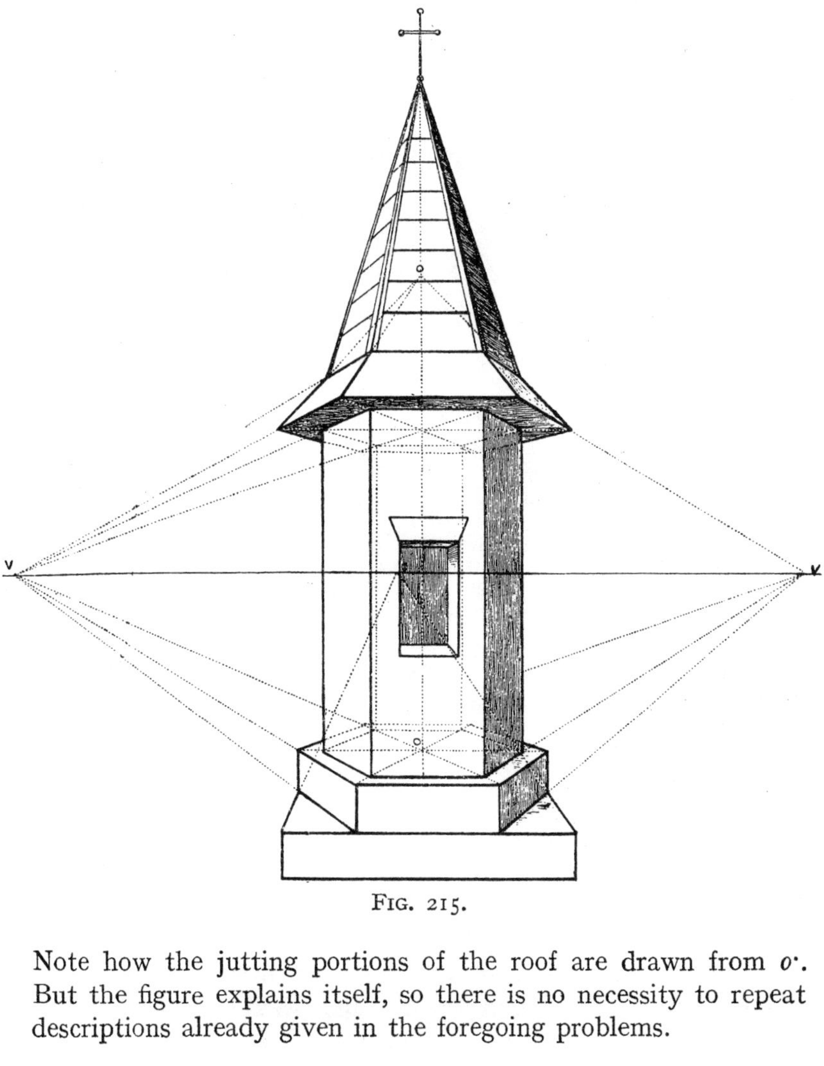

Fig. 215.

Note how the jutting portions of the roof are drawn from *o*·. But the figure explains itself, so there is no necessity to repeat descriptions already given in the foregoing problems.

CXX

THE PENTAGON

The pentagon is a figure with five equal sides, and if inscribed in a circle will touch its circumference at five equidistant points. With any convenient radius describe circle. From half this radius, marked 1, draw a line to apex, marked 2. Again, with 1 as centre and 1 2 as radius, describe arc 2 3. Now with 2 as

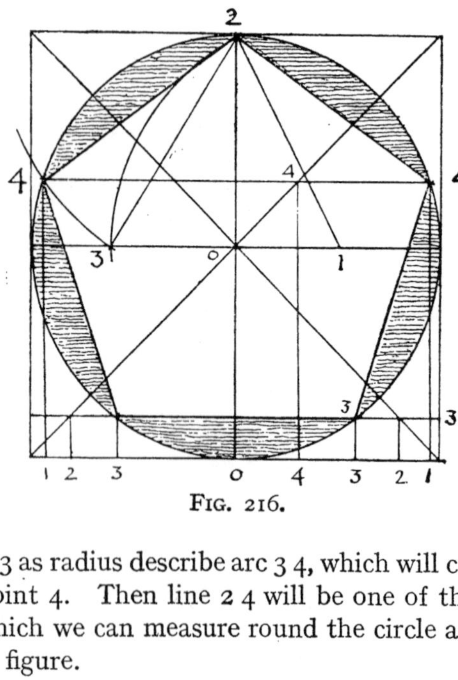

FIG. 216.

centre and 2 3 as radius describe arc 3 4, which will cut the circumference at point 4. Then line 2 4 will be one of the sides of the pentagon, which we can measure round the circle and so produce the required figure.

To put this pentagon into parallel perspective inscribe the circle in which it is drawn in a square, and from its five angles 4, 2, 4, &c., drop perpendiculars to base and number them as in the figure. Then draw the perspective square (Fig. 217) and transfer these measurements to its base. From these draw lines to point of sight, then by their aid and the two diagonals proceed to construct the pentagon in the same way that we did the triangles and other figures. Should it be required to place this

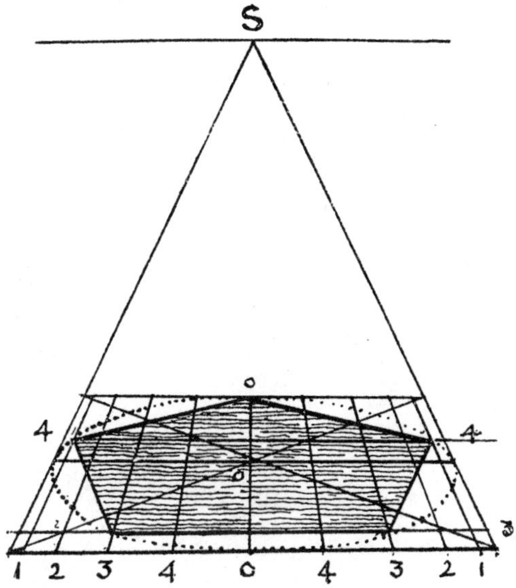

FIG. 217.

pentagon in the opposite position, then we can transfer our measurements to the far side of the square, as in Fig. 218.

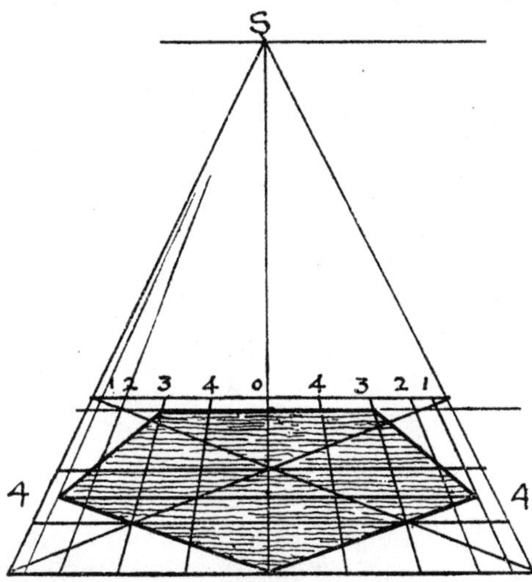

FIG. 218.

Or if we wish to put it into angular perspective we adopt the same method as with the hexagon, as shown at Fig. 219.

Another way of drawing a pentagon (Fig. 220) is to draw an isosceles triangle with an angle of 36° at its apex, and from centre

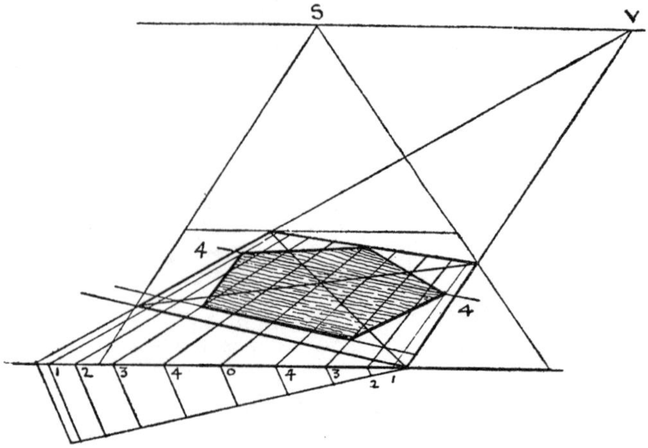

FIG. 219.

of each side of the triangle draw perpendiculars to meet at *o*, which will be the centre of the circle in which it is inscribed. From this centre and with radius OA describe circle A 3 2, &c.

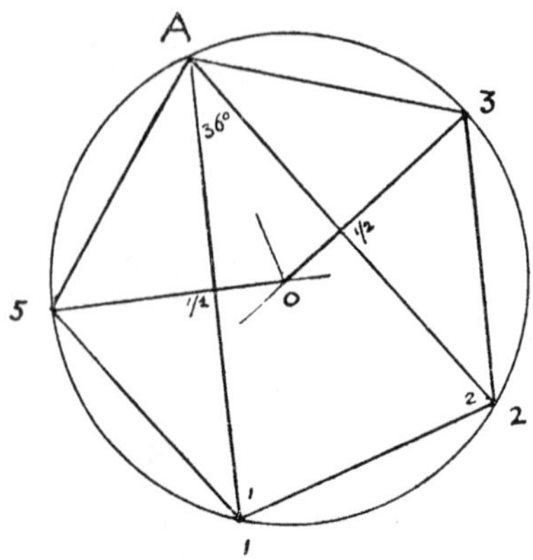

FIG. 220.

Take base of triangle 1 2, measure it round the circle, and so find the five points through which to draw the pentagon. The angles at 1 2 will each be 72°, double that at A, which is 36°.

CXXI

The Pyramid

Nothing can be more simple than to put a pyramid into perspective. Given the base (*abc*), raise from its centre a perpendicular (OP) of the required height, then draw lines from the corners of that base to a point P on the vertical line, and the thing is done. These pyramids can be used in drawing roofs, steeples, &c. The cone is drawn in the same way, so also is any other figure, whether octagonal, hexangular, triangular, &c.

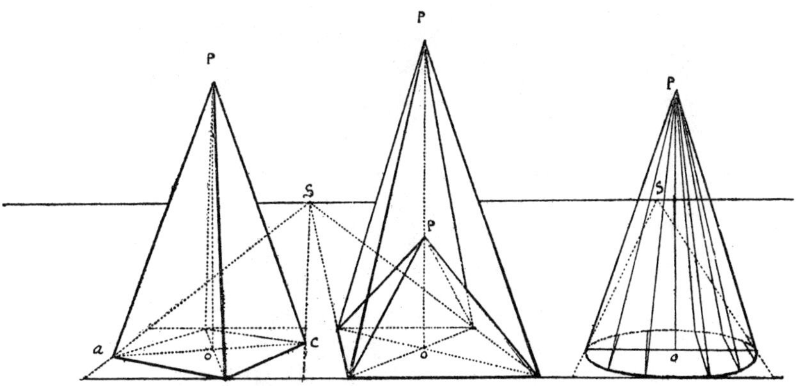

FIG. 221. FIG. 222. FIG. 223.

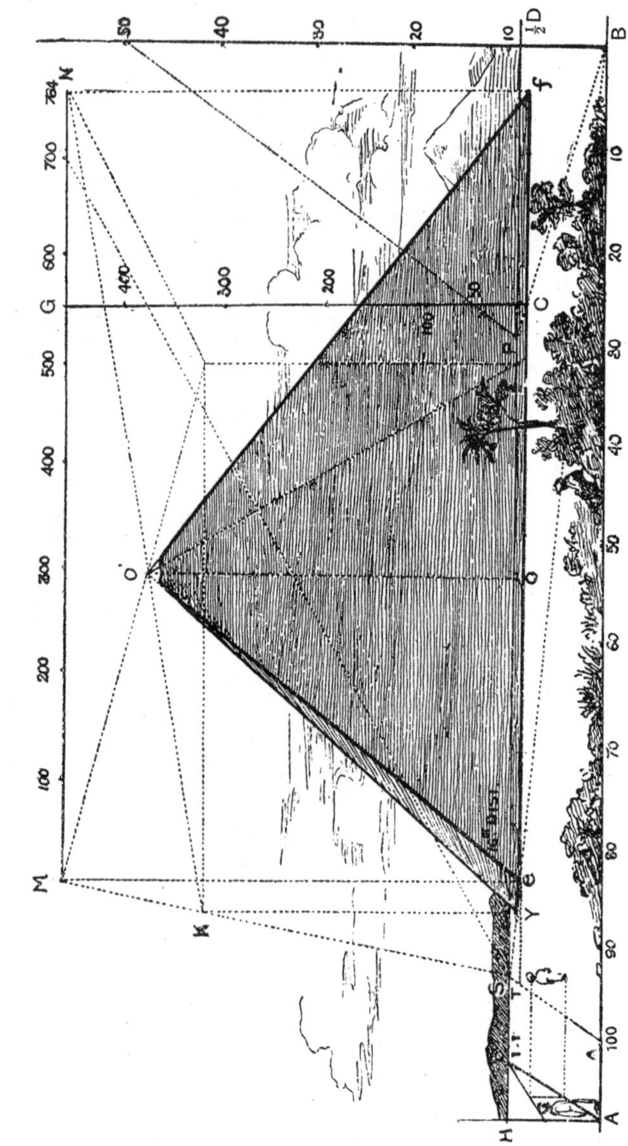

FIG. 224.

CXXII

The Great Pyramid

This enormous structure stands on a square base of over thirteen acres, each side of which measures, or did measure, 764 feet. Its original height was 480 feet, each side being an equilateral triangle. Let us see how we can draw this gigantic mass on our little sheet of paper.

In the first place, to take it all in at one view we must put it very far back, and in the second the horizon must be so low down that we cannot draw the square base of thirteen acres on the perspective plane, that is on the ground, so we must draw it in the air, and also to a very small scale.

Divide the base AB into ten equal parts, and suppose each of these parts to measure 10 feet. S, the point of sight, is placed on the left of the picture near the side, in order that we may get a long line of distance, S$\frac{1}{2}$D; but even this line is only half the distance we require. Let us therefore take the 16th distance, as shown in our previous illustration of the lighthouse (Fig. 92), which enables us to measure sixteen times the length of base AB, or 1,600 feet. The base *ef* of the pyramid is 1,600 feet from the base line of the picture, and is, according to our 10-foot scale, 764 feet long.

The next thing to consider is the height of the pyramid. We make a scale to the right of the picture measuring 50 feet from B to 50 at point where BP intersects base of pyramid, raise perpendicular CG and thereon measure 480 feet. As we cannot obtain a palpable square on the ground, let us draw one 480 feet above the ground. From *e* and *f* raise verticals *e*M and *f*N, making them equal to perpendicular G, and draw line MN, which will be the same length as base, or 764 feet. On this line form square MNK parallel to the perspective plane, find its centre O· by means of diagonals, and O· will be the central height of the pyramid and exactly over the centre of the base. From this point O· draw sloping lines O·*f*, O·*e*, O·Y, &c., and the figure is complete.

Note the way in which we find the measurements on base of pyramid and on line MN. By drawing AS and BS to point of sight we find T*e*, which measures 100 feet at a distance of 1,600 feet. We mark off seven of these lengths, and an additional 64 feet by the scale, and so obtain the required length. The position of the third corner of the base is found by dropping a perpendicular from K, till it meets the line *e*S.

Another thing to note is that the side of the pyramid that faces us, although an equilateral triangle, does not appear so, as its top angle is 382 feet farther off than its base owing to its leaning position.

CXXIII

The Pyramid in Angular Perspective

In order to show the working of this proposition I have taken a much higher horizon, which immediately detracts from the impression of the bigness of the pyramid.

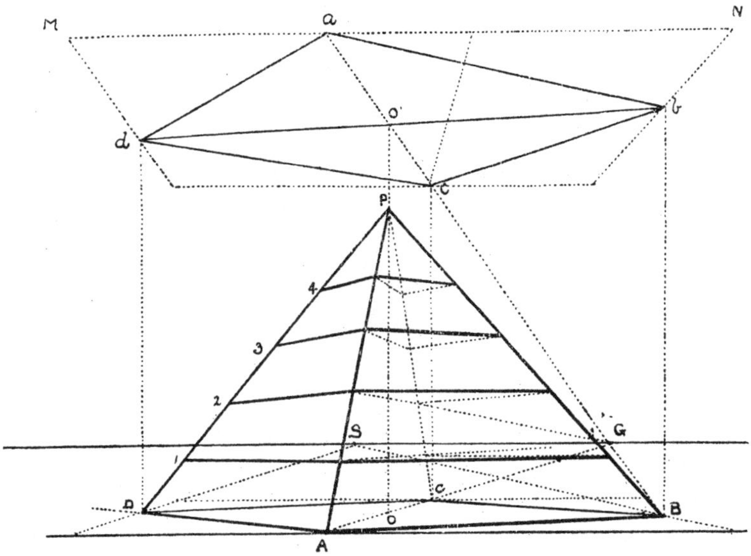

Fig. 225.

We proceed to make our ground-plan *abcd* high above the horizon instead of below it, drawing first the parallel square and then the oblique one. From all the principal points drop perpendiculars to the ground and thus find the points through which to draw the base of the pyramid. Find centres oo· and decide upon the height op. Draw the sloping lines from p to the corners of the base, and the figure is complete.

CXXIV

To Divide the Sides of the Pyramid Horizontally

Having raised the pyramid on a given oblique square, divide the vertical line *o*p into the required number of parts. From

A through C draw AG to horizon, which gives us G, the vanishing point of all the diagonals of squares parallel to and at the same angle as ABCD. From G draw lines through the divisions 2, 3, &c., on OP cutting the lines PA and PC, thus dividing them into the

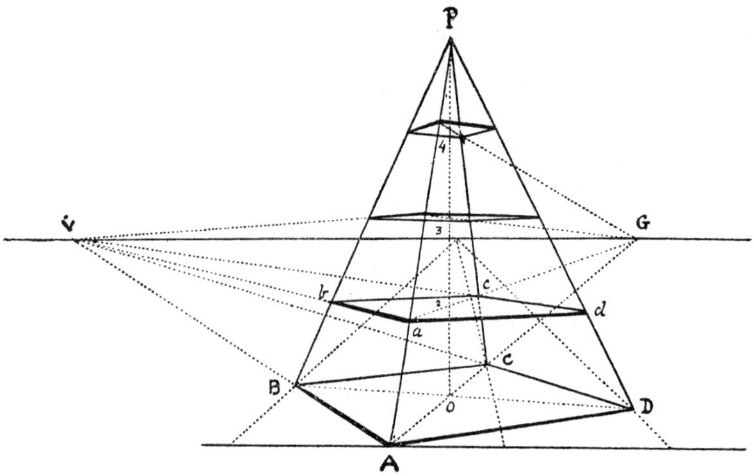

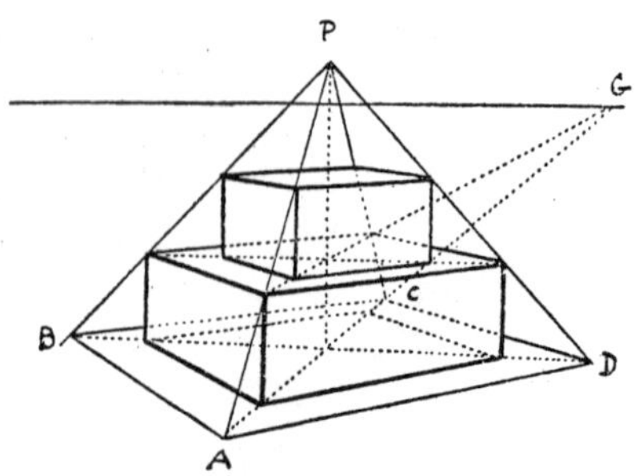

FIG. 227.

The same method will apply to drawing steps, square blocks, &c., as shown in Fig. 227, which is at the same angle as the above.

CXXV

Of Roofs

The pyramidal roof (Fig. 228) is so simple that it explains itself. The chief thing to be noted is the way in which the diagonals are produced beyond the square of the walls, to give the width of the eaves, according to their position.

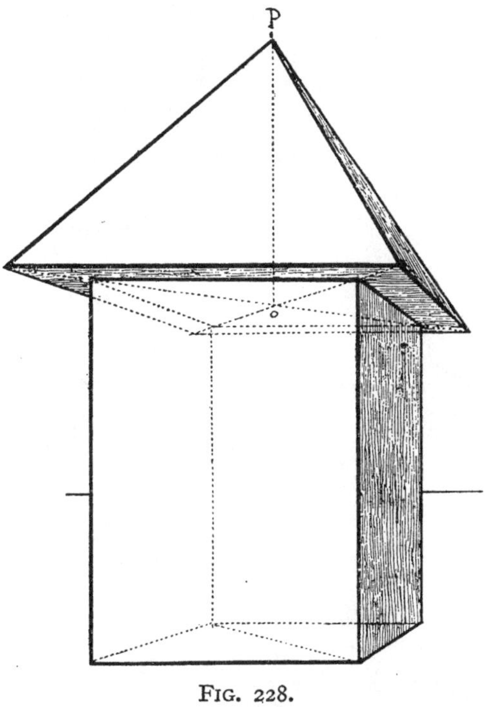

Fig. 228.

Another form of the pyramidal roof is here given (Fig. 229). First draw the cube *edcba* at the required height, and on the side facing us, *adcb*, draw triangle K, which represents the end of a gable roof. Then draw similar triangles on the other sides of the cube (see Fig. 159, LXXXIV). Join the opposite triangles at the apex, and thus form two gable roofs crossing each other at right angles. From *o*, centre of base of cube, raise vertical OP, and then from P draw sloping lines to each corner of base *a*, *b*, &c., and by means of central lines drawn from P to

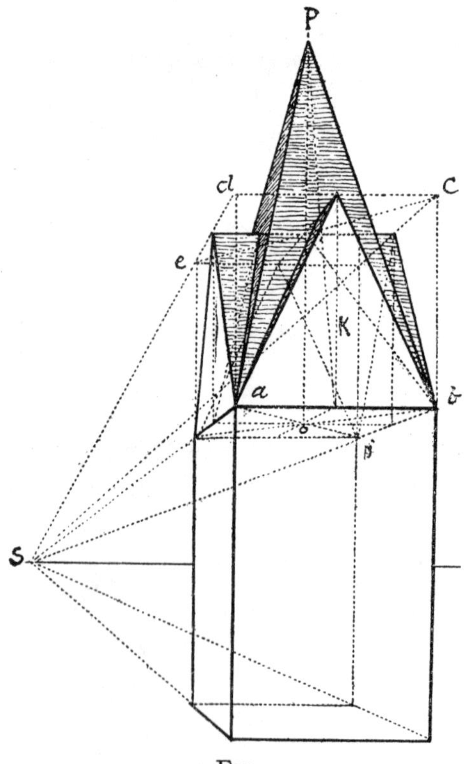

FIG. 229.

half base, find the points where the gable roofs intersect the central spire or pyramid. Any other proportions can be obtained by adding to or altering the cube.

To draw a sloping or hip-roof which falls back at each end we must first draw its base, CBDA (Fig. 230). Having found the centre O and central line SP, and how far the roof is to fall back at each end, namely the distance P*m*, draw horizontal line RB through *m*. Then from B through O draw diagonal BA, and from

A draw horizontal AD, which gives us point *n*. From these two points *m* and *n* raise perpendiculars the height required for the roof, and from these draw sloping lines to the corners of the base. Join *ef*, that is, draw the top line of the roof, which completes it. Fig. 231 shows a plan or bird's-eye view of the roof

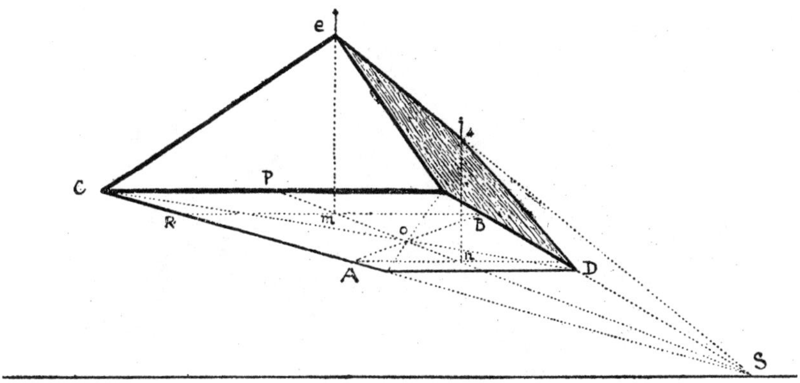

FIG. 230.

and the diagonal AB passing through centre O. But there are so many varieties of roofs they would take almost a book to themselves to illustrate them, especially the cottages and farm-

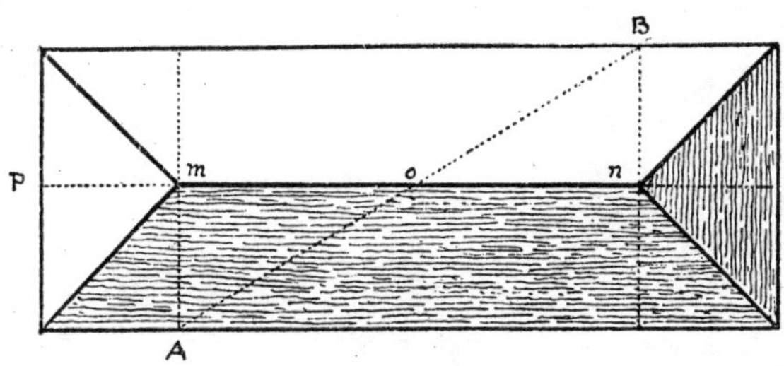

FIG. 231.

buildings, barns, &c., besides churches, old mansions, and others. There is also such irregularity about some of them that perspective rules, beyond those few here given, are of very little use. So that the best thing for an artist to do is to sketch them from the real whenever he has an opportunity.

CXXVI

Of Arches, Arcades, Bridges, &c.

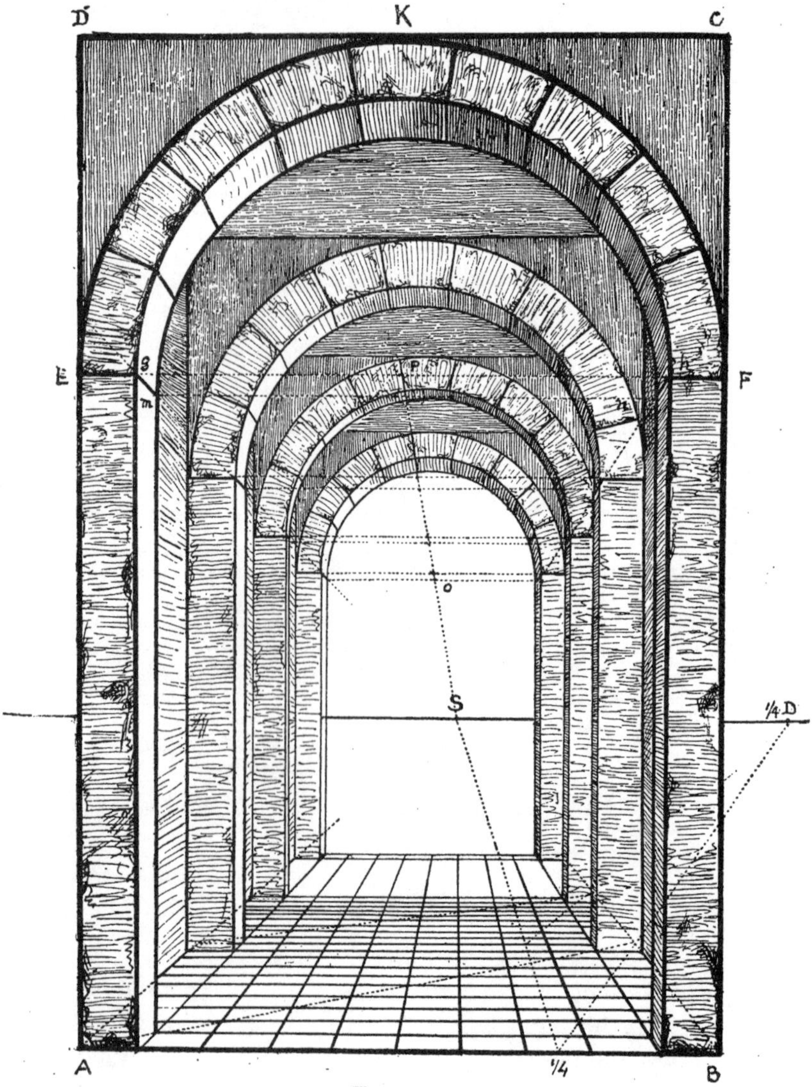

Fig. 232.

For an arcade or cloister (Fig. 232) first set up the outer frame ABCD according to the proportions required. For round arches the height may be twice that of the base, varying to one and a half. In Gothic arches the height may be about three times the width, all of which proportions are chosen to suit the different purposes and effects required. Divide the base AB into the desired number of parts, 8, 10, 12, &c., each part representing 1 foot. (In this case the base is 10 feet and the horizon 5 feet.) Set out floor by means of $\frac{1}{4}$ distance. Divide it into squares of 1 foot, so that there will be 8 feet between each column or pilaster, supposing we make them to stand on a square foot. Draw the first archway EKF facing us, and its inner semicircle *gh*, with also its thickness or depth of 1 foot. Draw the span of the archway EF, then central line PO to point of sight. Proceed to raise as many other arches as required at the given distances. The intersections of the central line with the chords *mn*, &c., will give the centres from which to describe the semicircles.

CXXVII

Outline of an Arcade with Semicircular Arches

This is to show the method of drawing a long passage, corridor, or cloister with arches and columns at equal distances, and is worked in the same way as the previous figure, using $\frac{1}{4}$ distance

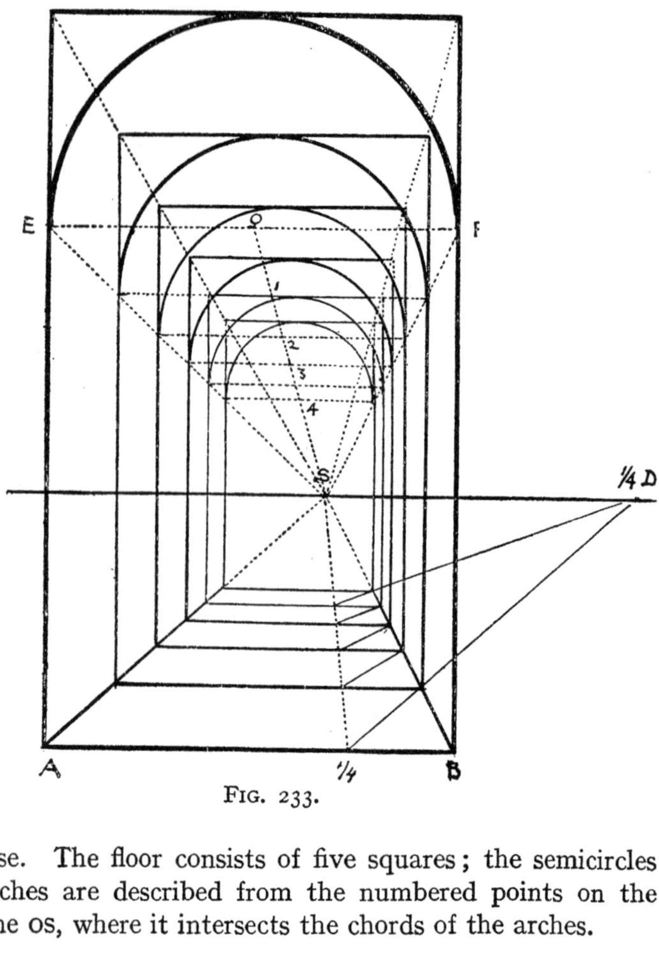

Fig. 233.

and $\frac{1}{4}$ base. The floor consists of five squares; the semicircles of the arches are described from the numbered points on the central line OS, where it intersects the chords of the arches.

CXXVIII

Semicircular Arches on a Retreating Plane

First draw perspective square *abcd*. Let *ae·* be the height of the figure. Draw *ae·f·b* and proceed with the rest of the outline. To draw the arches begin with the one facing us, E*o*·F enclosed in the quadrangle E*e·f·*F. With centre O describe the semicircle and across it draw the diagonals *e·*F, E*f·*, and through *nn*, where these lines intersect the semicircle, draw horizontal KK and also

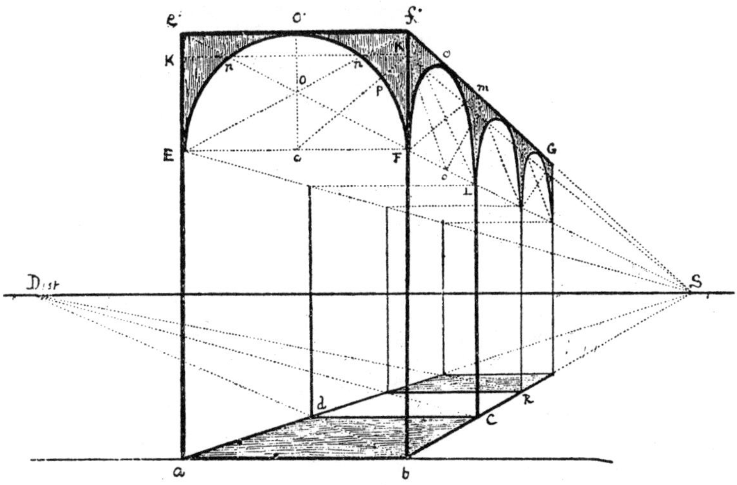

Fig. 234.

KS to point of sight. It will be seen that the half-squares at the side are the same size in perspective as the one facing us, and we carry out in them much the same operation; that is, we draw the diagonals, find the point O, and the points *nn*, &c., through which to draw our arches. See perspective of the circle (Fig. 165).

If more points are required an additional diagonal from O to

K may be used, as shown in the figure, which perhaps explains itself. The method is very old and very simple, and of course can be applied to any kind of arch, pointed or stunted, as in this drawing of a pointed arch (Fig. 235).

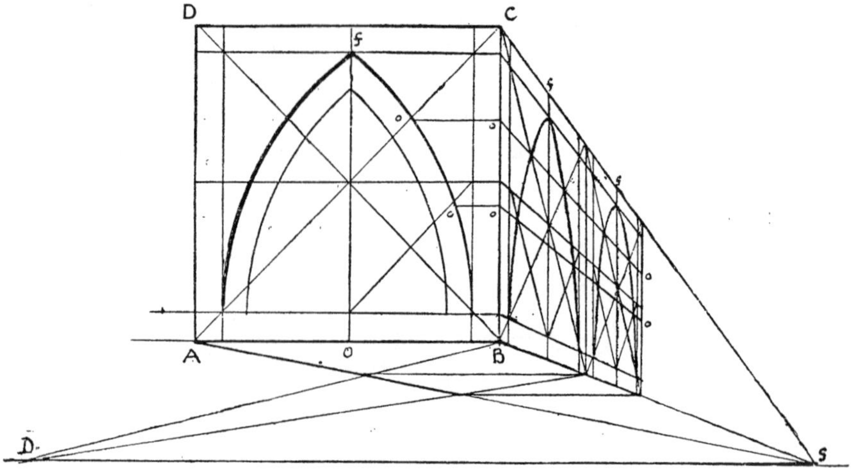

FIG. 235.

CXXIX

AN ARCADE IN ANGULAR PERSPECTIVE

First draw the perspective square ABCD at the angle required, by new method. Produce sides AD and BC to V. Draw diagonal BD and produce to point G, from whence we draw the other diagonals to *cfh*. Make spaces 1, 2, 3, &c., on base line equal to B 1 to obtain sides of squares. Raise vertical BM the height required. Produce DA to O on base line, and from O raise vertical OP equal to BM. This line enables us to dispense with the long vanishing point to the left; its working has been explained at Fig. 131. From P draw PRV to vanishing point V, which will intersect vertical AR at R. Join MR, and this line, if produced, would meet the horizon at the other vanishing point.

In like manner make O2 equal to B2'. From 2 draw line to V, and at 2, its intersection with AR, draw line 2 2, which will also

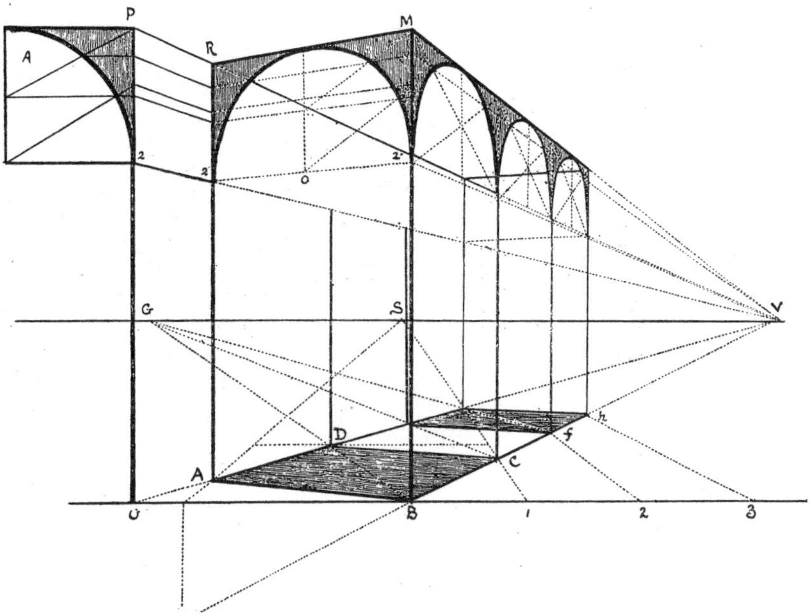

FIG. 236.

meet the horizon at the other vanishing point. By means of the quarter-circle A we can obtain the points through which to draw the semicircular arches in the same way as in the previous figure.

CXXX

A VAULTED CEILING

From the square ceiling ABCD we have, as it were, suspended two arches from the two diagonals DB, AC, which spring from the four corners of the square EFGH, just underneath it. The curves of these arches, which are not semicircular but elongated, are obtained by means of the vanishing scales *m*S, *n*S. Take any two convenient points P, R, on each side of the semicircle, and raise verticals P*m*, R*n* to AB, and on these verticals form the scales. Where *m*S and *n*S cut the diagonal AC drop perpendiculars

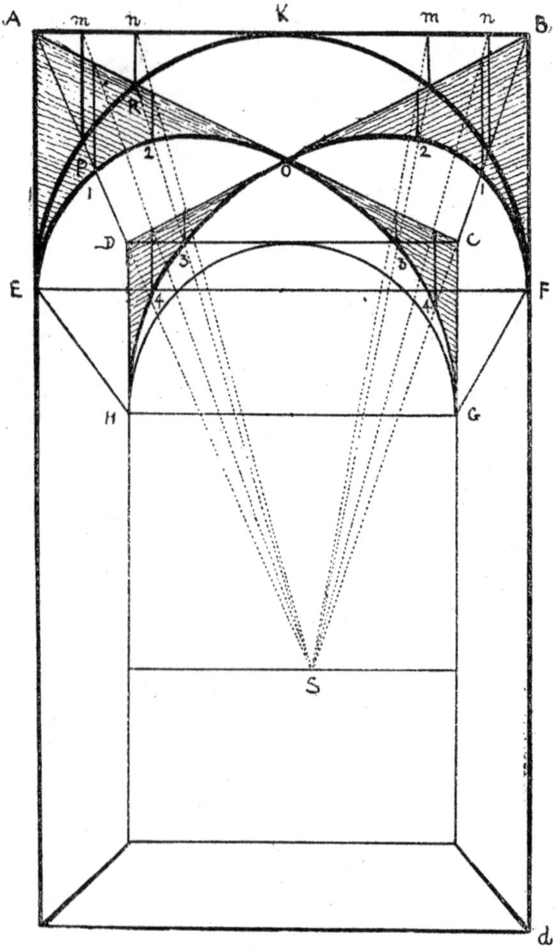

FIG. 237.

to meet the lower line of the scale at points 1, 2. On the other side, using the other scales, we have dropped perpendiculars in the same way from the diagonal to 3, 4. These points, together with EOG, enable us to trace the curve E 1 2 0 3 4 G. We draw the arch under the other diagonal in precisely the same way.

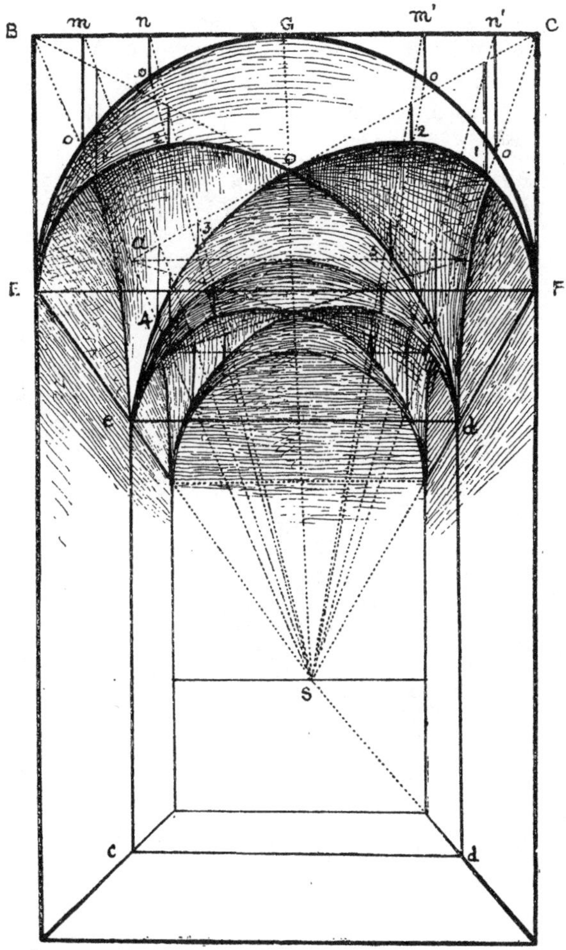

FIG. 238.

The reason for thus proceeding is that the cross arches, although elongated, hang from their diagonals just as the semicircular arch EKF hangs from AB, and the lines *mn*, touching the circle at PR, are represented by 1, 2, hanging from the diagonal AC.

Figure 238, which is practically the same as the preceding only differently shaded, is drawn in the following manner. Draw arch EGF facing us, and proceed with the rest of the corridor, but first finding the flat ceiling above the square on the ground AB*cd*. Draw diagonals *ac*, *bd*, and the curves pending from them. But we no longer see the clear arch as in the other drawing, for the spaces between the curves are filled in and arched across.

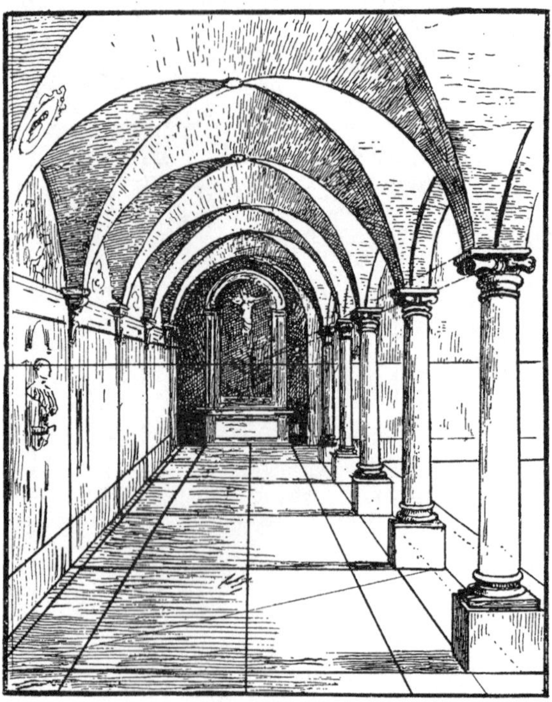

FIG. 239.

CXXXI

A Cloister, from a Photograph

This drawing of a cloister from a photograph shows the correctness of our perspective, and the manner of applying it to practical work.

CXXXII

The Low or Elliptical Arch

Let AB be the span of the arch and O*h* its height. From centre O, with OA, or half the span, for radius, describe outer semicircle.

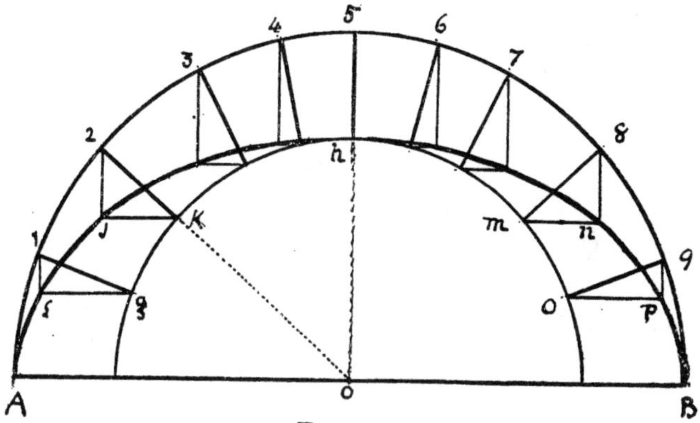

Fig. 240.

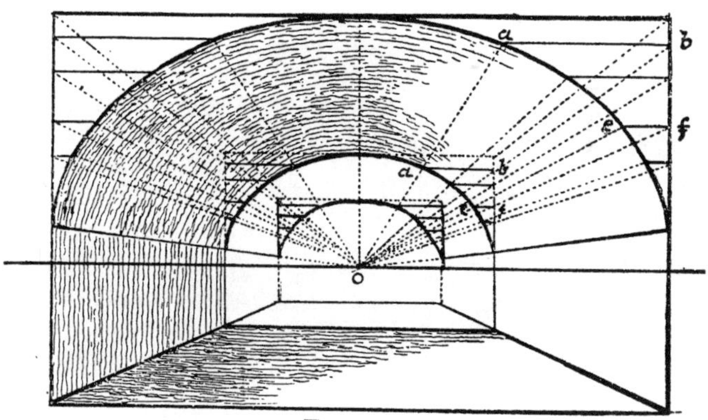

Fig. 241.

From same centre and *oh* for radius describe the inner semicircle. Divide outer circle into a convenient number of parts, 1, 2, 3, &c., to which draw radii from centre O. From each division drop perpendiculars. Where the radii intersect the inner circle, as at *gkmo*, draw horizontals *op*, *mn*, *kj*, &c., and through their intersections with the perpendiculars *f*, *j*, *n*, *p*, draw the curve of the flattened arch. Transfer this to the lower figure, and proceed to draw the tunnel. Note how the vanishing scale is formed on either side by horizontals *ba*, *fe*, &c., which enable us to make the distant arches similar to the near ones.

CXXXIII

Opening or Arched Window in a Vault

First draw the vault AEB. To introduce the window K, the upper part of which follows the form of the vault, we first decide on its width, which is *mn*, and its height from floor B*a*. On line

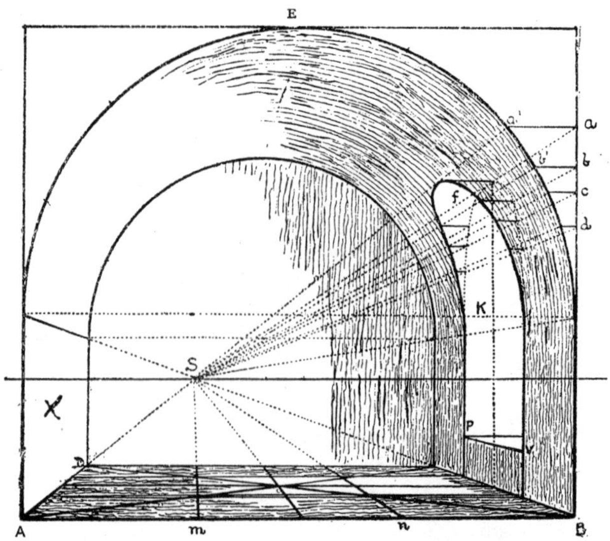

Fig. 242.

B*a* at the side of the arch form scales *aa*·s, *bb*·s, &c. Raise the semicircular arch K, shown by a dotted line. The scale at the side will give the lengths *aa*·, *bb*·, &c., from different parts of this dotted arch to corresponding points in the curved archway or window required.

Note that to obtain the width of the window K we have used

the diagonals on the floor and width *m n* on base. This method of measurement is explained at Fig. 144, and is of ready application in a case of this kind.

CXXXIV

STAIRS, STEPS, &c.

Having decided upon the incline or angle, such as CBA, at which the steps are to be placed, and the height B*m* of each step,

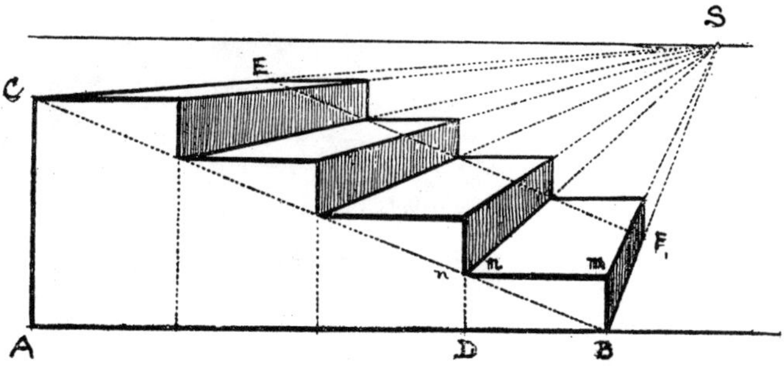

FIG. 243.

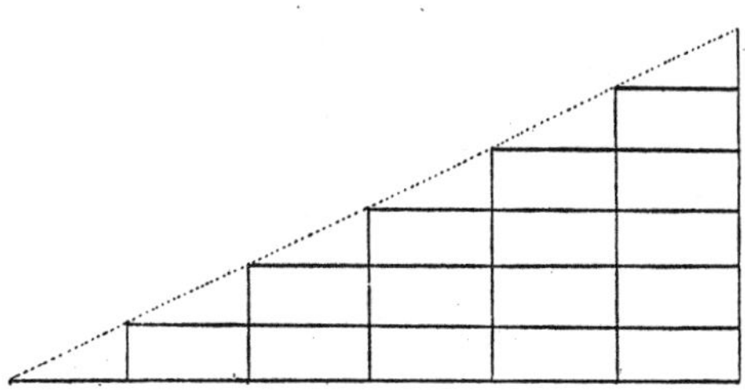

FIG. 244.

draw *mn* to CB, which will give the width. Then measure along base AB this width equal to DB, which will give that for all the other steps. Obtain length BF of steps, and draw EF parallel to CB. These lines will aid in securing the exactness of the figure.

CXXXV

Steps, Front View

In this figure the height of each step is measured on the vertical line AB (this line is sometimes called the line of heights),

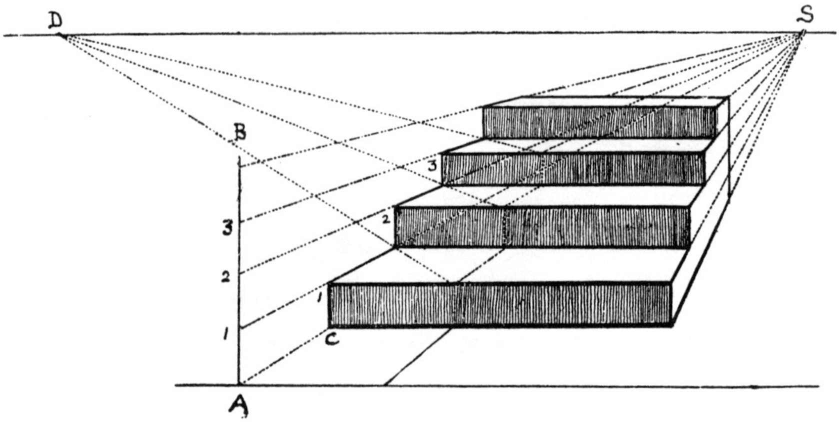

Fig. 245.

and their depth is found by diagonals drawn to the point of distance D. The rest of the figure explains itself.

CXXXVI

Square Steps

Draw first step ABEF and its two diagonals. Raise vertical AH, and measure thereon the required height of each step, and thus form scale. Let the second step CD be less all round than the

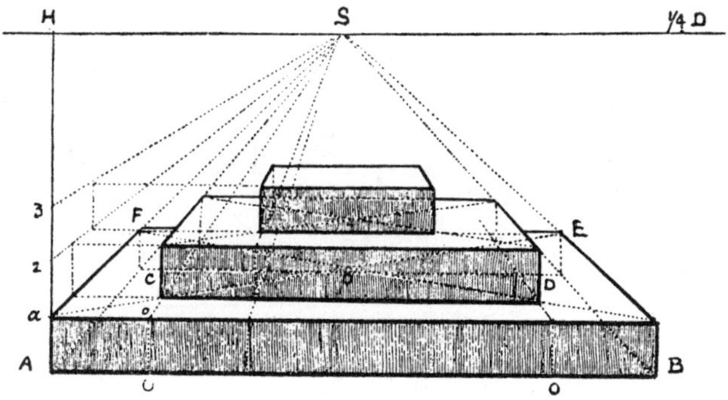

Fig. 246.

first by A*o* or B*o*. Draw *o*C till it cuts the diagonal, and proceed to draw the second step, guided by the diagonals and taking its height from the scale as shown. Draw the third step in the same way.

CXXXVII

To Divide an Inclined Plane into Equal Parts—such as a Ladder Placed against a Wall

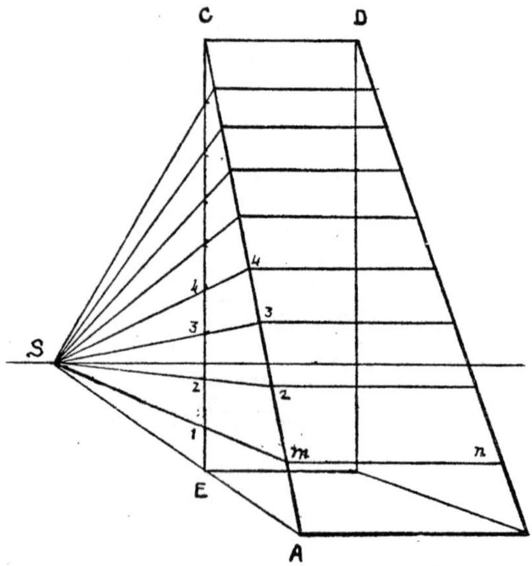

Fig. 247.

Divide the vertical EC into the required number of parts, and draw lines from point of sight S through these divisions 1, 2, 3, &c., cutting the line AC at 1, 2, 3, &c. Draw parallels to AB, such as *mn*, from AC to BD, which will represent the steps of the ladder.

CXXXVIII

Steps and the Inclined Plane

In Fig. 248 we treat a flight of steps as if it were an inclined plane. Draw the first and second steps as in Fig. 245. Then through 1, 2, draw 1V, AV to V, the vanishing point on the

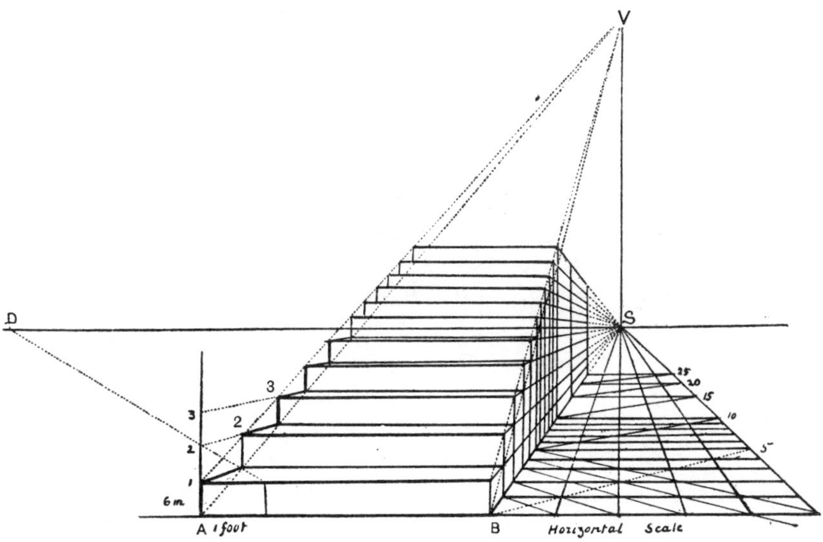

FIG. 248.

vertical line SV. These two lines and the corresponding ones at BV will form a kind of vanishing scale, giving the height of each step as we ascend. It is especially useful when we pass the horizontal line and we no longer see the upper surface of the step, the scale on the right showing us how to proceed in that case.

In Fig. 249 we have an example of steps ascending and descending. First set out the ground-plan, and find its vanishing point S (point of sight). Through S draw vertical BA, and make SA equal to SB. Set out the first step CD. Draw EA, CA, DA, and GA, for the ascending guiding lines. Complete the steps facing us, at central line OO. Then draw guiding line FB for the descending steps (see Rule 8).

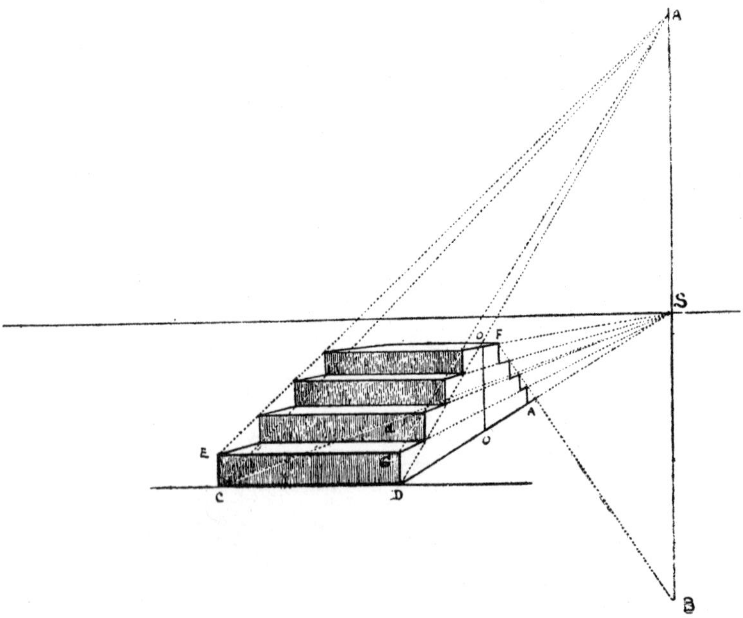

FIG. 249.

CXXXIX

STEPS IN ANGULAR PERSPECTIVE

First draw the base ABCD (Fig. 251) at the required angle by the new method (Fig. 250). Produce BC to the horizon, and thus find vanishing point V. At this point raise vertical VV'. Construct first step AB, refer its height at B to line of heights *h* I on left, and thus obtain height of step at A. Draw lines from A and F to

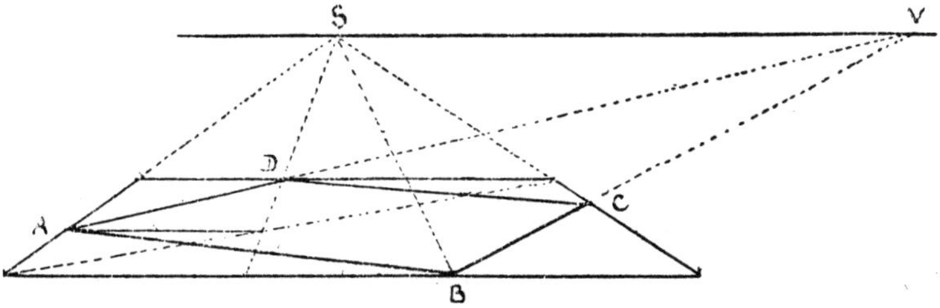

FIG. 250.

V'. From *n* draw diagonal through O to G. Raise vertical at O to represent the height of the next step, its height being determined

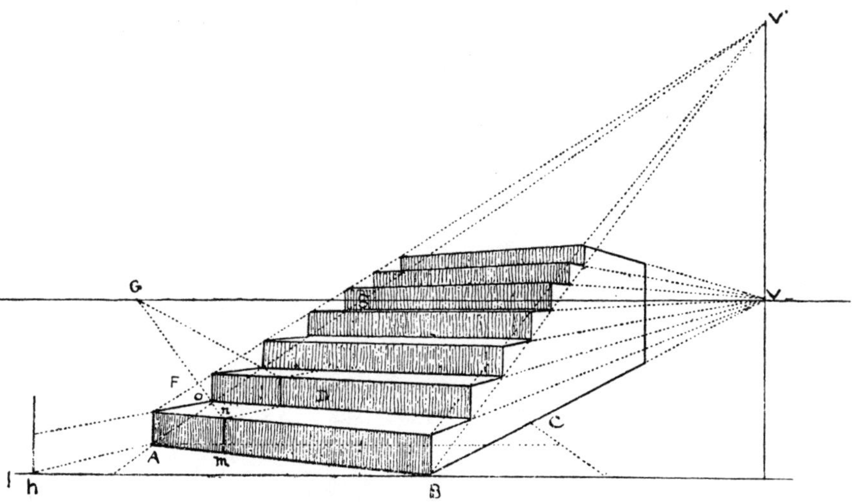

FIG. 251.

by the scale of heights at the side. From A and F draw lines to V', and also similar lines from B, which will serve as guiding lines to determine the height of the steps at either end as we raise them to the required number.

CXL

A Step Ladder at an Angle

First draw the ground-plan G at the required angle, using vanishing and measuring points. Find the height *h*H, and width at top HH', and draw the sides HA and H'E. Note that AE is wider than HH', and also that the back legs are not at the same angle as the front ones, and that they overlap them. From E

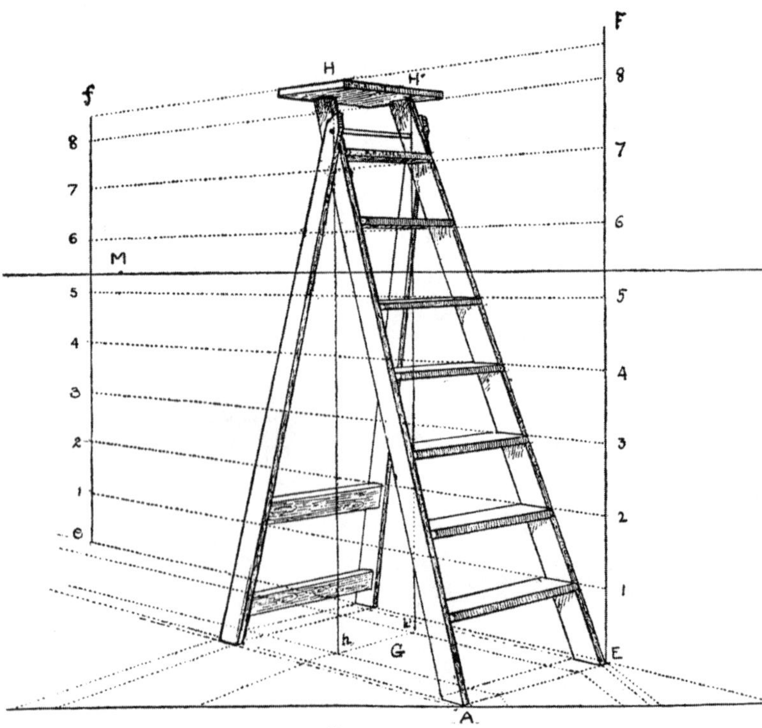

Fig. 252.

raise vertical EF, and divide into as many parts as you require rounds to the ladder. From these divisions draw lines 1 1, 2 2, &c., towards the other vanishing point (not in the picture), but

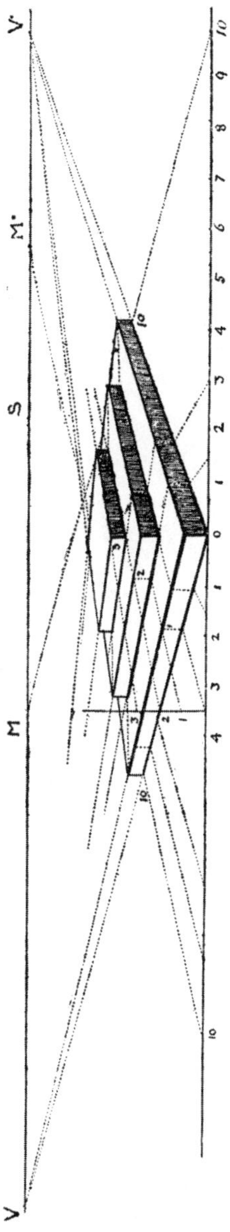

FIG. 253.

having obtained their direction from the ground-plan in perspective at line E*e*, you may set up a second vertical *ef* at any point on E*e* and divide it into the same number of parts, which will be in proportion to those on EF, and you will obtain the same result by drawing lines from the divisions on EF to those on *ef* as in drawing them to the vanishing point.

CXLI

SQUARE STEPS PLACED OVER EACH OTHER

This figure shows the other method of drawing steps, which is simple enough if we have sufficient room for our vanishing points.

The manner of working it is shown at Fig. 124.

CXLII

Steps and a Double Cross Drawn by Means of Diagonals and one Vanishing Point

Although in this figure we have taken a longer distance-point than in the previous one, we are able to draw it all within the page.

Begin by setting out the square base at the angle required.

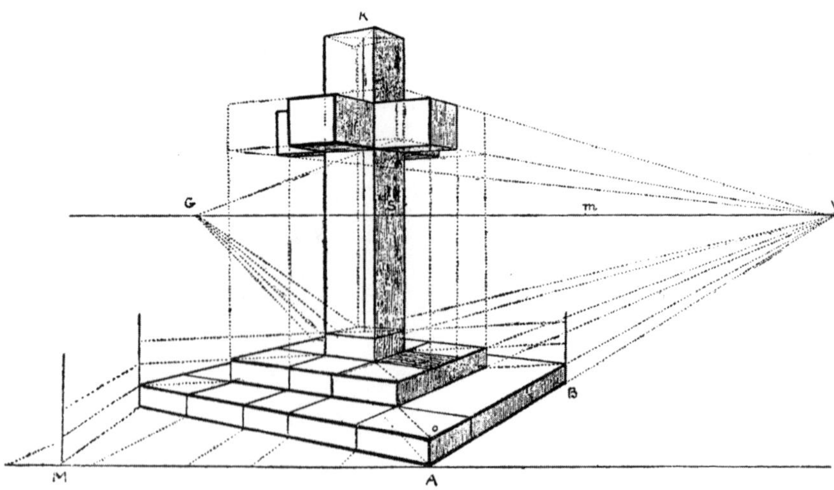

Fig. 254.

Find point G by means of diagonals, and produce AB to V, &c. Mark height of step A*o*, and proceed to draw the steps as already shown. Then by the diagonals and measurements on base draw the second step and the square inside it on which to stand the foot of the cross. To draw the cross, raise verticals from the four corners of its base, and a line K from its centre. Through any point on this central line, if we draw a diagonal from point G we cut the two opposite verticals of the shaft at *mn* (see Fig. 255), and by means of the vanishing point V we cut the other two

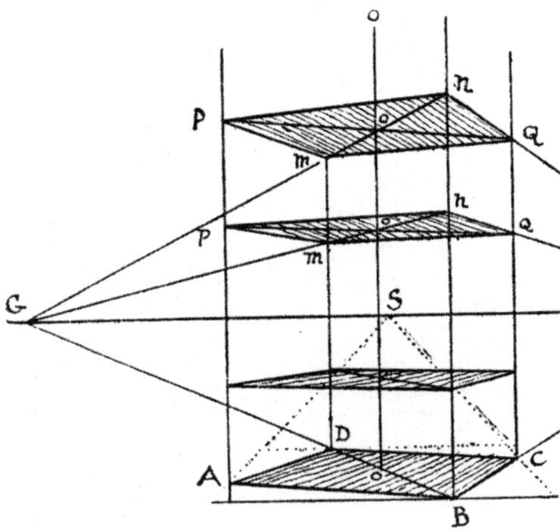

FIG. 255.

verticals at the opposite corners and thus obtain the four points through which to draw the other sides of the square, which go to the distant or inaccessible vanishing point. It will be seen by carefully examining the figure that by this means we are enabled to draw the double cross standing on its steps.

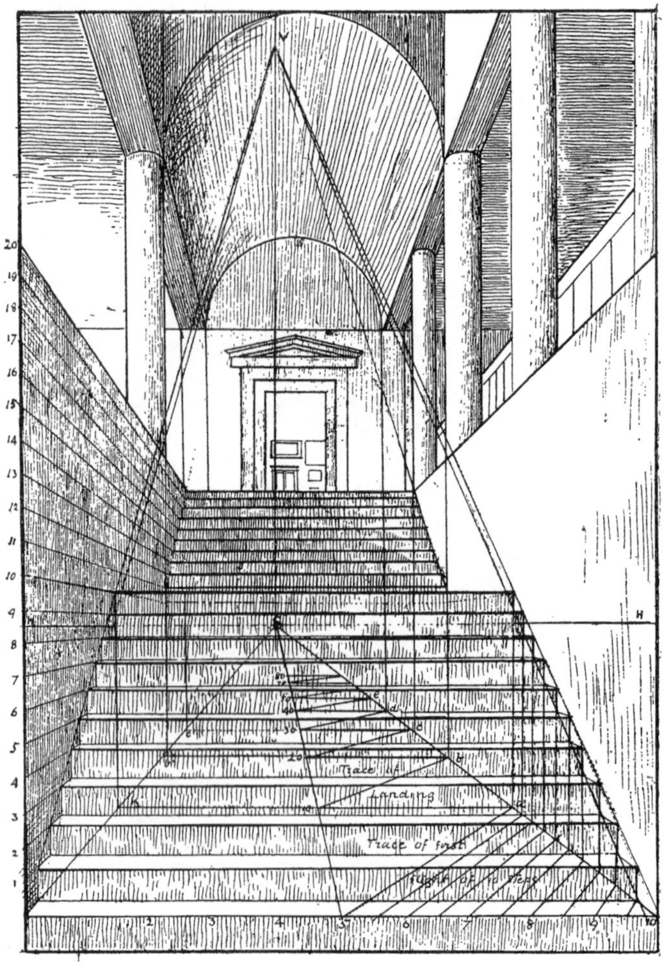

FIG. 256.

CXLIII

A Staircase Leading to a Gallery

In this figure we have made use of the devices already set forth in the foregoing figures of steps, &c., such as the side scale on the left of the figure to ascertain the height of the steps, the double lines drawn to the high vanishing point of the inclined plane, and so on; but the principal use of this diagram is to show on the perspective plane, which as it were runs under the stairs, the trace or projection of the flights of steps, the landings and positions of other objects, which will be found very useful in placing figures in a composition of this kind. It will be seen that these underneath measurements, so to speak, are obtained by the half-distance.

CXLIV

Winding Stairs in a Square Shaft

Draw square ABCD in parallel perspective. Divide each side into four, and raise verticals from each division. These verticals will mark the positions of the steps on each wall, four in number. From centre O raise vertical OP, around which the steps are to wind. Let AF be the height of each step. Form scale AB, which will give the height of each step according to its position. Thus at *mn* we find the height at the centre of the square, so if we transfer this measurement to the central line OP and repeat it upwards, say to fourteen, then we have the height of each step on the line where they all meet. Starting then with the first on the right, draw the rectangle *g*D1*f* the height of AF, then draw to the central line *go*, *f*1, and 1 1, and thus complete the first step. On DE, measure heights equal to D 1. Draw 2 2 towards central line, and 2*n* towards point of sight till it meets the second vertical *n*K. Then draw *n*2 to centre, and so complete the second step. From 3 draw 3*a* to third vertical, from 4 to fourth, and so on, thus obtaining the height of each ascending step on the wall to the right, completing them in the same way as numbers 1 and 2, when we come to the sixth step, the other end of which is against the wall opposite to us. Steps 6, 7, 8, 9 are all on this wall, and are therefore equal in height all along, as they are equally distant. Step 10 is turned towards us, and abuts on the wall to our left; its measurement is taken on the scale AB just underneath it, and on the same line to which it is drawn. Step 11 is just over the centre of base *mo*, and is therefore parallel to it, and its height is *mn*. The widths of steps 12 and 13 seem gradually to increase as they come towards us, and as they rise above the horizon we begin to see underneath them. Steps 13, 14, 15, 16 are against the wall on this side of the picture, which we may suppose has been removed to show the working of the drawing, or they might be an open flight as we sometimes see in shops and galleries, although in that case they are generally enclosed in a cylindrical shaft.

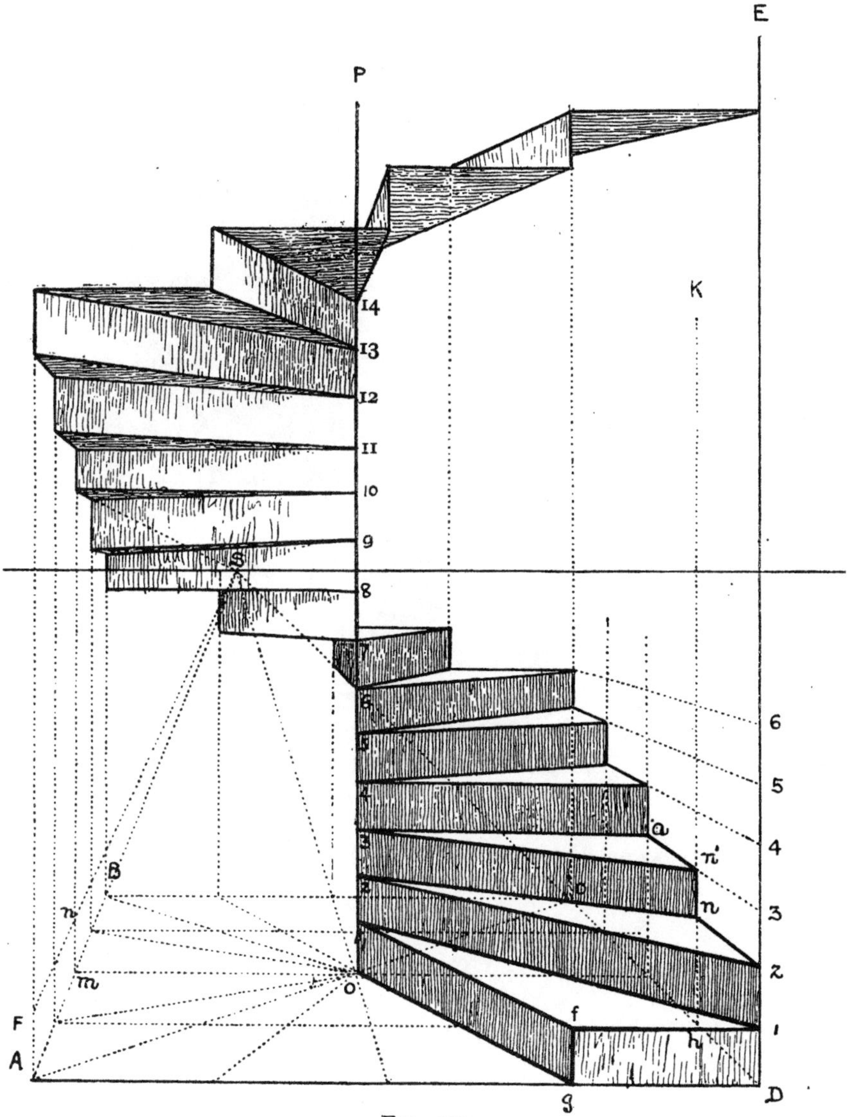

FIG. 257.

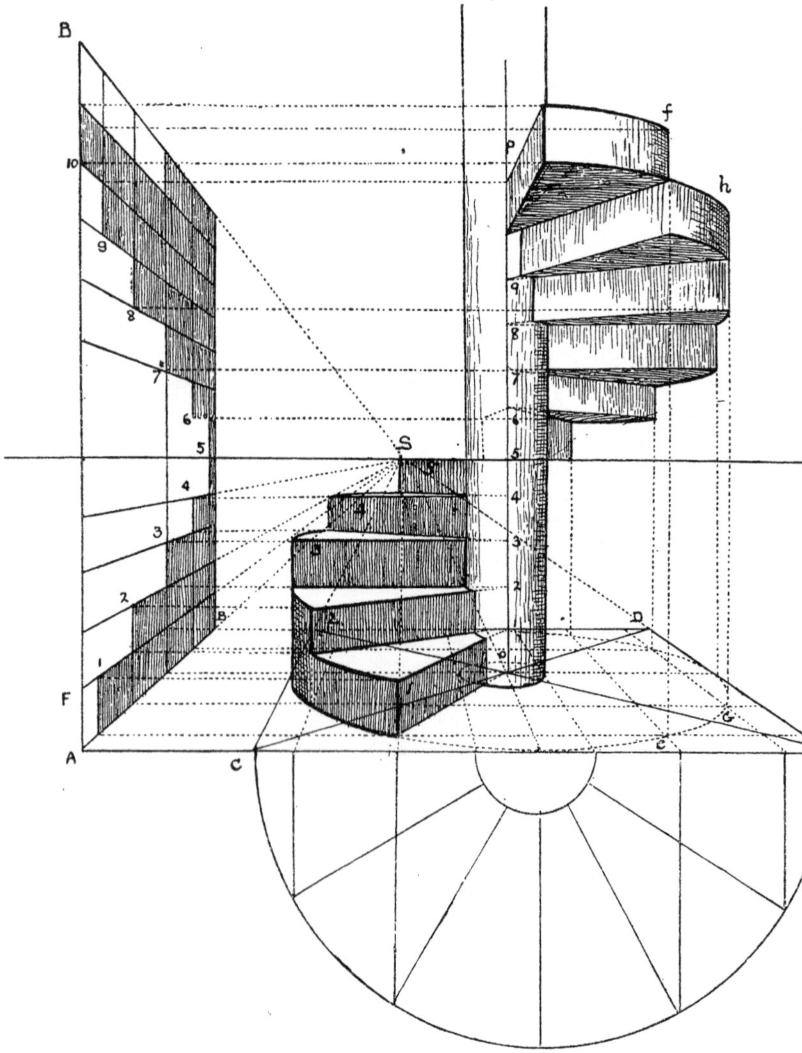

FIG. 258.

CXLV

Winding Stairs in a Cylindrical Shaft

First draw the circular base CD. Divide the circumference into equal parts, according to the number of steps in a complete round, say twelve. Form scale ASF and the larger scale ASB, on which is shown the perspective measurements of the steps according to their positions; raise verticals such as *ef*, G*h*, &c. From divisions on circumference measure out the central line OP, as in the other figure, and find the heights of the steps 1, 2, 3, 4, &c., by the corresponding numbers in the large scale to the left; then proceed in much the same way as in the previous figure. Note the central column OP cuts off a small portion of the steps at that end.

In ordinary cases only a small portion of a winding staircase is actually seen, as in this sketch.

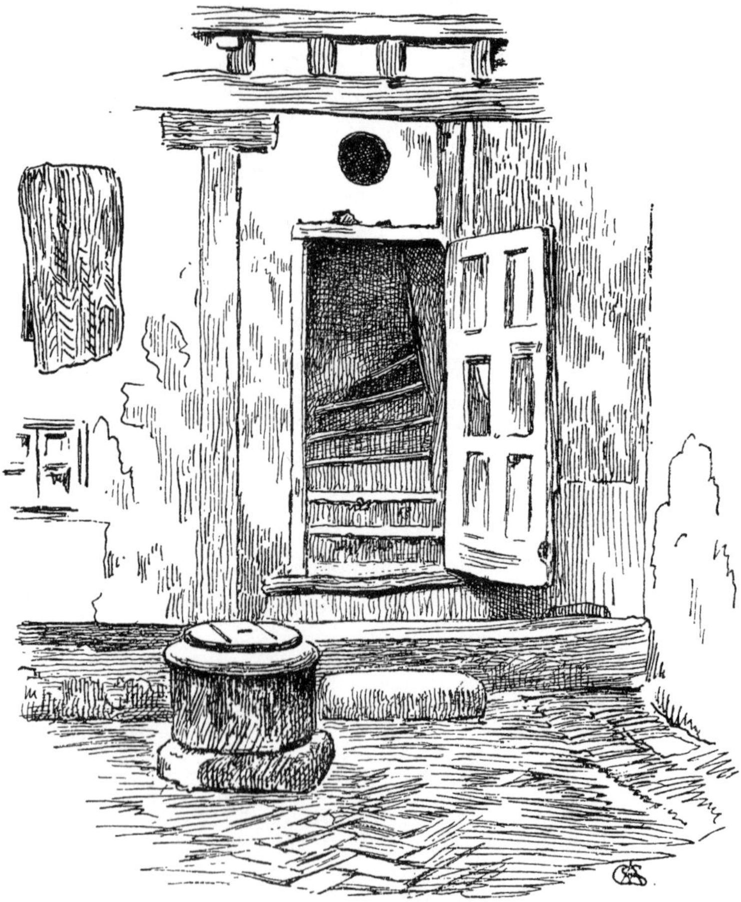

FIG. 259. Sketch of Courtyard in Toledo.

CXLVI

Of the Cylindrical Picture or Diorama

Although illusion is by no means the highest form of art, there is no picture painted on a flat surface that gives such a wonderful appearance of truth as that painted on a cylindrical canvas, such as those panoramas of 'Paris during the Siege', exhibited some

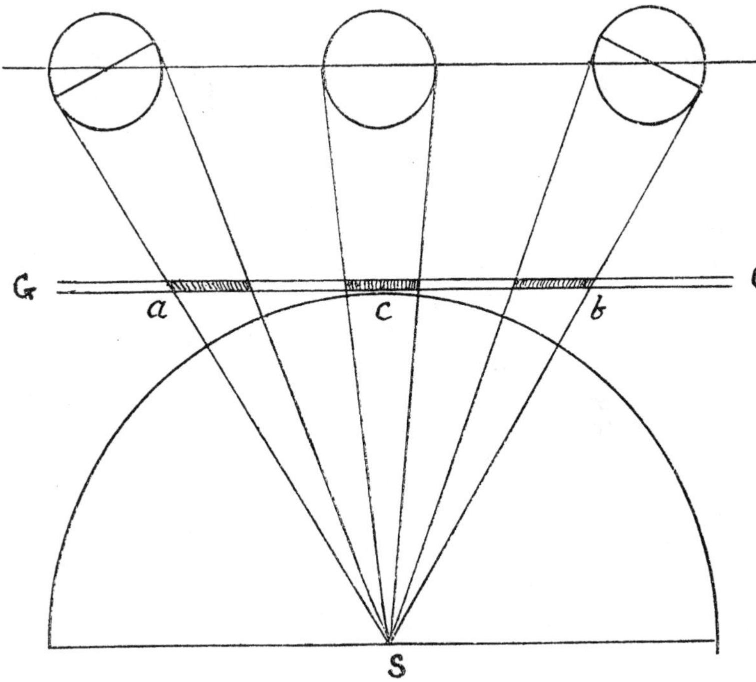

Fig. 260.

years ago; 'The Battle of Trafalgar', only lately shown at Earl's Court; and many others. In these pictures the spectator is in the centre of a cylinder, and although he turns round to look at the scene the point of sight is always in front of him, or nearly so. I believe on the canvas these points are from 12 to 16 feet apart.

The reason of this look of truth may be explained thus. If we place three globes of equal size in a straight line, and trace their apparent widths on to a straight transparent plane, those at the sides, as *a* and *b*, will appear much wider than the centre one at *c*. Whereas, if we trace them on a semicircular glass they will appear very nearly equal and, of the three, the central one *c* will be rather the largest, as may be seen by this figure.

We must remember that, in the first case, when we are looking at a globe or a circle, the visual rays form a cone, with a globe at its base. If these three cones are intersected by a straight glass GG, and looked at from point S, the intersection of C will be a circle, as the cone is cut straight across. The other two being intersected at an angle, will each be an ellipse. At the same time, if we look at them from the station point, with one eye only, then the three globes (or tracings of them) will appear equal and perfectly round.

Of course the cylindrical canvas is necessary for panoramas; but we have, as a rule, to paint our pictures and wall-decorations on flat surfaces, and therefore must adapt our work to these conditions.

In all cases the artist must exercise his own judgement both in the arrangement of his design and the execution of the work, for there is perspective even in the touch—a painting to be looked at from a distance requires a bold and broad handling; in small cabinet pictures that we live with in our own rooms we look for the exquisite workmanship of the best masters.

BOOK FOURTH

CXLVII

The Perspective of Cast Shadows

There is a pretty story of two lovers which is sometimes told as the origin of art; at all events, I may tell it here as the origin of sciagraphy. A young shepherd was in love with the daughter of a potter, but it so happened that they had to part, and were passing their last evening together, when the girl, seeing the shadow of her lover's profile cast from a lamp on to some wet plaster or on the wall, took a metal point, perhaps some sort of iron needle, and traced the outline of the face she loved on to the plaster, following carefully the outline of the features, being naturally anxious to make it as like as possible. The old potter, the father of the girl, was so struck with it that he began to ornament his wares by similar devices, which gave them increased value by the novelty and beauty thus imparted to them.

Here then we have a very good illustration of our present subject and its three elements. First, the light shining on the wall; second, the wall or the plane of projection, or plane of shade; and third, the intervening object, which receives as much light on itself as it deprives the wall of. So that the dark portion thus caused on the plane of shade is the cast shadow of the intervening object.

We have to consider two sorts of shadows: those cast by a luminary a long way off, such as the sun; and those cast by artificial light, such as a lamp or candle, which is more or less close to the object. In the first case there is no perceptible divergence of rays, and the outlines of the sides of the shadows of regular objects, as cubes, posts, &c., will be parallel. In the second case, the rays diverge according to the nearness of the light, and consequently the lines of the shadows, instead of being parallel, are spread out.

CXLVIII

THE TWO KINDS OF SHADOWS

In Figs. 261 and 262 is seen the shadow cast by the sun by parallel rays.

Fig. 263 shows the shadows cast by a candle or lamp, where the rays diverge from the point of light to meet corresponding diverging lines which start from the foot of the luminary on the ground.

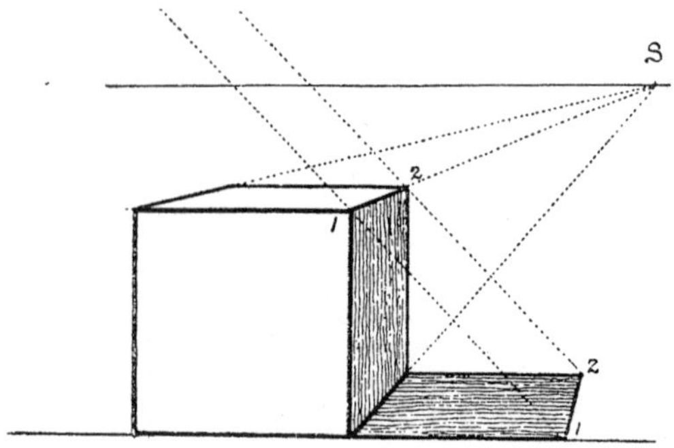

FIG. 261.

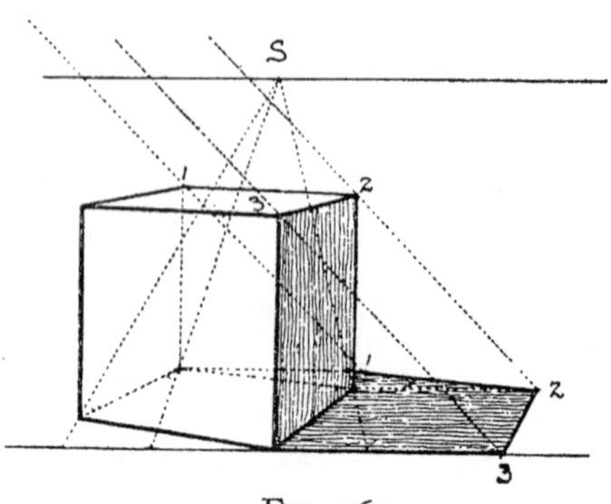

FIG. 262.

The simple principle of cast shadows is that the rays coming from the point of light or luminary pass over the top of the intervening object which casts the shadow on to the plane of shade to meet the horizontal trace of those rays on that plane, or the lines of light proceed from the point of light, and the lines of the shadow are drawn from the foot or trace of the point of light.

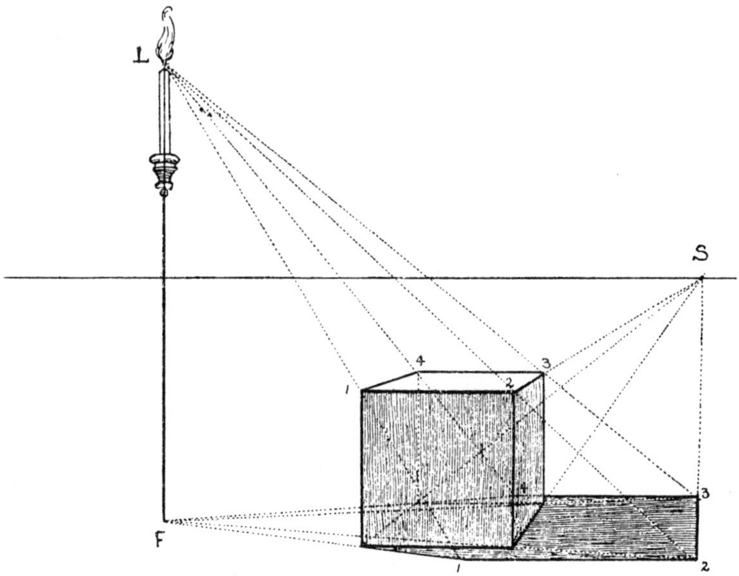

FIG. 263.

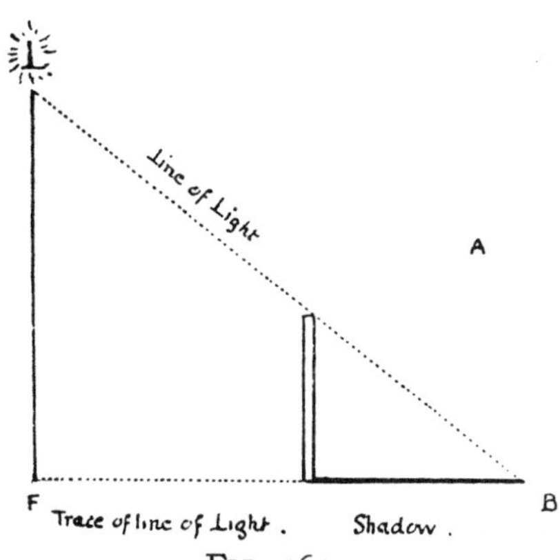

FIG. 264.

Fig. 264 shows this in profile. Here the sun is on the same plane as the picture, and the shadow is cast sideways.

Fig. 265 shows the same thing, but the sun being behind the

object, casts its shadow forwards. Although the lines of light are parallel, they are subject to the laws of perspective, and are therefore drawn from their respective vanishing points.

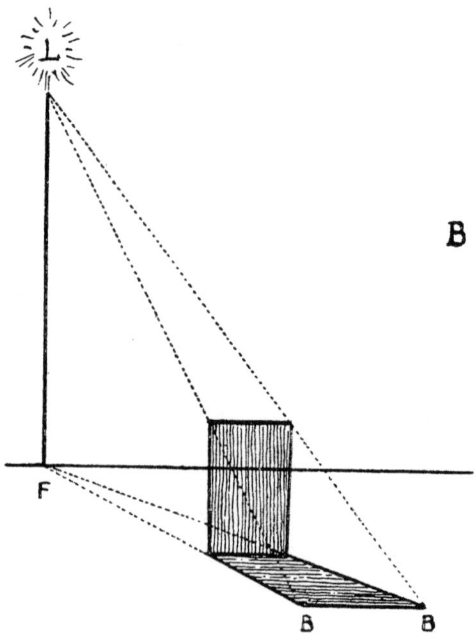

FIG. 265.

CXLIX

SHADOWS CAST BY THE SUN

Owing to the great distance of the sun, we have to consider the rays of light proceeding from it as parallel, and therefore subject to the same laws as other parallel lines in perspective, as already noted. And for the same reason we have to place the foot of the luminary on the horizon. It is important to remember this, as these two things make the difference between shadows cast by the sun and those cast by artificial light.

The sun has three principal positions in relation to the picture. In the first case it is supposed to be in the same plane either to the right or to the left, and in that case the shadows will be parallel with the base of the picture. In the second position it is on the other side of it, or facing the spectator, when the shadows of objects will be thrown forwards or towards him. In the third, the sun is in front of the picture, and behind the spectator, so that the shadows are thrown in the opposite direction, or towards the horizon, the objects themselves being in full light.

CL

The Sun in the Same Plane as the Picture

Besides being in the same plane, the sun in this figure is at an angle of 45° to the horizon, consequently the shadows will be the

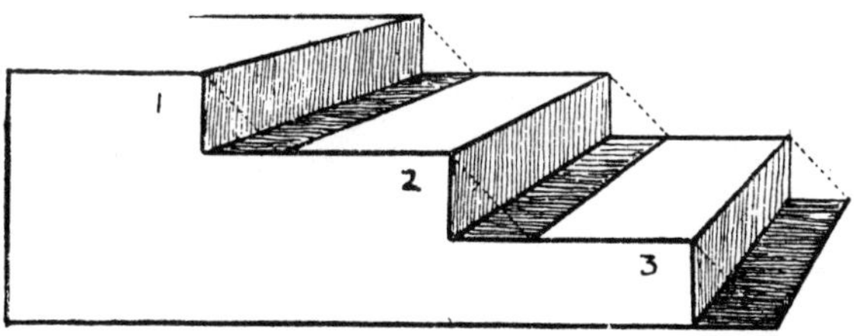

Fig. 266.

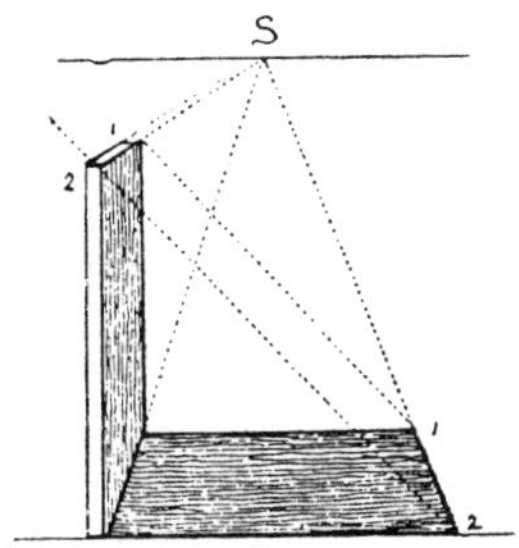

Fig. 267.

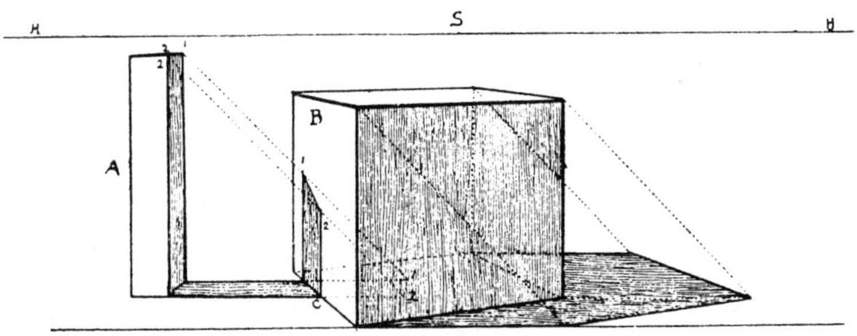

Fig. 268.

same length as the figures that cast them are high. Note that the shadow of step No. 1 is cast upon step No. 2, and that of No. 2 on No. 3, the top of each of these becoming a plane of shade.

When the shadow of an object such as A, Fig. 268, which would fall upon the plane, is interrupted by another object B, then the outline of the shadow is still drawn on the plane, but being interrupted by the surface B at C, the shadow runs up that plane till it meets the rays 1, 2, which define the shadow on plane B. This is an important point, but is quite explained by the figure.

Although we have said that the rays pass over the top of the object casting the shadow, in the case of an archway or similar figure they pass underneath it; but the same principle holds good, that is, we draw lines from the guiding points in the arch, 1, 2, 3, &c., at the same angle of 45° to meet the traces of those rays on the plane of shade, and so get the shadow of the archway, as here shown.

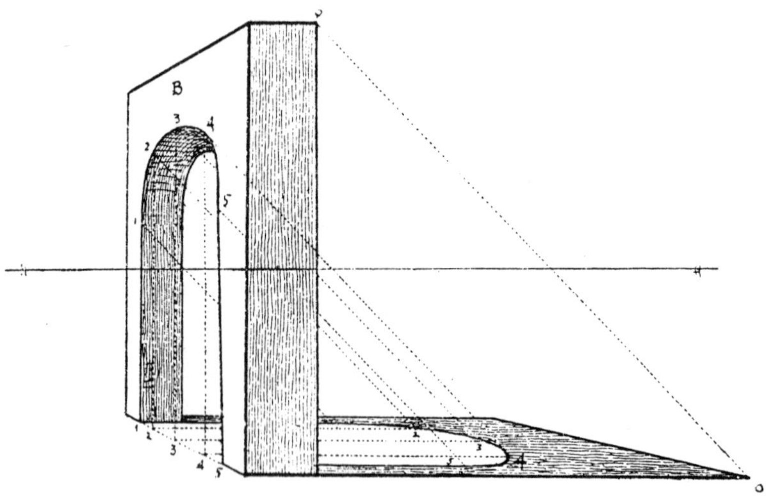

FIG. 269.

CLI

THE SUN BEHIND THE PICTURE

We have seen that when the sun's altitude is at an angle of 45° the shadows on the horizontal plane are the same length as the height of the objects that cast them. Here (Fig. 270), the sun still being at 45° altitude, although behind the picture, and consequently throwing the shadow of B forwards, that shadow must be the same length as the height of cube B, which will be seen is the case, for the shadow C is a square in perspective.

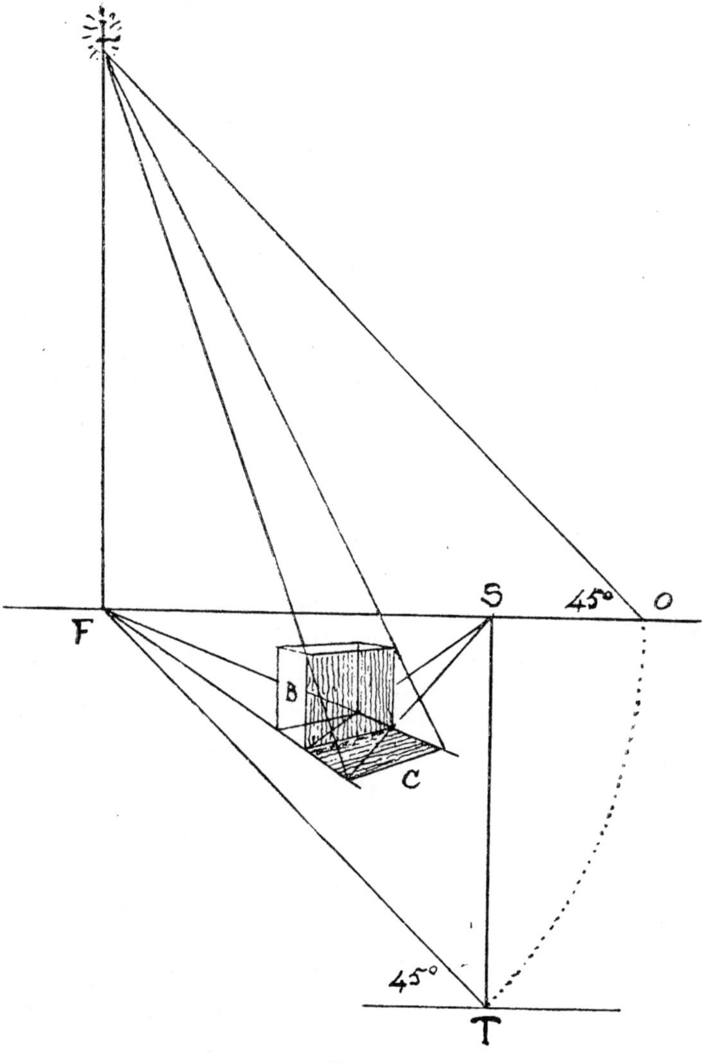

FIG. 270.

To find the angle of altitude and the angle of the sun to the picture, we must first find the distance of the spectator from the foot of the luminary.

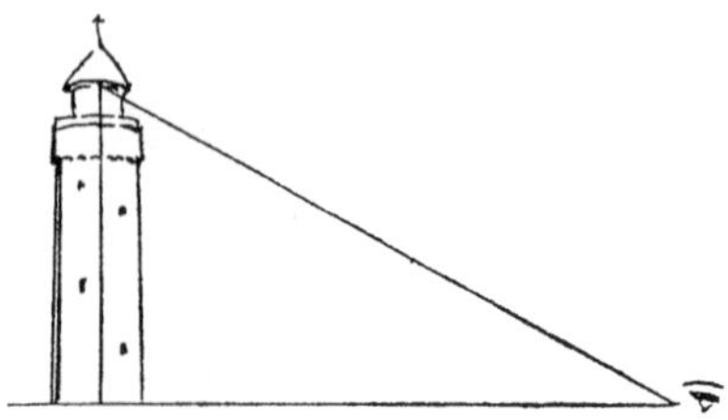

FIG. 271.

From point of sight S (Fig. 270) drop perpendicular to T, the station-point. From T draw TF at 45° to meet horizon at F. With radius FT make FO equal to it. Then O is the position of the spectator. From F raise vertical FL, and from O draw a line at 45° to meet FL at L, which is the luminary at an altitude of 45°, and at an angle of 45° to the picture.

Fig. 272 is similar to the foregoing, only the angles of altitude and of the sun to the picture are altered.

Note.—The sun being at 50° to the picture instead of 45°, is nearer the point of sight; at 90° it would be exactly opposite the spectator, and so on. Again, the elevation being less (40° instead of 45°) the shadow is longer. Owing to the changed position of the sun two sides of the cube throw a shadow. Note also that the outlines of the shadow, 1 2, 2 3, are drawn to the same vanishing points as the cube itself.

It will not be necessary to mark the angles each time we make a drawing, as it must be seen we can place the luminary in any position that suits our convenience.

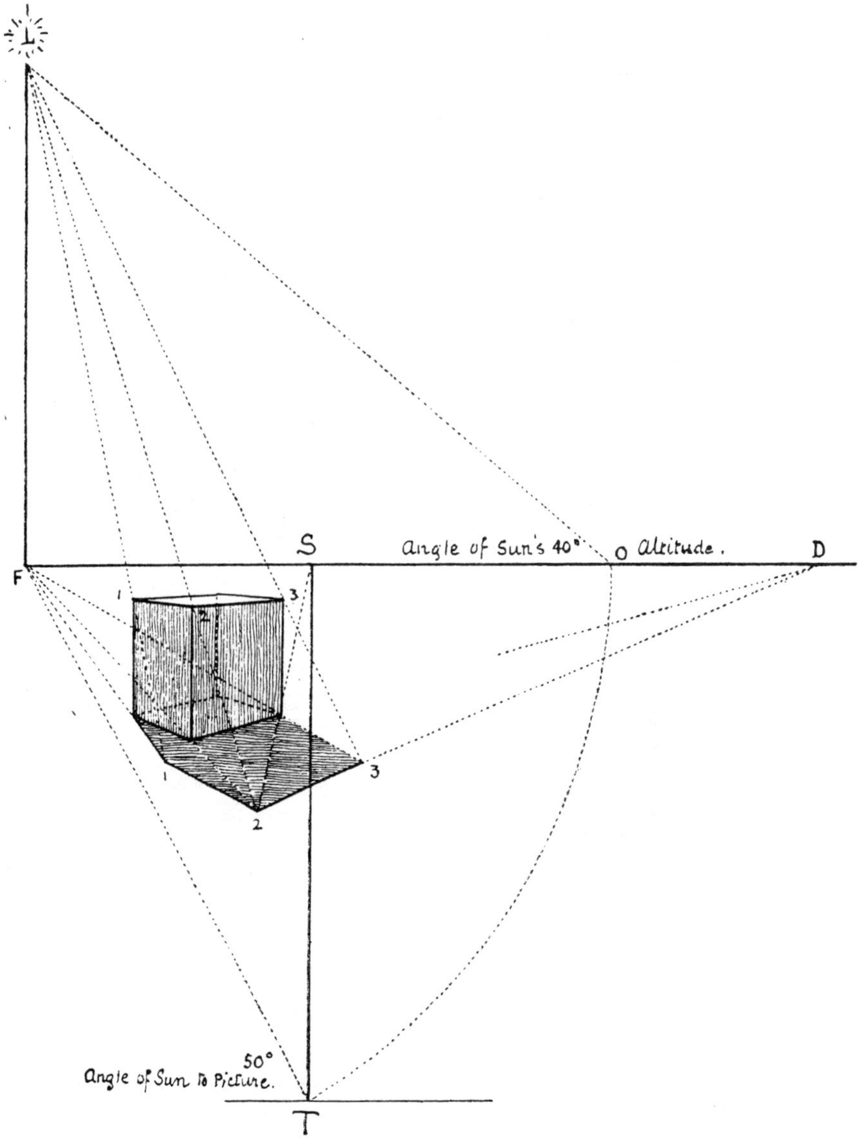
L
S
Angle of Sun's 40°
O
Altitude.
D
F
1
2
3
1
3
2
50°
Angle of Sun to Picture.
T

FIG. 272.

CLII

Sun Behind the Picture, Shadows Thrown on a Wall

As here we change the conditions we must also change our procedure. An upright wall now becomes the plane of shade, therefore as the principle of shadows must always remain the same we have to change the relative positions of the luminary and the foot thereof.

At S (point of sight) raise vertical SF·, making it equal to *f*L.

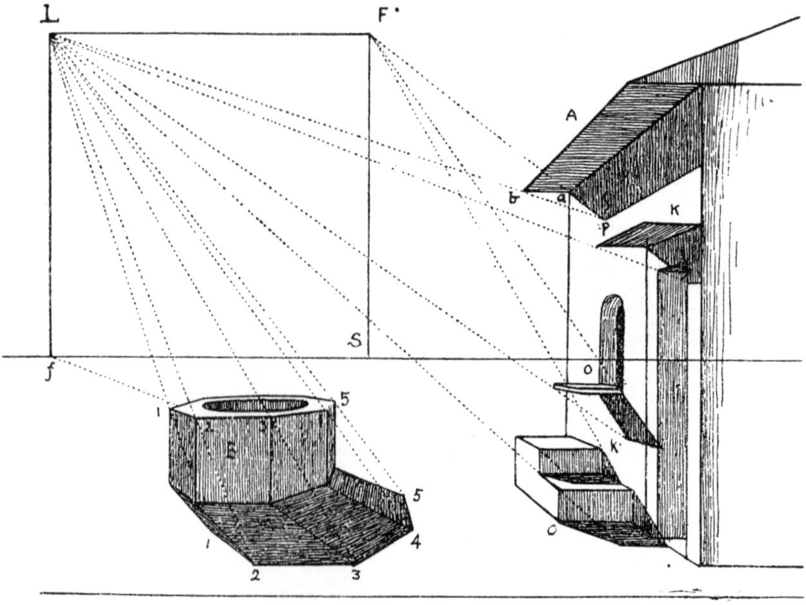

Fig. 273.

F· becomes the foot of the luminary, whilst the luminary itself still remains at L.

We have but to turn this page half round and look at it from the right, and we shall see that SF· becomes as it were the horizontal line. The luminary L is at the right side of point S instead of the left, and the foot thereof is, as before, the trace of the luminary, as it is just underneath it. We shall also see that by proceeding as in previous figures we obtain the same results on the wall as we did on the horizontal plane. Fig. B being on the horizontal plane is treated as already shown. The steps have their shadows partly on the wall and partly on the horizontal plane, so that the shadows on the wall are outlined from F· and those on the ground from *f*. Note shadow of roof A, and how the line drawn from F· through A is met by the line drawn from the luminary L, at the point P, and how the lower line of the shadow is directed to point of sight S.

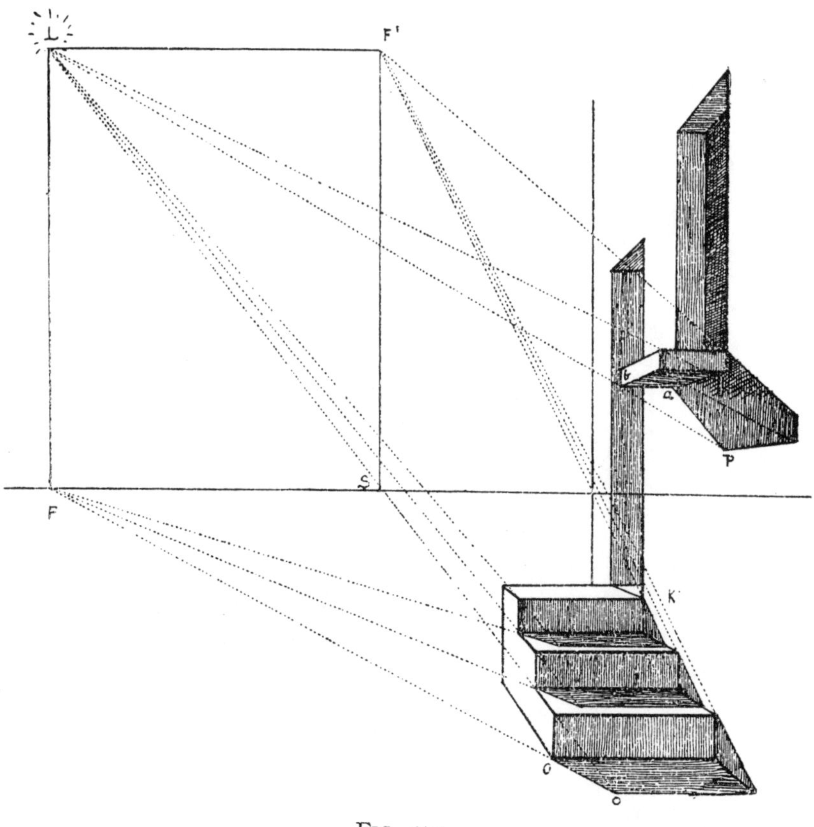

FIG. 274.

Fig. 274 is a larger drawing of the steps, &c., in further illustration of the above.

CLIII

Sun Behind the Picture Throwing Shadow on an Inclined Plane

The vanishing point of the shadows on an inclined plane is on a vertical dropped from the luminary to a point (F) on a level

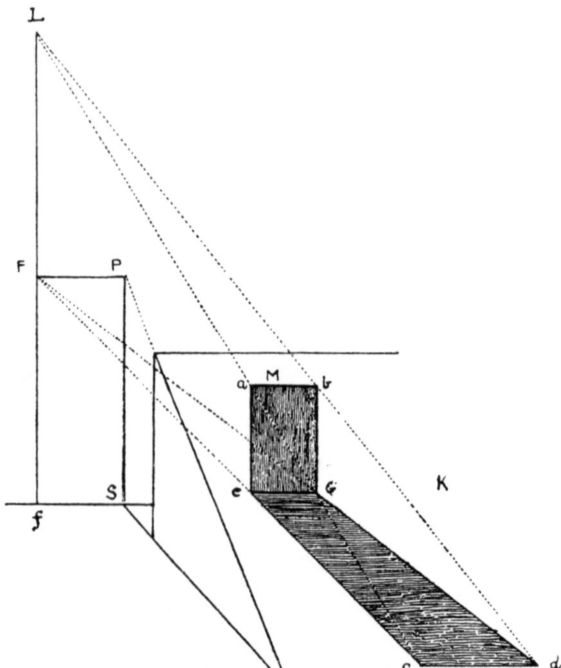

Fig. 275.

with the vanishing point (P) of that inclined plane. Thus P is the vanishing point of the inclined plane K. Draw horizontal PF to meet *f*L (the line drawn from the luminary to the horizon). Then F will be the vanishing point of the shadows on the inclined plane. To find the shadow of M draw lines from F through the base *eg* to *cd*. From luminary L draw lines through *ab*, also to *cd*, where they will meet those drawn from F. Draw CD, which determines the length of the shadow *egcd*.

CLIV

The Sun in Front of the Picture

When the sun is in front of the picture we have exactly the opposite effect to that we have just been studying. The shadows,

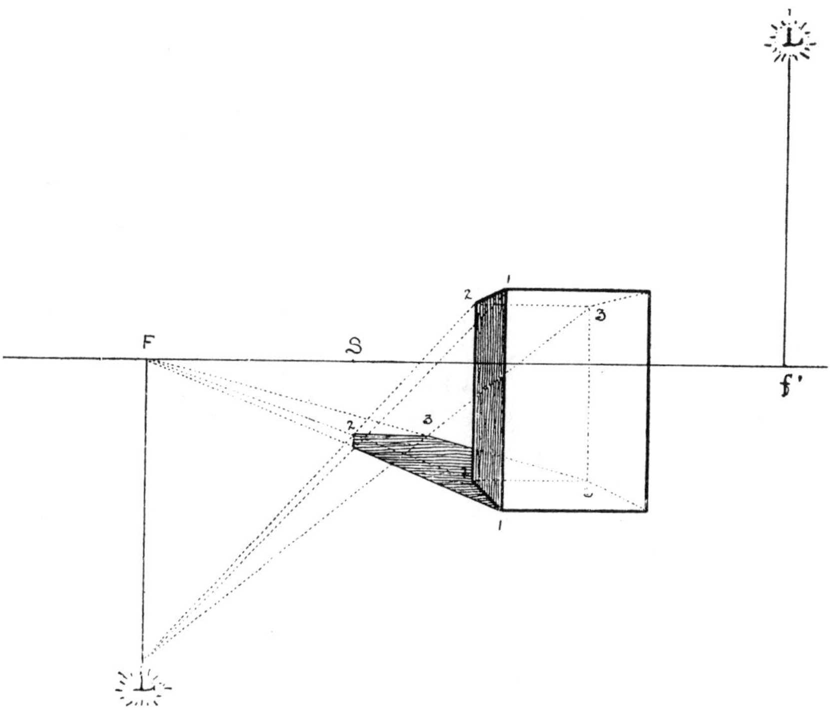

Fig. 276.

instead of coming towards us, are retreating from us, and the objects throwing them are in full light, consequently we have to reverse our treatment. Let us suppose the sun to be placed above the horizon at L·, on the right of the picture and behind the spectator (Fig. 276). If we transport the length L·*f*· to the opposite side and draw the vertical downwards from the horizon, as at FL, we can then suppose point L to be exactly opposite the sun, and if we make that the vanishing point for the sun's rays we shall find that we obtain precisely the same result. As in

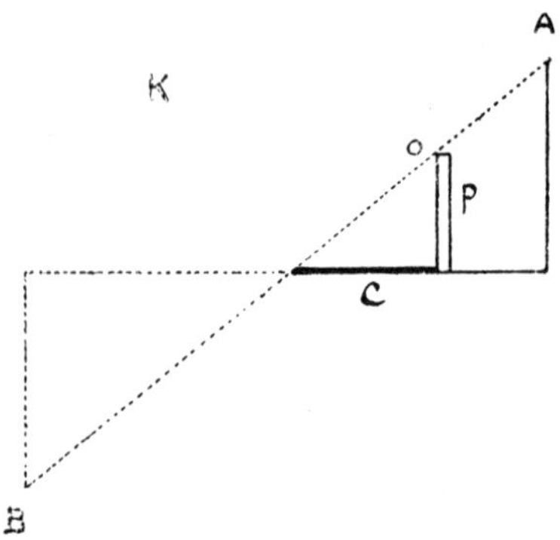

FIG. 277.

Fig. 277, if we wish to find the length of C, which we may suppose to be the shadow of P, we can either draw a line from A through O to B, or from B through O to A, for the result is the same. And as we cannot make use of a point that is behind us and out of the picture, we have to resort to this very ingenious device.

In Fig. 276 we draw lines L1, L2, L3 from the luminary to the top of the object to meet those drawn from the foot F, namely F1, F2, F3, in the same way as in the figures we have already drawn.

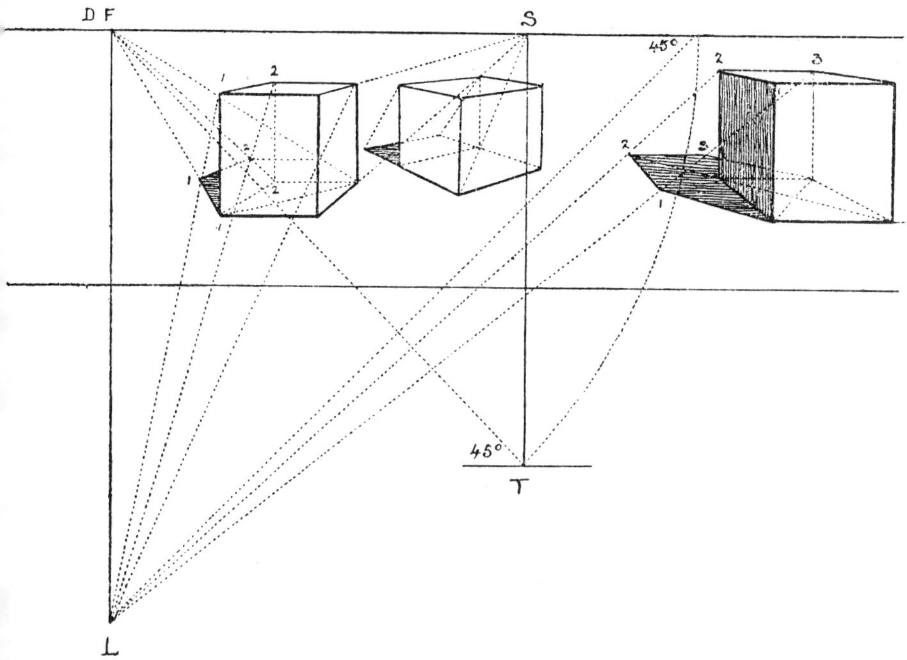

FIG. 278.

Fig. 278 gives further illustration of this problem.

CLV

The Shadow of an Inclined Plane

The two portions of this inclined plane which cast the shadow are first the side *fbd*, and second the farther end *abcd*. The points we have to find are the shadows of *a* and *b*. From luminary

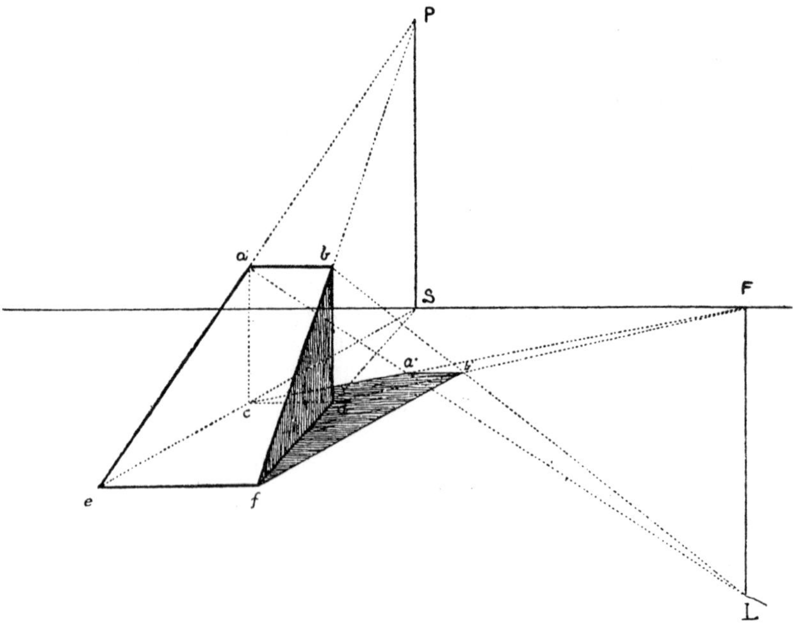

Fig. 279.

L draw L*a*, L*b*, and from F, the foot, draw F*c*, F*d*. The intersection of these lines will be at *a·b·*. If we join *fb·* and *db·* we have the shadow of the side *fbd*, and if we join *ca·* and *a·b·* we have the shadow of *abcd*, which together form that of the figure.

CLVI

Shadow on a Roof or Inclined Plane

To draw the shadow of the figure M on the inclined plane K (or a chimney on a roof). First find the vanishing point P of the inclined plane and draw horizontal PF to meet vertical raised

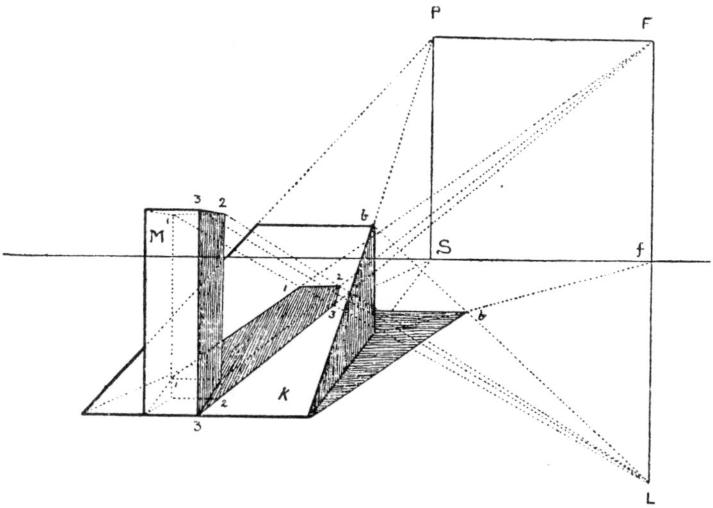

Fig. 280.

from L, the luminary. Then F will be the vanishing point of the shadow. From L draw L1, L2, L3 to top of figure M, and from the base of M draw 1F, 2F, 3F to F, the vanishing point of the shadow. The intersections of these lines at 1, 2, 3 on K will determine the length and form of the shadow.

CLVII

To Find the Shadow of a Projection or Balcony on a Wall

To find the shadow of the object K on the wall W, drop verticals OO till they meet the base line B·B· of the wall. Then from the point of sight S draw lines through OO, also drop verticals D*d*·,

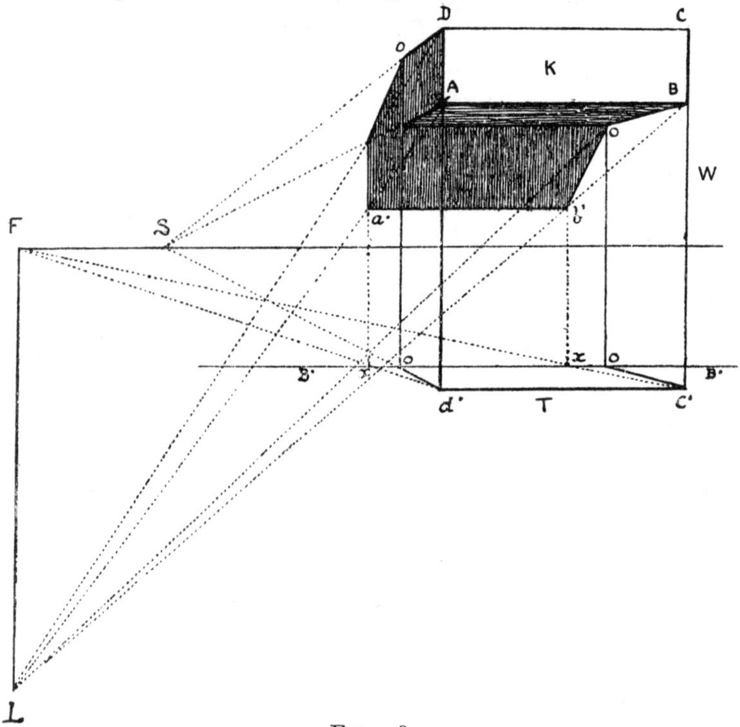

Fig. 281.

C*c*·, to meet these lines in *d*·*c*·; draw *c*·F and *d*·F to foot of luminary. From the points *xx* where these lines cut the base B raise perpendiculars *xa*·, *xb*·. From D, A, and B draw lines to the luminary L. These lines or rays intersecting the verticals raised from *xx* at *a*·*b*· will give the respective points of the shadow.

The shadow of the eave of a roof can be obtained in the same way. Take any point thereon, mark its trace on the ground, and then proceed as above.

CLVIII

SHADOW ON A RETREATING WALL, SUN IN FRONT

Let L be the luminary. Raise vertical LF. F will be the vanishing point of the shadows on the ground. Draw L*f*·

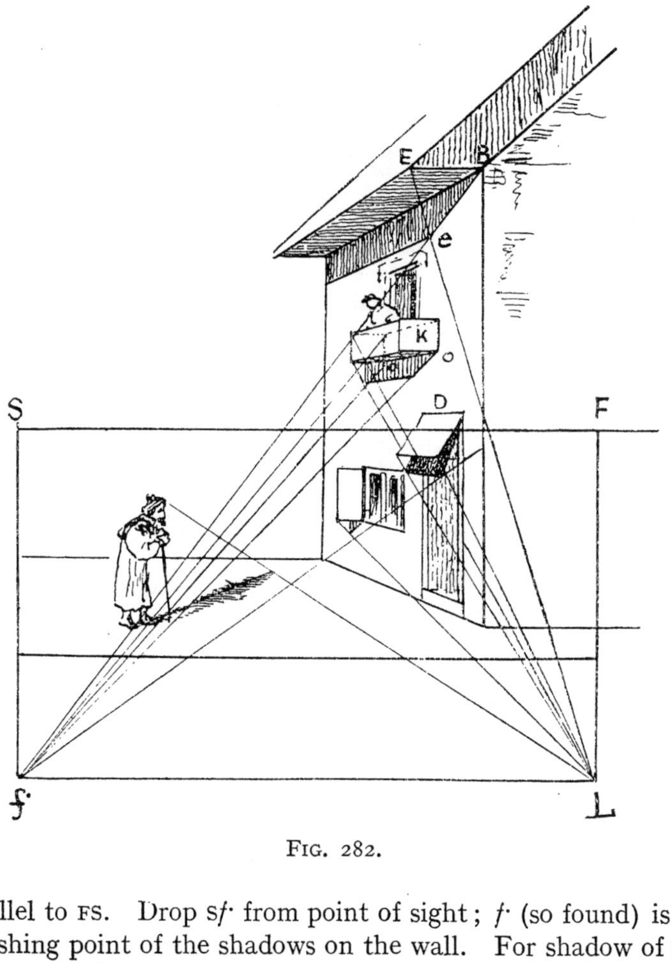

FIG. 282.

parallel to FS. Drop S*f*· from point of sight; *f*· (so found) is the vanishing point of the shadows on the wall. For shadow of roof draw LE and *f*·B, giving us *e*, the shadow of E. Join B*e*, &c., and so draw shadow of eave of roof.

For shadow of K draw lines from luminary L to meet those from *f*· the foot, &c.

The shadow of D over the door is found in a similar way to that of the roof.

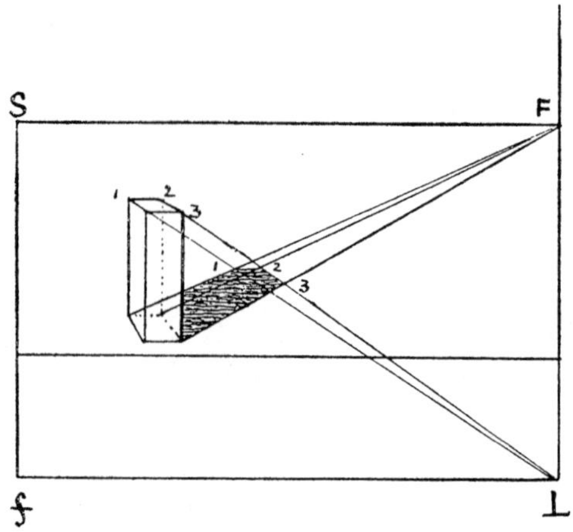

FIG. 283.

Figure 283 shows how the shadow of the old man in the preceding drawing is found.

CLIX

Shadow of an Arch, Sun in Front

Having drawn the arch, divide it into a certain number of parts, say five. From these divisions drop perpendiculars to

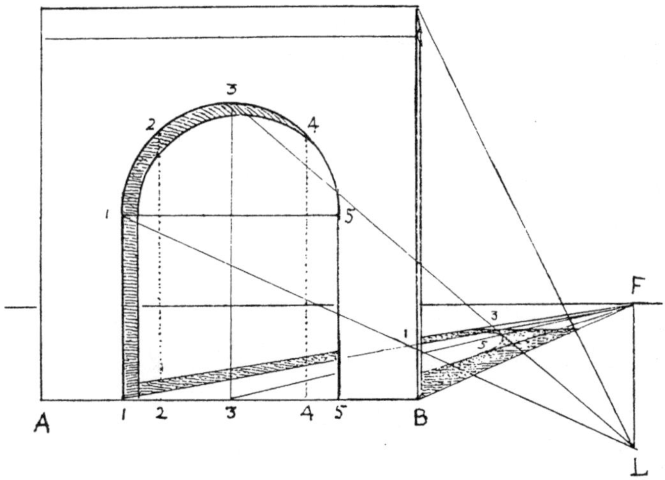

Fig. 284.

base line. From divisions on AB draw lines to F the foot, and from those on the semicircle draw lines to L the luminary. Their intersections will give the points through which to draw the shadow of the arch.

CLX

Shadow in a Niche or Recess

In this figure a similar method to that just explained is adopted. Drop perpendiculars from the divisions of the arch 1 2 3 to the base. From the foot of each draw 1s, 2s, 3s to foot of luminary

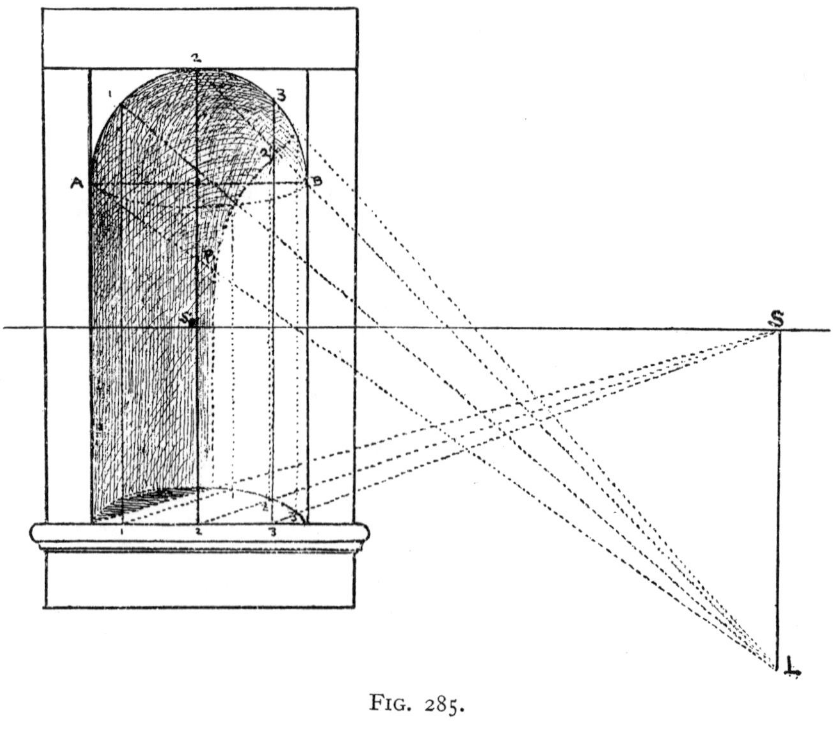

Fig. 285.

s, and from the top of each, A 1 2 3 B, draw lines to L as before. Where the former intersect the curve on the floor of the niche raise verticals to meet the latter at P 1 2 B, &c. These points will indicate about the position of the shadow; but the niche being semicircular and domed at the top the shadow gradually loses itself in a gradated and somewhat serpentine half-tone.

CLXI

Shadow in an Arched Doorway

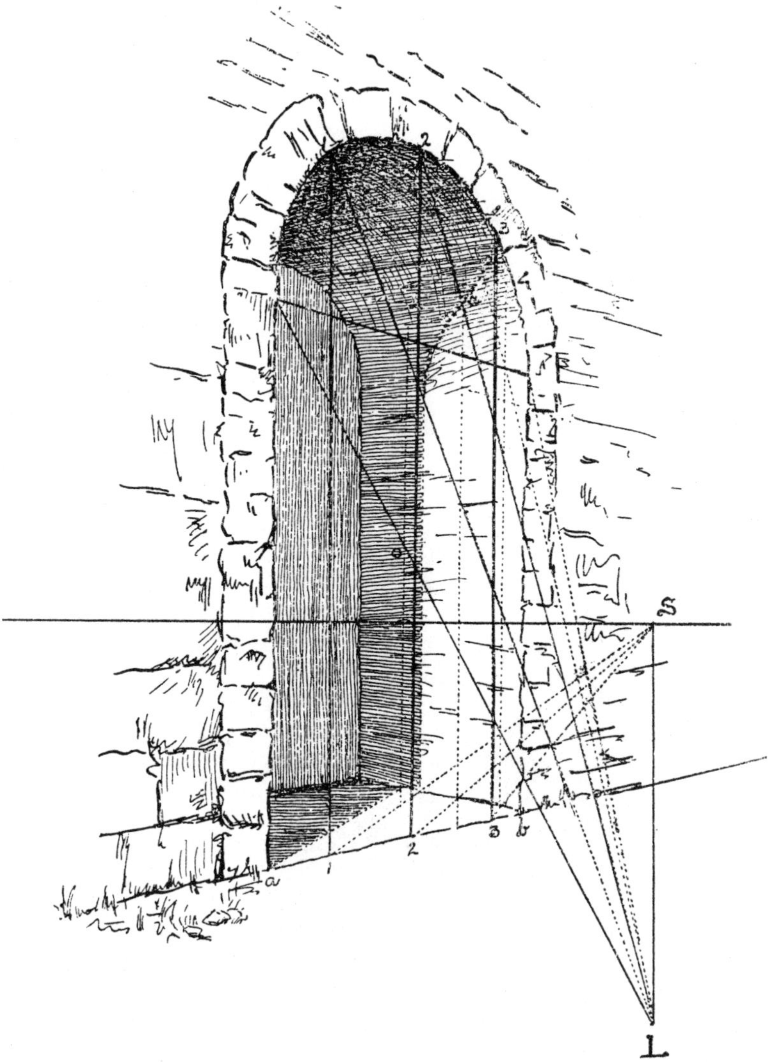

Fig. 286.

This is so similar to the last figure in many respects that I need not repeat a description of the manner in which it is done. And surely an artist after making a few sketches from the actual thing will hardly require all this machinery to draw a simple shadow.

CLXII

Shadows Produced by Artificial Light

Shadows thrown by artificial light, such as a candle or lamp, are found by drawing lines from the seat of the luminary through

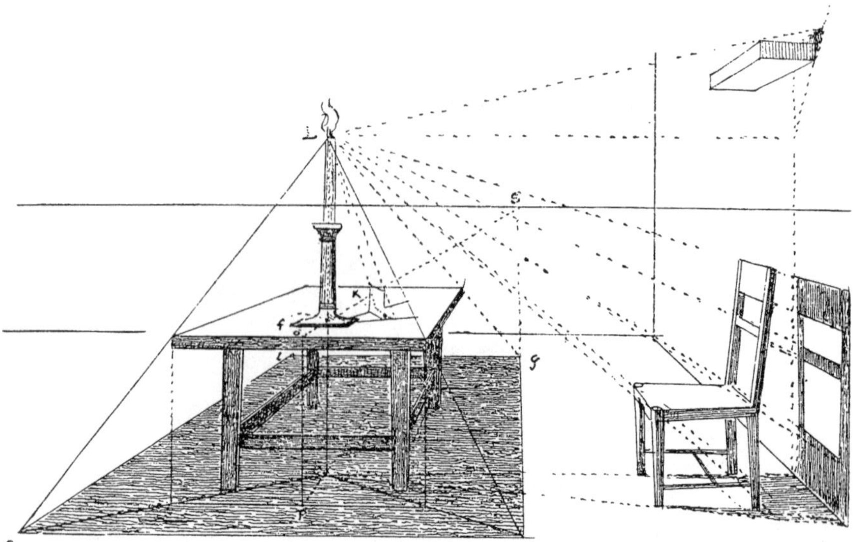

Fig. 287.

the feet of the objects to meet lines representing rays of light drawn from the luminary itself over the tops or the corners of the objects ; very much as in the cases of sun-shadows, but with this difference, that whereas the foot of the luminary in this latter case is supposed to be on the horizon an infinite distance away, the foot in the case of a lamp or candle may be on the floor or on a table close to us. First draw the table and chair, &c. (Fig. 287), and let L be the luminary. For objects on the table such as K the foot will be at *f* on the table. For the shadows on the floor, of the chair and table itself, we must find the foot of the luminary on the floor. Draw S*o*, find trace of the edge of the table, drop vertical *o*P, draw PS to point of sight, drop vertical from foot of candlestick to meet PS in F. Then F is the foot of the luminary on the floor. From this point draw lines through the feet or traces of objects such as the corners of the table, &c., to meet other lines drawn from the point of light, and so obtain the shadow.

CLXIII

Some Observations on Real Light and Shade

Although the figures we have been drawing show the principles on which sun-shadows are shaped, still there are so many more laws to be considered in the great art of light and shade that it is better to observe them in Nature herself or under the teaching of the real sun. In the study of a kitchen and scullery in an old house in Toledo (Fig. 288) we have an example of the many things to be considered besides the mere shapes of shadows of regular forms. It will be seen that the light is dispersed in all directions, and although there is a good deal of half-shade there are scarcely any cast shadows except on the floor; but the light on the white walls in the outside gallery is so reflected into the cast shadows that they are extremely faint. The luminosity of this part of the sketch is greatly enhanced by the contrast of the dark legs of the bench and the shadows in the roof. The warm glow of all this portion is contrasted by the grey door and its frame.

Note that the door itself is quite luminous, and lighted up by the reflection of the sun from the tiled floor, so that the bars in the upper part throw distinct shadows, besides the mystery

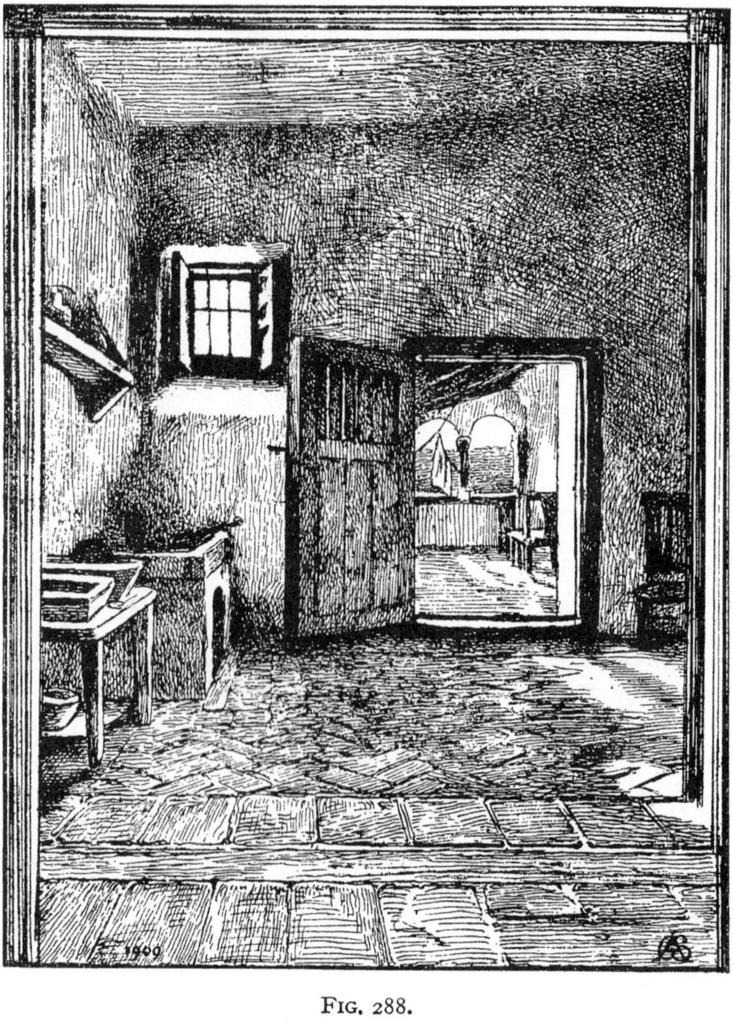

FIG. 288.

of colour thus introduced. The little window to the left, though not admitting much direct sunlight, is evidence of the brilliant glare outside; for the reflected light is very conspicuous on the top and on the shutters on each side; indeed they cast distinct shadows up and down, while some clear daylight from the blue sky is reflected on the window-sill. As to the sink, the table, the wash-tubs, &c., although they seem in strong light and shade they really receive little or no direct light from a single point; but from the strong reflected light re-reflected into them from the wall of the doorway. There are many other things in such effects as this which the artist will observe, and which can only be studied from real light and shade. Such is the character of reflected light, varying according to the angle and intensity of the luminary and a hundred other things. When we come to study light in the open air we get into another region, and have to deal with it accordingly, and yet we shall find that our sciagraphy will be a help to us even in this bewilderment; for it will explain in a manner the innumerable shapes of sun-shadows that we observe out of doors among hills and dales, showing up their forms and structure; its play in the woods and gardens, and its value among buildings, showing all their juttings and abuttings, recesses, doorways, and all the other architectural details. Nor must we forget light's most glorious display of all on the sea and in the clouds and in the sunrises and the sunsets down to the still and lovely moonlight.

These sun-shadows are useful in showing us the principle of light and shade, and so also are the shadows cast by artificial light; but they are only the beginning of that beautiful study, that exquisite art of tone or *chiaro-oscuro*, which is infinite in its variety, is full of the deepest mystery, and is the true poetry of art. For this the student must go to Nature herself, must study her in all her moods from early dawn to sunset, in the twilight and when night sets in. No mathematical rules can help him, but only the thoughtful contemplation, the silent watching, and the mental notes that he can make and commit to memory, combining them with the sentiments to which they in turn give rise. The *plein air*, or broad daylight effects, are but one item of the great range of this ever-changing and deepening mystery—from the hard reality to the soft blending of evening when form almost disappears, even to the merging of the whole landscape, nay, the whole world, into a dream—which is felt rather than seen, but possesses a charm that almost defies the pencil of the painter, and can only be expressed by the deep and sweet notes of the poet and the musician. For love and reverence are necessary to appreciate and to present it.

There is also much to learn about artificial light. For here, again, the study is endless : from the glare of a hundred lights—electric and otherwise—to the single lamp or candle. Indeed a whole volume could be filled with illustrations of its effects. To those who aim at producing intense brilliancy, refusing to acknowledge any limitations to their capacity, a hundred or a thousand lights commend themselves ; and even though wild splashes of paint may sometimes be the result, still the effort is praiseworthy. But those who prefer the mysterious lighting of a Rembrandt will find, if they sit contemplating in a room lit with one lamp only, that an endless depth of mystery surrounds them, full of dark recesses peopled by fancy and sweet thought, whilst the most beautiful gradations soften the forms without distorting them; and at the same time he can detect the laws of this science of light and shade a thousand times repeated and endless in its variety.

Note.—Fig. 288 must be looked upon as a rough sketch which only gives the general effect of the original drawing; to render all the delicate tints, tones and reflections described in the text would require a highly-finished reproduction in half-tone or in colour.

As many of the figures in this book had to be re-drawn, not a light task, I must here thank Miss Margaret L. Williams, one of our Academy students, for kindly coming to my assistance and volunteering her careful co-operation.

CLXIV

Reflection

Reflections in still water cán best be illustrated by placing some simple object, such as a cube, on a looking-glass laid horizontally on a table, or by studying plants, stones, banks, trees, &c., reflected in some quiet pond. It will then be seen that the reflection is the counterpart of the object reversed, and having the same vanishing points as the object itself.

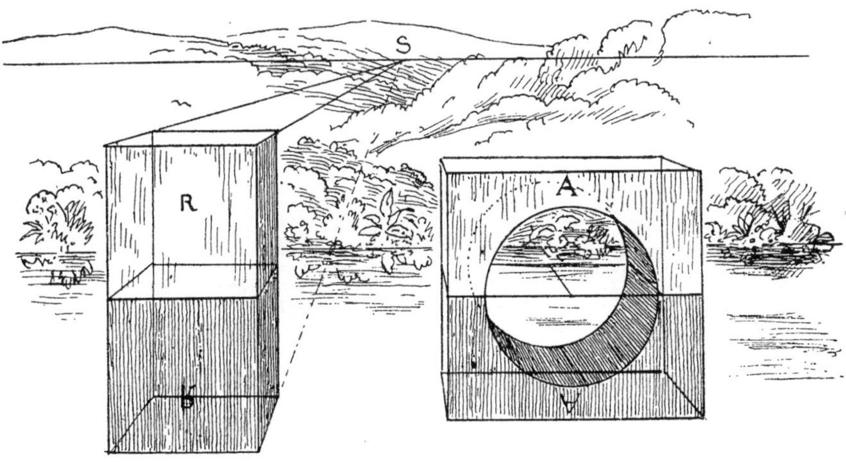

Fig. 289.

Let us suppose R (Fig. 289) to be standing on the water or reflecting plane. To find its reflection make square ꓤ equal to the original square R. Complete the reversed cube by drawing its other sides, &c. It is evident that this lower cube is the reflection of the one above it, although it differs in one respect, for whereas in figure R the top of the cube is seen, in its reflection ꓤ it is hidden, &c. In figure A of a semicircular arch we see the underneath portion of the arch reflected in the water, but we do not see it in the actual object. However, these things are obvious. Note that the reflected line must be equal in length to the actual one, or the reflection of a square would not be a square, nor that of a semicircle a semicircle. The apparent lengthening of reflections in water is owing to the surface being broken by wavelets, which, leaping up near to us, catch some of the image of the tree, or whatever it is, that it is reflected.

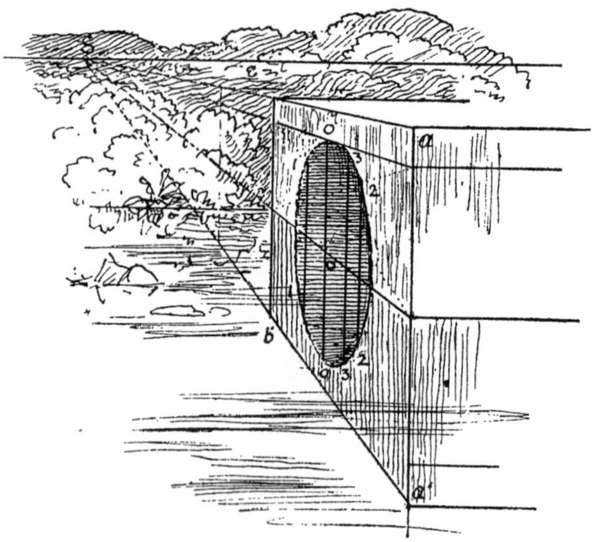

FIG. 290.

In this view of an arch (Fig. 290) note that the reflection is obtained by dropping perpendiculars from certain points on the arch, 1, 0, 2, &c., to the surface of the reflecting plane, and then measuring the same lengths downwards to corresponding points, 1, 0, 2, &c., in the reflection.

CLXV

Angles of Reflection

In Fig. 291 we take a side view of the reflected object in order to show that at whatever angle the visual ray strikes the reflecting surface it is reflected from it at the same angle.

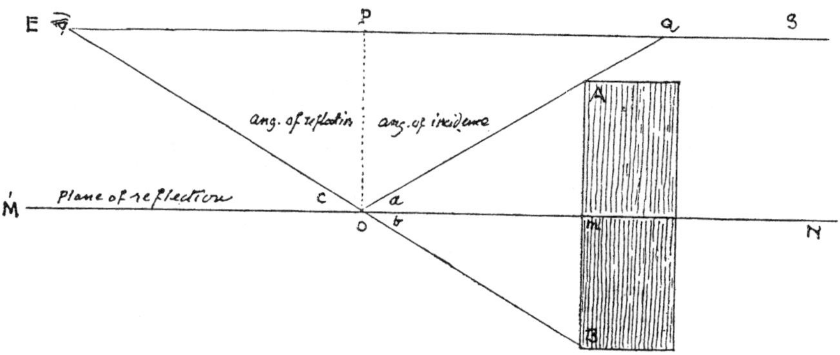

Fig. 291.

We have seen that the reflected line must be equal to the original line, therefore *m*B must equal M*a*. They are also at right angles to MN, the plane of reflection. We will now draw the visual ray passing from E, the eye, to B, which is the reflection of A; and just underneath it passes through MN at O, which is the point where the visual ray strikes the reflecting surface. Draw OA. This line represents the ray reflected from it. We have now two triangles, OA*m* and O*m*B, which are right-angled triangles and equal, therefore angle *a* equals angle *b*. But angle *b* equals angle *c*. Therefore angle E*c*M equals angle A*am*, and the angle at which the ray strikes the reflecting plane is equal to the angle at which it is reflected from it.

CLXVI

Reflections of Objects at Different Distances

In this sketch the four posts and other objects are represented standing on a plane level or almost level with the water, in order to show the working of our problem more clearly. It will be seen that the post A is on the brink of the reflecting plane, and therefore is entirely reflected; B and C being farther back are only

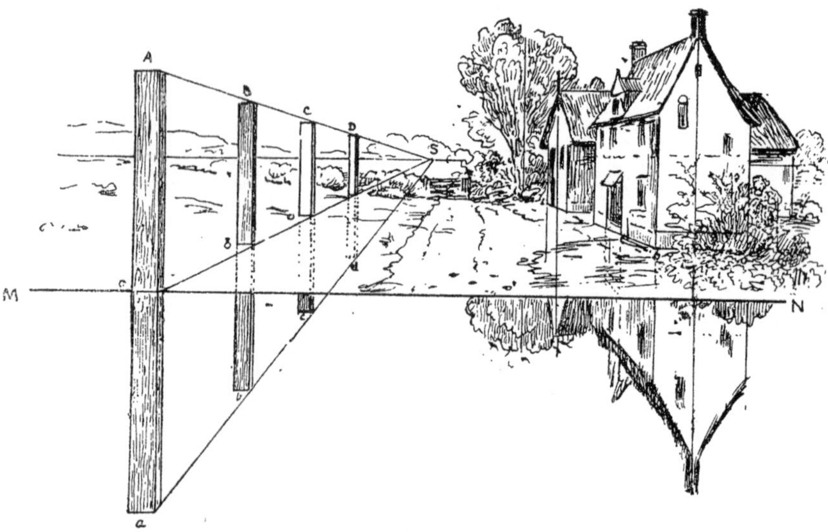

Fig. 292.

partially seen, whereas the reflection of D is not seen at all. I have made all the posts the same height, but with regard to the houses, where the length of the vertical lines varies, we obtain their reflections by measuring from the points *oo* upwards and downwards as in the previous figure.

Of course these reflections vary according to the position they are viewed from; the lower we are down, the more do we see of the reflections of distant objects, and vice versa. When the figures are on a higher plane than the water, that is, above the plane of reflection, we have to find their perspective position, and drop a perpendicular AO (Fig. 293) till it comes in contact with the plane of reflection, which we suppose to run under the ground, then measure the same length downwards, as in this

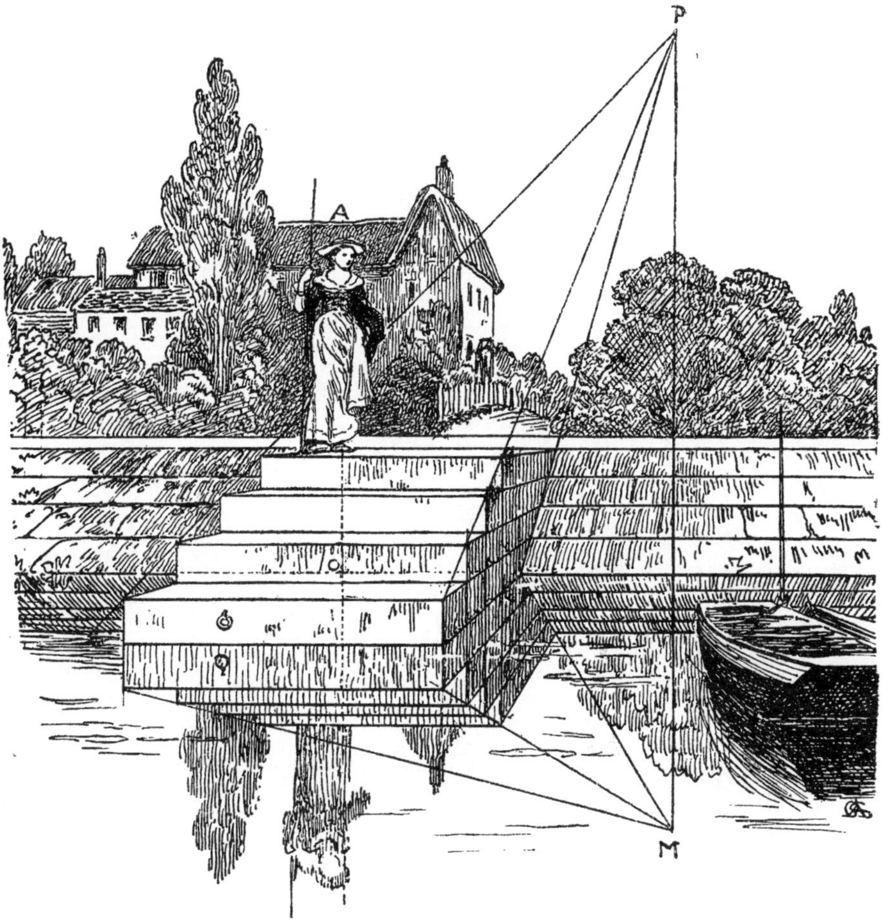

FIG. 293.

figure of a girl on the top of the steps. Point *o* marks the point of contact with the plane, and by measuring downwards to *a* we get the length of her reflection, or as much as is seen of it. Note the reflection of the steps and the sloping bank, and the application of the inclined plane ascending and descending.

CLXVII

Reflection in a Looking-glass

I had noticed that some of the figures in Titian's pictures were only half life-size, and yet they looked natural; and one day, thinking I would trace myself in an upright mirror, I stood at arm's length from it and with a brush and Chinese white, I made a rough outline of my face and figure, and when I measured it I found that my drawing was exactly half as long and half as

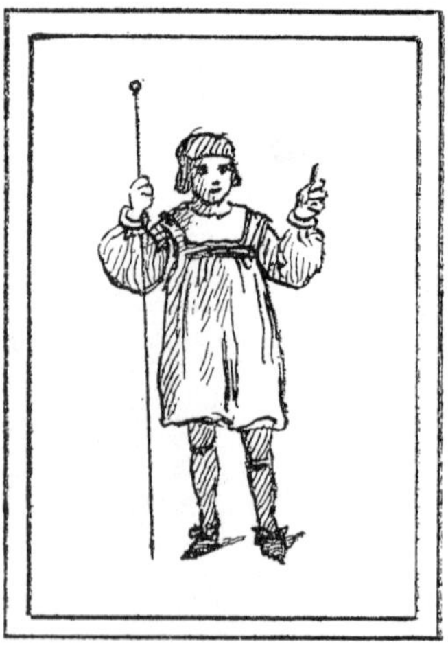

Fig. 294.

wide as nature. I went closer to the glass, but the same outline fitted me. Then I retreated several paces, and still the same outline surrounded me. Although a little surprising at first, the reason is obvious. The image in the glass retreats or advances exactly in the same measure as the spectator.

Suppose him to represent one end of a parallelogram *e·s·*, and his image *a·b·* to represent the other. The mirror AB is a perpendicular half-way between them, the diagonal *e·b·* is the visual ray passing from the eye of the spectator to the foot of his image, and is the diagonal of a rectangle, therefore it cuts AB in the centre *o*, and AO represents *a·b·* to the spectator. This is an

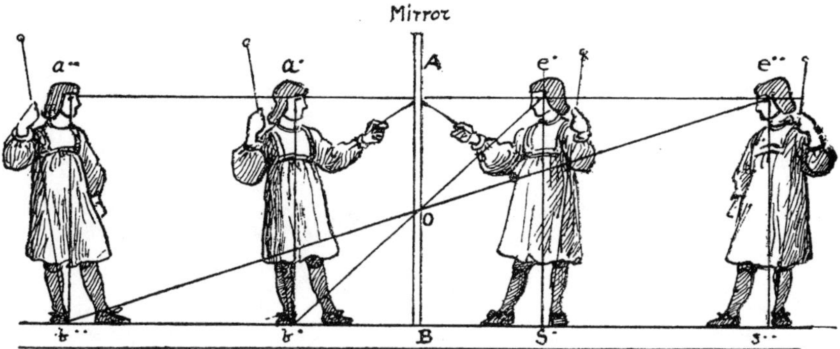

FIG. 295.

experiment that any one may try for himself. Perhaps the

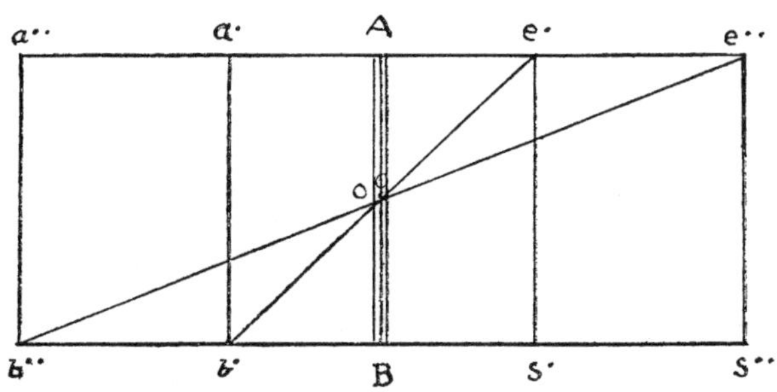

FIG. 296.

above fact may have something to do with the remarks I made about Titian at the beginning of this chapter.

CLXVIII

The Mirror at an Angle

If an object or line AB is inclined at an angle of 45° to the mirror RR, then the angle BAC will be a right angle, and this angle is exactly divided in two by the reflecting plane RR. And whatever the angle of the object or line makes with its reflection that angle will also be exactly divided.

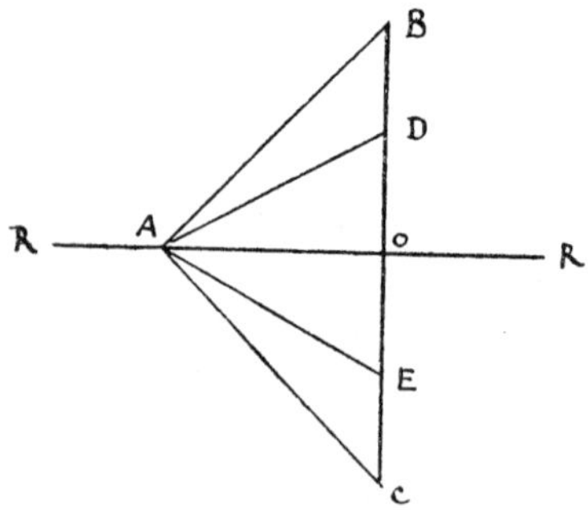

Fig. 297.

Now suppose our mirror to be standing on a horizontal plane and on a pivot, so that it can be inclined either way. Whatever

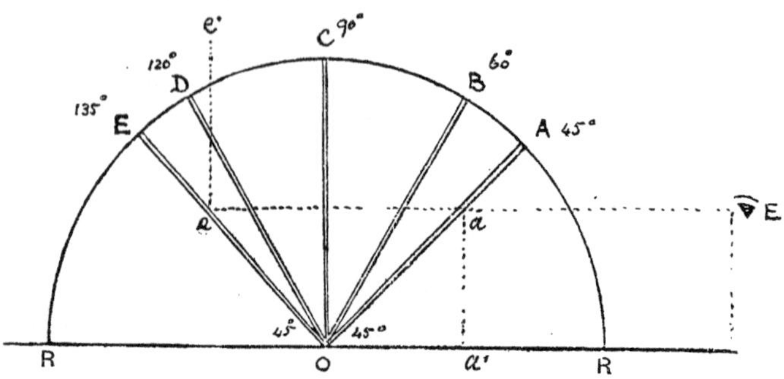

Fig. 298.

angle the mirror is to the plane the reflection of that plane in the mirror will be at the same angle on the other side of it, so that if the mirror OA (Fig. 298) is at 45° to the plane RR then the reflection of that plane in the mirror will be 45° on the other side of it, or at right angles, and the reflected plane will appear perpendicular, as shown in Fig. 299, where we have a front view of a mirror leaning forward at an angle of 45° and reflecting the square *aob* with a cube standing upon it, only in the reflection the cube appears to be projecting from an upright plane or wall.

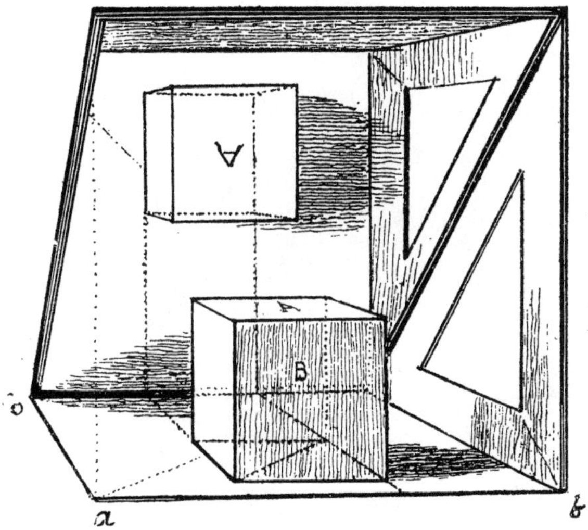

FIG. 299.

If we increase the angle from 45° to 60°, then the reflection of the plane and cube will lean backwards as shown in Fig. 300. If we place it on a level with the original plane, the cube will be standing upright twice the distance away. If the mirror is still farther tilted till it makes an angle of 135° as at E (Fig. 298), or 45° on the other side of the vertical O*c*, then the plane and cube would disappear, and objects exactly over that plane, such as the ceiling, would come into view.

In Fig. 300 the mirror is at 60° to the plane *mn*, and the plane itself at about 15° to the plane *an* (so that here we are using angular perspective, V being the accessible vanishing point). The reflection of the plane and cube is seen leaning back at an angle of 60°. Note the way the reflection of this cube is found by the dotted lines on the plane, on the surface of the mirror, and also on the reflection.

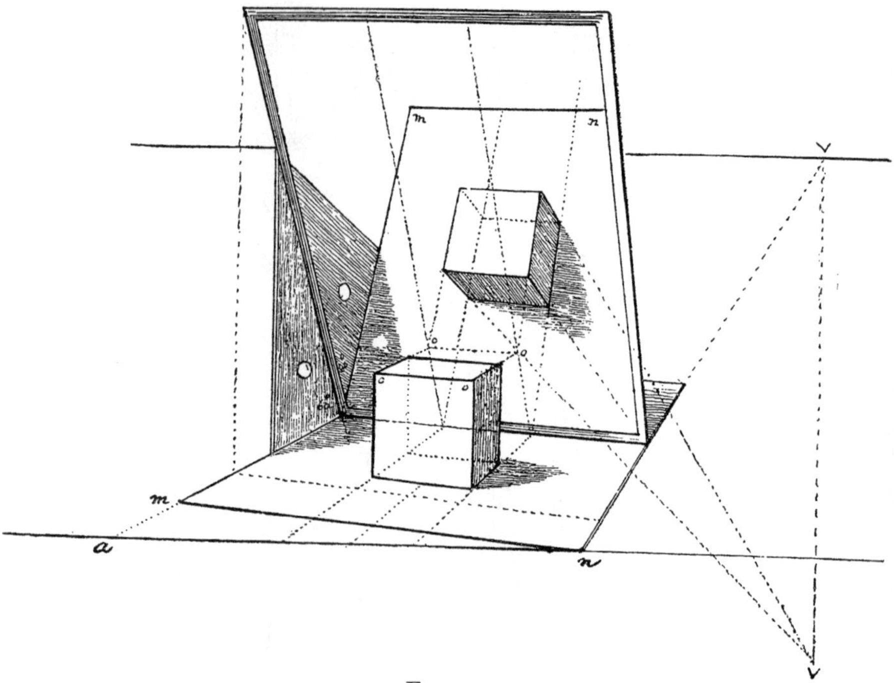

FIG. 300.

CLXIX

THE UPRIGHT MIRROR AT AN ANGLE OF 45° TO THE WALL

In Fig. 301 the mirror is vertical and at an angle of 45° to the wall opposite the spectator, so that it reflects a portion of that wall as though it were receding from us at right angles; and the wall with the pictures upon it, which appears to be facing us, in reality is on our left.

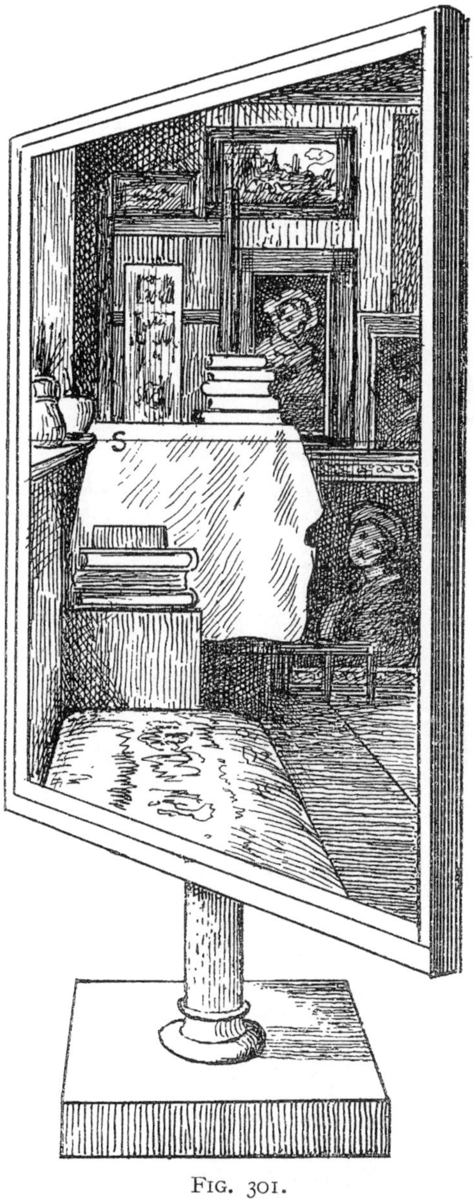

FIG. 301.

An endless number of complicated problems could be invented of the inclined mirror, but they would be mere puzzles calculated rather to deter the student than to instruct him. What we chiefly have to bear in mind is the simple principle of reflections. When a mirror is vertical and placed at the end or side of a room it reflects that room and gives the impression that we are in one double the size. If two mirrors are placed opposite to each other at each end of a room they reflect and reflect, so that we see an endless number of rooms.

Again, if we are sitting in a gallery of pictures with a hand mirror, we can so turn and twist that mirror about that we can bring any picture in front of us, whether it is behind us, at the side, or even on the ceiling. Indeed, when one goes to those old palaces and churches where pictures are painted on the ceiling, as in the Sistine Chapel or the Louvre, or the palaces at Venice, it is not a bad plan to take a hand mirror with us, so that we can see those elevated works of art in comfort.

There are also many uses for the mirror in the studio, well known to the artist. One is to look at one's own picture reversed, when faults become more evident ; and another, when the model is required to be at a longer distance than the dimensions of the studio will admit, by drawing his reflection in the glass we double the distance he is from us.

The reason the mirror shows the fault of a work to which the eye has become accustomed is that it doubles it. Thus if a line that should be vertical is leaning to one side, in the mirror it will lean to the other ; so that if it is out of the perpendicular to the left, its reflection will be out of the perpendicular to the right, making a double divergence from one to the other.

CLXX

Mental Perspective

Before we part, I should like to say a word about mental perspective, for we must remember that some see farther than others, and some will endeavour to see even into the infinite. To see Nature in all her vastness and magnificence, the thought must supplement and must surpass the eye. It is this far-seeing that makes the great poet, the great philosopher, and the great artist. Let the student bear this in mind, for if he possesses this quality or even a share of it, it will give immortality to his work.

To explain in detail the full meaning of this suggestion is beyond the province of this book, but it may lead the student to think this question out for himself in his solitary and imaginative moments, and should, I think, give a charm and virtue to his work which he should endeavour to make of value, not only to his own time but to the generations that are to follow. Cultivate, therefore, this mental perspective, without forgetting the solid foundation of the science I have endeavoured to impart to you.

INDEX